AN ARGUMENT FOR MIND

AN

Argument for Mind

JEROME KAGAN

YALE UNIVERSITY PRESS NEW HAVEN AND LONDON

Published with assistance from the foundation established in memory of
Amasa Stone Mather of the Class of 1907, Yale College.

Printed in the United States of America by R. R. Donnelley, Harrisonburg, Virginia.

Library of Congress Cataloging-in-Publication Data
Kagan, Jerome.
An argument for mind / Jerome Kagan.
p.   cm.
Includes bibliographical references (p.   ) and index.
ISBN-13: 978-0-300-11337-2 (clothbound : alk. paper)
ISBN-10: 0-300-11337-4 (clothbound : alk. paper)
1. Psychology—History—20th century. I. Title.
BF105.K34 2006
150.9′045—dc22   2005033441

A catalogue record for this book is available from the British Library.

The paper in this book meets the guidelines for permanence and
durability of the Committee on Production Guidelines for
Book Longevity of the Council on Library Resources.

10   9   8   7   6   5   4   3   2   1

For Steve

Names are noise and smoke; the important point is to have a clear and adequate conception of the facts signified by a name.
—T. H. Huxley, *Evolution and Ethics* (1893)

But it is significant that the meaning of historical events has frequently been obscured, not by the real historian but by social scientists who sought abortively to bring history into the realms of nature and thus deny the characteristically historical aspects of the human scene. In short, our culture has been intent upon equating history with nature at the precise moment when history revealed the dangerous possibilities of human freedom which were not at all like nature.
—Reinhold Niebuhr, *Time*, April 25, 1988

CONTENTS

This book, like an unplanned infant born to an older couple, was not supposed to be written. I had not regarded my life as sufficiently different
from, or more interesting than, other social scientists in my age cohort to
warrant a personal narrative. A stroll on a beach with my son-in-law, Steven
Reznick, in the summer of 2004 put the bee in the proverbial bonnet. When
he asked what project I had planned for the fall and I told him that I had no
puzzle pressing for a lengthy analysis, he suggested I write a summary of the
extraordinary changes in psychology over the past half century, arguing that
the paradigm shifts over this interval would be of general interest, especially
if this history were part of a tapestry that contained the seminal elements of
my research career. Although I rejected his suggestion that afternoon, several
weeks later, on a bright September morning with no pressing responsibilities
before me, I began to outline the manuscript he had urged.

I had also been brooding over the comments of a friend, Robert Pozen,
who wanted me to state, in nontechnical prose, my current beliefs about the
relation of mind to brain because he felt that the attraction to the influence
of biology late in my career was misunderstood.

This book tries to orchestrate three themes—a selective history of psychology from my graduate years to the present, the questions I put to nature and
the replies, and a critique of contemporary social science, especially an analysis of the current romance between psychology and biology. I am critical of
a number of popular ideas in contemporary psychology. I hope that those

friendly to these concepts, many of whom are respected friends, will interpret my comments as an invitation for constructive dialogue and not as ad hominem criticism. Psychology will continue to make important contributions to human welfare, and I do not wish to injure its precarious position among the natural sciences. These comments are thus affectionate suggestions to beloved friends. James Secord, who has written a masterful history of how the Victorians received Robert Chambers's *Vestiges*, noted that every act of reading involves a forgetting of what came before. Each retrieval of the past distorts the memory exploited. The memories that bind this text are neither a personal memoir nor the book a historian of psychology would have penned. Nonetheless, I hope that this three-part fugue will generate in readers some of the pleasure I have taken from its composition.

ACKNOWLEDGMENTS

I t is not possible to list all the students, colleagues, and friends who have shaped my ideas, and I apologize to those from whom I have profited whose names do not appear in the alphabetic list below. To all I am grateful. Doreen Arcus, Rosa Arriaga, Abigail Baird, Joyce Benenson, Joseph Biederman, Gilbert Brim, Joseph Campos, Wendy Coster, Joseph Coyle, Richard Davidson, Virginia Demos, Adele Diamond, Peter Ellison, Robert Emde, Kai Erikson, Gordon Finley, Kurt Fischer, Nathan Fox, Ellen Frank, Howard Freeman, Cynthia Garcia-Coll, Howard Gardner, Norman Garmezy, Marshall Haith, Sydney Hans, Anne Harrington, Marc Hauser, Stuart Hauser, Barbara Henker, Ellen Herbener, Norbert Herschkowitz, Philip Holzman, Steven Hyman, Sandra Jacobson, Vali Kahn, Alan Kazdin, Richard Kearsley, Daniel Kilburn, Dennis Kinney, Robert Klein, Arthur Kleinman, Stephen Kosslyn, Milton Kotelchuck, David Kupfer, John and Beatrice Lacey, Sharon Lamb, Deborah Lapidus, Janet Levine, Michael Lewis, Susan Linn, Lewis Lipsitt, Kenneth Livingston, Eric Loken, David Magnusson, Robert McCall, Mark McManis, Richard McNally, Stanley Messer, Cheri Minton, Kazuo Miyake, David Moore, Michael Moore, Fred Morrison, Robin Mount, Mary Mullen, Charles Nelson, Nora Newcombe, Elizabeth Nolan, Michael Novey, Kevin Nugent, Eric Peterson, Rachel Pollock, Robert Pozen, Marion Radke-Yarrow, Maureen Rezendes, J. Steven Reznick, Charles Richmond, Sara Rimm-Kaufman, Barbara Rogoff, A. K. Romney, Robert Rose, Jerrold Rosenbaum, Allison Rosenberg, Donald Rubin, Michael Rutter, Robin Schacht, Jay

Schulkin, Carl Schwartz, Martha Sellers, Heidi Sigal, Irving Sigel, Jordan Smoller, Nancy Snidman, Debra Sorenson, Elizabeth Spelke, Frank Sulloway, Charles and Sara Super, Edward Tronick, Wang Yu Feng, Paul Whalen, Sue Woodward, Regina Yando, and Philip R. Zelazo. Thanks also to Laura Jones Dooley for her careful editing.

My research over the past forty-five years has been supported by the National Institutes of Health, John D. and Catherine T. MacArthur Foundation, Carnegie Foundation, Spencer Foundation, William T. Grant Foundation, Foundation for Child Development, Lilly Endowment, Office for Naval Research, Harvard University, Bial Foundation, Metanexus Institute, and the COUQ Foundation. I am grateful to the officers and staff of these institutions.

And of course the path has been made infinitely easier by my wife, Cele, whose affection, encouragement, and loyalty have never failed to dispel the shadows of doubt that have darkened many moments in the past half-century.

AN ARGUMENT FOR MIND

ONE

Choice and Indoctrination

The second week of September 1950 was warm and humid when I arrived in New Haven, Connecticut, to begin graduate work at what the chairman of my psychology department at Rutgers had told me was the best psychology department in the world. I was twenty-one. That autumn the *New York Times* announced that President Harry Truman had threatened China with an atomic bomb if it attacked Formosa, the first modern credit card was introduced, and Senator Joseph McCarthy began his witch hunt of Americans suspected of being communists. Hundreds of thousands of men and women who had served in the armed forces during World War II were taking advantage of both the nation's gratitude and Congress's passage of the G.I. Bill of Rights, enabling them to choose careers that required a college education rather than returning to the blue-collar jobs held by their parents and grandparents. Americans felt confident of their egalitarian receptivity to reducing class distinctions without disrupting the economic philosophy and practices of competitive capitalism. Education, honesty, and perseverance would be rewarded with material comforts, a loving family, and, perhaps, a few moments of praise for discoveries, outstanding performances, or acts of kindness that struck some as commendable. Many different journeys in this version of Oz were possible. Although a few might be blocked by obstacles, many more would eventually capture the happiness they were told was the prize for sustained effort.

The five significant categories to which I belonged, and whose values I felt obligated to honor, were male, Jewish, middle-class, American, and white in that order. Members of this symbolic quintet assumed that a mind exploiting its talents to gain financial security and status was the icon to bow before when deciding how to exploit the talents, desires, and energies that genes, family history, and schools had cobbled together. Medicine and law were two obvious choices. Writer, painter, or composer required special, somewhat mysterious abilities most adolescents assumed they did not possess, and their less certain economic futures moved them into the shadows. A scientist at a university seemed both attractive and realizable. I remember the glittering halo my adolescent imagination placed on the college professor's life after seeing Robert Donat in the film *Goodbye, Mr. Chips*. The gentle setting of academia and the opportunity to reflect and nurture the young struck a chord in my incoherently articulated sense of self, even though my later decision to apply to graduate school was discrepant from the preferences of the peers and relatives I had used as buoys when deciding where to place the next brushstroke on my bare mural.

I had rejected law as an option, even though an uncle, a relatively successful lawyer in my hometown, had urged me to do so and to join his office. I was not attracted to the law because it was made by people rather than by nature, but I could not articulate the deeper bases for this prejudice. For reasons I did not understand, nature roused my feelings, and it still does, whereas human artifacts, whether Roman ruins, Baroque churches, Chinese porcelain vases, jeweled swords, or the law, did not. This judgment was a bit inconsistent with my reverence for the human artifacts that took the form of books, poems, paintings, and symphonies. But the human mind has no difficulty rationalizing such inconsistencies. The artist, writer, and composer were trying to create objects of lasting beauty. This intention distinguished these products from the law, which I saw as devoid of beauty because its propositions seemed arbitrary declarations with short lives.

My attraction to nature was more passionate for living forms than for stars or fossils. Many leading cosmologists remembered that, as adolescents, they remained awake many nights staring at the stars with a profound curiosity and awe.[1] Adolescents who have had a strong emotional experience try to find ways to relive that precious moment. One undergraduate had his epiphany at a symphony concert when the audience applauded the conductor for many minutes after the performance. So many people celebrating a single person generated a moment of envy. He wanted to be on that stage, washed in the admiration of so many strangers. No one understands why a small number of adolescents have such powerful experiences and why these feelings are restricted to such specific events. I attended concerts but never felt the desire to be a conductor; I often looked at the night sky but never had a feeling of *agape*.

My curiosity was pricked by things that were alive. I remember walking home one afternoon—I was about twelve—when I saw a dead squirrel that had recently been struck by a car. Here was an opportunity to look inside the animal to see what unknown things resided there. I wrapped the animal in paper and took it to my bedroom—I may have felt there was something illicit in this activity—and with a kitchen knife sliced open its belly to examine its moist viscera. I found the gentle probing of the life-giving organs exciting and, in a sense, sacred. The glistening intestines evoked a feeling that may have resembled the state of a future cosmologist staring at the Milky Way at two in the morning.

I am not certain why life-forms possessed this power. Each time I silently pose that question, the same voice, whose source seems to lie midway between head and heart, whispers sexuality. One need not be loyal to Freudian ideas, of which only a few remain roughly correct a century after their announcement, to suggest that boys find the unselfishness of mothers puzzling and the female body mysterious. Why are women gentler and kinder than men, and what was hidden beneath that mound of hair that was always covered? Today's parents worry over the Internet pornography their adolescents might be watching. My father, and the fathers of my friends, hid sexually explicit paperbacks in the top drawer of a dresser beneath a high pile of handkerchiefs. When a boy was lucky enough to find one of these treasures, he immediately shared it with his friends, like an early forager bringing back to camp a gazelle he had managed to kill. Sex excites, and only living forms engage in sex. Although I might be wildly wrong, perhaps my exploration of the moist organs of the squirrel lying on the floor of my bedroom brought me closer to understanding the mystery of women. François Jacob, a Nobel Laureate in biology, recalls his mother: "Tender, sweet perfume, warmth. Safe harbor from all fears and all violence . . . maman, who rocked me to sleep,

3

bathed me, wiped me, blew my nose, disciplined me, tucked me in, caressed me, scolded me, watched over me . . . maman . . . who, when I was a medical student and would get back late at night, always left a snack on the table with a note as tender as a kiss."[2]

A career in medicine, which promised economic security, status, and an understanding of human bodies, seemed the right choice. The imagined routines of this role, however, competed with a penetrating interest in human thought and, especially, the puzzling roots of prejudice. Rahway, New Jersey, a town twenty miles south of New York City, with a population of about twenty thousand in my childhood, had a relatively large working-class population and a small group of Jewish merchants, including my father. Like many Americans during the 1930s, some adolescent boys could be virulently anti-Semitic, hurling muted versions of Hitler's harsher rhetoric. I did not understand why I, who had white skin, broke no laws, did my homework, bullied no one, and lived in a modest home without ostentation, should have been selected as a target of hatred. What illogical ideas were tumbling around in the minds of those who disliked me without provocation? Could it be only the arbitrary symbolic category to which I belonged?

A second, quite different foundation for my curiosity about mind had a more internal origin. I was conscious of frequent feelings of uneasiness that today's clinicians would call generalized anxiety. The persona I displayed to others—a good school record, close friendships, and passable skill at touch football—did not rest on a firm foundation. It seemed that these thin outer layers would dissolve if challenged by my friends' more forceful personalities. John Widemann, an African-American writer who grew up in a poor black ghetto in Pittsburgh, combined great talent, a warm, encouraging family, nurturing teachers, and a little luck to become a respected writer and beloved professor. In his memoir, *Brothers and Keepers*, Widemann revealed that each morning when he awoke he feared that this would be the day others would discover that he was a fraud.[3] George F. Kennan, one of America's most influential diplomats, confessed to a similar unsureness, for he was shy, without athletic talent, and embarrassed because his family was less wealthy and his childhood experiences were less worldly than most of his friends in Princeton's Class of 1925.[4] My feelings were not as strong as those of Widemann or Kennan, but they lay on that continuum. I was a shy six-year-old who stuttered and occasionally woke with my sheets wet with urine — a fact that worried my mother, who was told by a pediatrician that I would outgrow it.

It is hard to ignore the uneasiness that pierces consciousness in the minutes between assignments, and I wondered why I felt this way. What crooked thoughts produced a gnawing doubt that none of my friends seemed to harbor. Adolescents who have these feelings today might be told that they were born with a temperamental bias. But the popular explanation in the 1940s was that parents were the unwitting villains. My mother was protective, emotionally labile, hypercritical of her husband, and effective at generating guilt. My father was bitter over his crippling arthritis and failure to make as much money as his younger brother and some of his friends. On occasion, his frustration could be ignited by a slightly critical comment from his wife. Thus, I attributed the uneasiness to a mother who restrained my independence, a father who could become unpredictably angry, and the jeers of my Christian peers. The desire to understand how these events came together, like the elements of a perfect storm, to create these tensions in a fourteen-year-old was as strong as was my interest in human bodies.

One more fact made psychology attractive. Despite a resentment of my mother's restrictiveness, I felt confident in her love for me, and I held a deep affection for her. She reminded me regularly that her father, whom I never knew, was always reading books, many concerned with human nature. I was told hundreds of times that, as a late adolescent returning home, my mother found her father dead of a heart attack, an open book on his chest. The mother whom I desperately wanted to please revered a man who loved to read books on human nature. If I were able to find out how the mind worked I would be carrying on his tradition and, perhaps, replacing him in my mother's eyes. George Kennan chose the Foreign Service because a close relative with the same name and birthday was a celebrated statesman who specialized in the politics of Russia. Kennan became a Russian specialist.

Because my interest in the mind was nourished by penetrating emotions, I was vulnerable when a professor teaching abnormal psychology asked me to walk with him across the Rutgers campus at the end of class. As we strolled he said, "You know, you would make a good psychologist," because of a comment I had made in class that afternoon. I have no memory of the comment, only his suggestion that, in his opinion, there was the possibility of my achiev-

5

ing a creative career in this profession. No stranger had ever told me that I might be an unusually skilled physician, chemist, lawyer, or astronomer. Most young people live with continual doubt. So when a stranger who has no reason to flatter offers a heady prediction of the future, a rational analysis of the accuracy of the prophecy is foolish. Relish it and run.

Most college seniors wondering about their future want a challenge that, with effort, they can meet. Humans enjoy the unique feeling that accompanies the successful exploitation of an uncommon competence. A successful neurosurgeon once told me that he chose this specialty because he felt he had "talented hands." I still feel a twinge of guilt over a comment I made more than twenty years ago: I told a dozen students training for a career in clinical psychology that although they believed their primary motive was to help those with mental problems, they would become bored in less than a year if they had a magic wand that cured every patient they touched. What they really wanted was to use their talents to alleviate distress. I interpreted their long silence as a sign that they were brooding about the reasons for their choice. John Stuart Mill had a similar epiphany in 1826 when he realized, with sadness, that he not would experience great joy if all of his wishes were suddenly granted.

Psychology was not especially attractive to many of my peers because its activities did not seem to require any special abilities that were not already in the repertoire of most college seniors. Recording the behavior of rats traversing a maze or of college students memorizing words did not tax one's intelligence excessively. The attractiveness of psychology lay in the hope that its discoveries would illuminate the human mind and, as a dividend, suggest ways to alleviate suffering. The first task used to belong to philosophers and novelists. Plato, Michel de Montaigne, and Immanuel Kant, as well as Fyodor Dostoyevsky, Eugene O'Neill, and Jean-Paul Sartre, believed that their sentences contained answers to perennial queries about the essence of human nature. I recall an afternoon when, as a thirteen-year-old, I had borrowed Dostoyevsky's *The Brothers Karamazov* from the town library and could not wait to get home to discover its insights. Far fewer of today's thirteen-year-olds believe that reading novels will reveal universal truths. The television programs *Nova* and *Nature* now serve that function because people have become persuaded that philosophers and writers brooding about life, self, and society in a quiet room are less likely than scientists to arrive at the correct answers. Young people who would have chosen philosophy had they been born in the seventeenth century were drawn to psychology in the twentieth.

If psychological research helped us understand why some children cannot learn to read and some become criminals, we might eventually prevent or cure these afflictions. Psychology was a moral enterprise, and many in my age group who selected this discipline did so because of this altruistic concern. I chose psychology, instead of biochemistry or the law, not only because I wanted to understand why I was easily intimidated and a target of prejudice but also to improve social conditions so that fewer people might experience the shame of school failure, the indignity of imprisonment, and the psychic pain of depression.

It may thus have been inevitable that, when forced to decide between graduate training in biochemistry at the University of Texas (I had learned of my acceptance in early April) and studying psychology at Yale, I chose psychology. Although I would probably have accepted Yale anyway, two improbable events contributed to the resolution. The first occurred one afternoon during a chemistry laboratory exercise in which we had to estimate the amount of barium sulfate in an analysis that in 1948 took about six hours. I had just turned in my estimate when a friend who was walking to the balance to weigh his tiny pile of white powder stumbled and the barium sulfate fell on the floor in a heap. In no mood to redo the work, he asked the other students to estimate the amount of barium sulfate in the pile. He computed an average of the guesses and turned that value in as his answer. I was troubled the following week when he received an A and I was given a B. I interpreted this injustice as a warning to avoid chemistry.

The second event was even less probable. I had borrowed the recently published book *Organization of Behavior*, by the McGill University psychologist Donald Hebb, from the town library.[5] This small public library should not have had Hebb's book on its shelves because it was highly technical and written for a professional audience. While reading Hebb, I received a letter from Frank A. Beach announcing that I had been accepted at Yale and that, if I came, I would be his research assistant. I turned to the bibliography of Hebb's book and saw with delight that the first page was full of references to Beach. The reasoning that followed was rapid and persuasive. Hebb appeared to be

7

a brilliant scientist; he thought that Beach was equally brilliant, and Beach wanted me to study with him. I suspect that my future was sealed in that moment. One afternoon in the summer of 2004, when my wife and I were visiting Lewis Lipsitt and his wife in Marion, Massachusetts, I learned that Lew—a distinguished psychologist at Brown University—had chosen psychology after hearing Hebb lecture at the University of Chicago the same month I was reading the *Organization of Behavior*. Psychology in New Haven, not biochemistry in Texas, was the direction that some invisible power had chosen as best suited to my uneven profile of qualities.

Yale Psychology

Psychology is the child of two quarreling parents, a fact that may account for its unsureness. The philosophical side of the family seeks to understand the qualities that are unique to humans, especially conscience, language, logic, inference, consciousness, and the symbolic categories that transform the products of perception into a version of reality no other animal could understand. This distinguished pedigree includes Plato, Montaigne, David Hume, Kant, John Locke, Charles Sanders Peirce, William James, and, more recently, Willard Van Orman Quine, Hilary Putnam, Stuart Hampshire, Richard Rorty, John Searle, and Daniel Dennett. The biological side of the family, with Charles Darwin as its eminent grandparent, searches for universal principles rooted in biology that might explain the psychological features unique to humans as well as those shared with animals.

The origins of American psychology are found in the historical resolution of two conflicting nineteenth-century interests: a concern with character and morality, on one hand, and an equally strong belief in pragmatism, technology, and a materialist explanation of behavior implied by the Darwinian thesis, on the other. These two ideas were incompatible at the end of the nineteenth century. How could anyone defend an idealistic description of humans as loyal, altruistic, cooperative, and spiritual and simultaneously accept the extreme individualism and pursuit of self-interest society demanded and biology rationalized? It took a little over a century for E. O. Wilson to try to resolve the dissonance by arguing, in *Sociobiology*, that human morality grew out of biology.[6] Humans were nurturant to kin because they shared some of the same genes, and they strove to perfect and to satisfy the self in order to attract the healthiest mates in the service of producing the most children. Although it is impossible to understand the premises and practices of the first psychologists without acknowledging the profound influence of evolutionary theory, it is also necessary to appreciate that, without industrialization, mass migration from small towns to urban centers made easier by rail travel, and an increasingly confident middle class wanting to be free of the restrictions of Christian ethics, Darwin's ideas would not have been adopted so quickly or eagerly.

The first academic psychologists, many working in German universities during the late nineteenth century, identified with the philosophical side of the family in their studies of human consciousness, perception, and memory. Then Ivan Pavlov, a physiologist working in Saint Petersburg at the turn of the twentieth century, expanded the vision by conditioning dogs to salivate to the sound of a metronome.[7] The conditioned reflex, Pavlov suggested, was the fundamental psychological unit in animals as well as humans—he even posited a freedom reflex. Conditioned reflexes were psychology's atoms. It usually takes about fifty years for a fruitful idea to penetrate a scientific discipline. The magnetic moment of hydrogen was discovered in 1941; half a century later hundreds of scientists were using fMRI scanners, which rely on this fact, to measure the brain. Conditioning became the central focus of psychological research about fifty years after Pavlov's discovery, and it was the central idea in Yale's department.

The history of the natural sciences reveals that dramatic progress often follows attempts to explain a highly reliable fact. Physics supplies a classic example. Early-twentieth-century scientists had discovered that each chemical element, when heated, released a distinct spectrum of light frequencies that was its unique signature. The attempts to explain this robust fact in the 1920s led to the first formulations of quantum mechanics. Classical and instrumental conditioning were equally firm observations, and attempts to explain them led, in time, to an appreciation of the importance of unexpected events, the receptivity of a species to a specific conditioned stimulus, and the brain circuits that were responsible for a select set of conditioned reactions.

Most, but not all, American faculty in psychology in 1950 were loyal to one of two traditions. Although both groups asked different questions, they held the same fundamental premise, not unlike the members of the fragmented Puritan sects in colonial New England. The politically dominant group, seeking universal truths, wanted to understand how animals and humans learned new habits. Rats, for example, were required to learn a new, usually simple, motor habit (for example, pressing a lever or making the correct turn at the intersection of a T-maze) to obtain food, get water, escape from electric shock, or have an opportunity for sex. College students had to memorize lists of words, often meaningless nonsense syllables, or improve their skill on a simple motor response. Hidden within the daily round of experiments was the hope that conditioned habits, like a mirror directed at mind, provided a faithful reflection of a person's history.

The second group wanted to understand why adults differed in intellectual abilities, capacity for anxiety and guilt, and vulnerability to schizophrenia, depression, and psychopathy; at Yale, this group consisted of faculty loyal to Freudian ideas. The two communities gathered different evidence and described their findings with distinctive vocabularies, but both chanted the catechism that change and variation in thought and behavior were due primarily to experience and they would remain unchanged until events altered them. Although there was tacit acceptance of the assumption that the products of experience were instantiated somewhere in the nervous system, the impossibility of measuring the brain made it easy to ignore its contribution. This perspective married Locke's insistence on the power of sensory events to Darwin's emphasis on adaptations but for the moment was indifferent to biology because European immigration to the United States had made arguments for a biological contribution to human variation politically incorrect. Essentially, these scientists, like diners at a smorgasbord, carefully selected from existing ideologies those beliefs that suited their intellectual and ethical appetites.

Frank Beach was the distinctive outsider in the Yale department, for he was skeptical of both the behaviorists and the Freudians. Beach was one of five psychologists (Norman Maier, T. C. Schneirla, David Krech, and Donald Hebb were the other four) mentored by Karl Lashley at the University of Chicago during the early 1930s who believed that mind/brain was a book and not a dictionary and should be described as sets of organized patterns rather than collections of associations.[8] This view is now a central tenet, but in 1950 Beach stood at the periphery watching the behaviorists trying to infer big principles from tiny facts.

The status hierarchy among the natural sciences resembles the relations among siblings, with later-borns envying the power and privileges of their older brothers and sisters. Physics is the beloved firstborn in the scientific academy; psychology is the envious toddler aping the eldest. Many psychologists would love to write equations with the power of Isaac Newton's terse statement that force is the product of mass and acceleration. Here was an equation with only three terms that applied to an asteroid striking the Earth, a boulder rolling down a mountain, and a tree falling on a house. Psychologists lusted for equally simple, rigorous, profound laws that explained the behavior of living things. Clark Hull, one of Yale's eminent psychologists, aspired to be the discipline's Newton and wrote the influential *Principles of Behavior* (1943), which posited laws with abstract terms like "habit strength" and "drive."[9] Unfortunately, Hull's laws did not distinguish among a rat running down an alley to turn right at an intersection, an adolescent learning to play soccer, and a music student trying to master the cello.

The anthropologist Geoffrey Gorer unabashedly wrote in 1955 that a unified theory of the social sciences could be summarized in twelve postulates. The second was: "Human behavior is predominately learned. Although the human infant may be born with some instincts and is born with some basic drives whose satisfaction is necessary to its survival, it is the treatment which the infant undergoes from the other members of the society into which it is born, and its experiences in its environment, which are of importance in molding adult behavior." The fifth and sixth postulates were consistent with this statement: "Habits are established by differential reward and punishment, chiefly meted out by other members of the society. . . . [T]he habits established early in the life of the individual influence all subsequent learning and, therefore, the experiences of early childhood are of predominant importance."[10]

This high-flying mood wafted through the halls of Yale's psychology department. At the same time, about 120 miles to the north, social scientists in Harvard's Department of Social Relations, especially Clyde Kluckhohn and Talcott Parsons, were equally optimistic, but their answers required broad concepts that promised to explain society and culture.[11] Kluckhohn's book

Mirror for Man (1949) was as ambitious as Hull's *Principles of Behavior,* but *Mirror for Man* gazed up at abstract symbolic meanings shared by thousands, whereas the *Principles of Behavior* stared down at the concreteness of a rat's paw striking a lever to obtain a pellet of food.

Most psychologists wanted their concepts to be imaginable because it is easier to persuade an audience of the validity of an interpretation if the audience can imagine the elements and the causal processes in which they participated. Associations between stimuli and responses resembled a network of connected roads or wires in a telephone exchange. On reflection, it seems bizarre that so many of us believed that all the complexities of human thought, feeling, and behavior could be explained with only one hypothetical entity—an acquired association between an event and a reaction. A dog could be taught to salivate to a tone; a child could learn to cry to a spider; a student could learn to divide fractions. Although salivation, crying, and dividing fractions were different responses, this variety was chaff. All one needed to know was that new links could be established if one arranged the right conditions. The construction of a mind was compared to a child with an Erector set assembling an infinitely large number of structures.

Psychologists begin their work with two incontrovertible facts: behaviors change with time, and at every age, there is psychological variation. American psychologists trying to explain these facts swore allegiance to two forms of continuity—a biological continuity between animals and humans and a psychological continuity between the infant and the adult. The biological view maintained that all animals relied on very similar processes when they learned new habits and exploited them in behavior. The hope that study of the white rat could reveal basic psychological processes that applied to all animals first surfaced in the 1890s and became dogma by 1950. Loyalty to this idea required a denial of the many examples of biological discontinuity in evolution. Respiration, for example, is accomplished with gills in fish but with lungs in mammals. More relevant is that, compared with apes and humans, laboratory rats and mice have no convolutions in their cortex, possess poor vision, and do not form social groups with a dominance hierarchy. These and many other dramatic differences imply that rats and humans might learn new habits in different ways.

The behaviorists also argued that behaviors that appeared to be instincts in mice, rats, and birds might be early origins of voluntary actions in primates and humans. Konrad Lorenz, who challenged the smoothness of the transition between species, insisted that the chirping of birds bore no relation to a child's speech and that nest building by a pregnant rat was not an early form of a human mother's nurture of her infant.[12] Lorenz's claim that responses that appeared to be "instinctive" were, in fact, reactions restricted to a species and released by very particular incentives threatened the Pavlovian model. Daniel Lehrman rescued the behaviorists from the German's skepticism in 1953 by demonstrating that experience was necessary for Lorenz's automatic instincts. Continuity across species had been saved, and the behaviorists could return to their laboratories assured that the mechanisms of learning were essentially similar in all species. This victory had political overtones, for Lorenz was regarded as sympathetic toward Nazi ideology. A challenge to his views was thus also a way to discredit Hitler and his storm troops.[13]

The commitment to a biological continuity across species, which is alive and well today, is revealed in an experiment in which human speech varying in rhythm and timbre—called prosody—was presented to rats. The rats, like children, could discriminate speech segments with different prosodic features. But surprisingly, the authors implied that the process involved was the same in both species.[14] The truth of this claim is not obvious. Children can tell the difference between the songs of a finch and a meadowlark, but it is not obvious that they use the same mechanisms as birds do to make this discrimination. Children who walked various distances between their homes and candy stores in their neighborhood could discriminate between distances of one hundred and three hundred yards. But honeybees, which can make the same discrimination, use a very different mechanism when they visit flowers at varying distances from the hive.

The problem is that similarity between two outcomes does not guarantee that the processes that mediate the behaviors are identical. Alan Turing argued that if an expert cannot tell the difference between the output of a computer and a person playing chess, it is reasonable to conclude that the "processes" are similar in machine and person.[15] Physicists are one source of this bold statement, for they argue that if two outcomes can be described with the same mathematics, they can be regarded as equivalent. The mathematics that describes the motion of water in a bowl is the same whether the bowl is rotated or the Earth rotates. But this rationale for equivalence is dangerous in the life sciences. The equivalence argument makes no sense in a moral context. If a child struggling in a lake dies, either because a bystander does nothing or because he tries to save the child and, in so doing, both he and the child drown, few would say that the two outcomes were equivalent in psychological terms. The deaths of a hundred thousand people following an earthquake, a flood, a flu epidemic, or war are not equivalent, either in the conditions that produced the deaths or in the psychological consequences for those in the community who survived.

The premise of psychological continuity asserts that every experience is stored somewhere in brain/mind and that every response or thought has its origin somewhere in the past. There are no breaks in the chain and no sudden discontinuities. Freud assumed that the delusions of a paranoid who thought he was Napoleon could be traced to his nursing experiences. Jean Piaget claimed that the knowledge that a ball cannot be in two places at the same time was a derivative of experiences twenty years earlier when an infant reached for a rattle. Perfectly respectable nineteenth-century psychologists wrote that adult greed could be seen in the infant's automatic grasping of a pencil placed on the palm. Only a hundred years ago, psychologists warned American parents to keep their infants away from the new art form of the movie because emotional reactions to the aggressive or romantic scenes portrayed on film could have a malevolent outcome decades later.

Psychological continuity is a pretty idea because it renders early forms useful. If the origins of adult enthusiasm or despair were in late childhood, the first years of life would appear to have no important purpose. The possibility that the products of early development could be temporary bothered those who believed that mothers must remain close to and vigilant with their infants. A faith in continuity has the added advantage of seeming mechanistic. It is easier to invent cause-and-effect sequences when a new phenomenon is preceded by one that makes a contribution to it than if a property emerges suddenly.

There is a third basis for the attractiveness of continuity from the first days of life to old age. A historical era is often marked by a dominating philosophical position that scholars are reluctant to confront—an intellectual electric fence. European philosophers, from the Renaissance to the nineteenth century, resisted inferences or deductions that contradicted the Bible. Although few social scientists today worry about the implications of their work for religious tenets, they are concerned with the implications of their ideas for the ethic of egalitarianism. Continuity in the growth of human properties is in closer accord with egalitarian principles because discontinuities imply maturational changes in the brain and, therefore, the need to award power to biology. A faith in continuous development both orients the investigator to the experiences that gradually establish new properties and suggests, but of course does not prove, that one could arrange similar growth-enhancing experiences for all children and as a result approach similar levels of dignity for all adults. The appeal of Jared Diamond's admirable book *Guns, Germs, and Steel* (1997) profits from this premise.[16] Diamond suggests that the primary reason that cultures in the Middle East developed tools, writing, and social institutions before societies in other regions rests with the ecology of the Fertile Crescent about ten thousand years ago, which made it easy to domesticate plants and animals—a stroke of good luck. The possibility that thousands of years of migration from Africa to the Fertile Crescent might have created a population with distinct values and perhaps a special biology that contributed to their early domestication of plants and animals is simply ignored. Diamond, like the behaviorists, gave the environment all the power.

My generation had also decided, with embarrassingly meager evidence, that social experiences were the primary causes of, and potential cures for, the habits, attitudes, and feelings that produced psychic distress. The origins of depression, academic failure, and criminality were stimulus-response units established over the years through encounters with family members, peers, and teachers.

The need for tidiness—scientists use the word "parsimony"—allowed the behaviorists to ignore other conditions that induced psychological change. They blithely denied that animals and humans acquire new actions simply by watching others. The plethora of television shows devoted to cooking and home improvement is sufficient proof of this claim. The behaviorists were also indifferent to the changes demanded by environmental disasters, such as earthquakes and floods. And they dogmatically refused to acknowledge the power of thought. An adolescent boy's happy mood is altered when he learns that his father was imprisoned years earlier for armed robbery. Arthur

Miller exploited this phenomenon when he had Biff discover his father with a prostitute in *Death of a Salesman*. But perhaps the most egregious error was a reluctance to award the brain any place in the explanations of human differences in talents or adaptation. To do so required acknowledging that some variation might not be reparable with experience. Recognition of that possibility diminished the autonomy of the young discipline we had chosen to nurture and prevented us from appreciating that most behaviors can be likened to a piece of homogeneously gray cloth woven from the thin black threads of biology and the equally thin white threads of experience.

The exclusion of biology can be traced to John Locke's declaration that all minds are essentially alike at birth and that later variation is due to what children heard and saw and which habits were praised and punished. Locke's position was attractive because a growing proportion of eighteenth-century Britons desired a more egalitarian society in which neither religion nor family pedigree was a basis for legitimacy. The newly ascendant middle class wished to challenge the notion that princes and priests were inherently more virtuous than paupers. Legitimate power should belong to those who exploited their experiences intelligently.

This meritocratic ideal became the foundation of American behaviorism two centuries later. John Watson, a psychologist at the Johns Hopkins University in the 1920s, effectively disseminated Pavlov's discovery because many Americans with liberal views looked to science to quiet a strident eugenics movement that was pressing for the sterilization of the retarded and laws restricting foreign immigration and the further "tainting" of the pure Mayflower pedigree.[17] A resolution of this political crisis required an unquestioned faith that human talents and character were learned and were independent of the biology children inherited. The chant among most social scientists in the 1920s was that humans, unlike animals, had no instincts. One dogmatic behaviorist even denied that sexuality had a foundation in biology. The postures of lovemaking were learned, and an infatuation was no different in fundamental mechanism from the excitement experienced during a baseball game. The behaviorists were loyal to the credo of the biologists in their search for universals, but they had thrown out the biology.

With vaulting ambitions the behaviorists felt justified in applying their ideas to classrooms, families, autistic children, and adults fearful of flying because they were certain that they possessed a principle that could explain almost every psychological phenomenon. This confidence created an evangelical mood among the graduate students. The faculty created the illusion that our small band of talented students who had the good fortune of studying in the most enlightened department had an obligation to move psychology forward. Beach gave a final examination during my first year that consisted of reading several current issues of the *Journal of Comparative and Physiological Psychology* and criticizing some of the papers. My initial feeling was despair. How could a first-year graduate student find serious defects in papers that had passed professional judgment? But when I quieted my fear and began the assignment, I was alternately delighted and appalled by how easy the assignment was to complete. The message Beach intended had been assimilated.

The behaviorists never assumed that the infant mind was a "blank slate."[18] They acknowledged that every child was born with a set of reflexes and sensory capacities. All infants had the ability to sneeze, suck, babble, smile, reach, feel pain, taste food, see objects, and hear sound. But experiences could manipulate those inherited elements to create almost any skill, attitude, or emotion desired. The clever manipulation of events could shape the instructions genes had written and, like ancient alchemists, turn lead into gold.

The ambience of confidence intimidated some of the students training to be clinical psychologists who had little interest in animals and conditioning. Many, however, felt that they had to prove to the faculty, and to themselves, that they were authentic scientists by conducting an experiment with rats that demonstrated a form of learning. This work was an initiation rite allowing entrance into a sacred club. The relation of brain function to behavior holds a similar position of centrality in contemporary psychology, and some students feel obligated to conduct a study that requires the use of a brain-scanning machine. One graduate student whose parents had not attended college announced that his thesis would involve the measurement of brain activity. I told him this was not a good idea because he knew little about the brain and even less about the electronics of the apparatus he would have to use. After acknowledging both weaknesses, he confessed that he had to work on a problem that would "transcend his childhood background." Neuroscience was High Church, and studying the brain was a required ritual for anyone who wished to be ordained into a holy order.

Some of the Impressionists assumed an attitude of superiority toward their peers by linking their new painting technique with science. Discoveries in the physiology of vision had suggested rational rules that, if followed, would produce canvases that had unique perceptual effects on viewers. Georges Seurat and Vincent Van Gogh felt "intellectually ahead" of the unsophisticated Parisian artists who were unaware of these scientific advances. One reason why the composer Arnold Schoenberg, who had read about biological evolution, invented the twelve-tone scale was his desire to enhance the public's aesthetic sense by exposing them to a new form of music. Some philosophers legitimate their claims about mind by citing the evidence of cognitive psychologists; some cognitive psychologists seek legitimacy in the discoveries of the neuroscientists; some neuroscientists look for support in the research of molecular biologists; some molecular biologists explain the electrical activity of neurons with the concepts of the physicists; and all stand gazing in awe at the mathematicians, who, staring straight ahead, worry occasionally about the shaky foundations of their elegant equations. The members of each scientific discipline, like children trying to join a more powerful group, seek to persuade others by announcing who their friends are.

A Pair of Premises

Two related assumptions penetrated the research on learning. First, any result found with any group of animals probably had a generality that went beyond the species observed, actions taught, and rewarding events administered. Inferences based on rats learning a maze to obtain food had implications for children learning to read. With few exceptions, the biology of the learner was irrelevant because of the presumed biological continuity between animals and humans. This assumption remains vital today, although there is a keener appreciation that species inherit different sets of biologically prepared properties. A few lone voices insisted that studies of humans required some knowledge of their prior history to predict whether, and what, each would learn. But most psychologists did not want to hear this skeptical restriction on their ambitions. I assure readers who find this description exaggerated that my friends and I were certain of the power of conditioning to create almost any desired outcome. We even believed that a mother who was cold and aloof could create the symptoms of autism in her child. If one wishes to believe, it takes precious little to produce a commitment.

A second, more important issue centered on the meaning of the term "reward," or reinforcement, and why rewarding events (food, praise, sex, or escape from punishment) had the mysterious power to establish new associations and sustain an action that delivered the event, if even for a limited time. A resolution of this question was important because explanation is the goal of inquiry. Darwin, not Robert Chambers, is praised because he supplied the mechanism of natural selection to explain evolution. The idea that no one would do anything unless they were rewarded went unchallenged, even though it did not match daily experience. Anyone can learn the name of a new neighbor simply by being told this information. Nothing else happens! No reward is administered, yet the listener might remember the name for years. The assumption that an animal will not establish a new association unless it receives something material for behaving (notice the hidden value judgment) shares a feature with Isaac Newton's principle that all objects remain at rest until a force is imposed. Why would an animal or child do anything unless it received something for the effort? I recall an afternoon when Neal Miller, one of America's most respected psychologists, began his graduate seminar by confessing that he did not understand why his three-year-old son had turned on the garden hose the previous day. Miller seemed genuinely puzzled by his inability to imagine what the reward for that action might have been because he was not ready to acknowledge that at least three very different types of events can function as rewards. The most obvious class refers to events that satisfy biological needs or are universally pleasant because of their sensory foundation, like food when hungry, water when thirsty, and sweet tastes and sexual release. This class also includes the termination of an aversive state. Although these events have a biological foundation, they do not rest on the same brain state.

The second class is defined functionally as any event that can establish an association and sustain behaviors aimed at obtaining the event. Stated simply, a reward is anything an animal is willing to work to attain. Unexpected events

that are not aversive are one member of this class. The consequences of turn-
ing on a hose belong to this category. That is why monkeys in a boring cage
will work to see some interesting things in the world outside the cage.

The third class, which applies only to humans, refers to experiences that
are desired because they are symbolic of an enhanced conception of self.
Some energetic souls fly a thousand miles to climb a snow-covered mountain in subfreezing temperatures; others travel as far to watch a blood-red
sunset over a tropical beach. Notice that an event belonging to one of these
categories need not belong to the other two. The taste of chocolate cake is
inherently pleasant, but dieters avoid this delightful experience. Unexpected
events are sought if they can be understood but avoided if they generate a
level of uncertainty that can not be coped with effectively. Working eighteen
hours a day, seven days a week, to accumulate money or power fits neither
of the first two definitions of reward. The pleasures derived from these rewards have a unique feature, for they require a comparison with an alternative, prior, or ideal state of affairs. I recall a walk along a beach on Vineyard
Sound with a chilly breeze on my left and a hot sun on my right. My judgment that this stroll was pleasant required knowing that the temperature in
Boston that afternoon was 95 degrees and the humidity 75 percent. If the sensations from the breeze, sun, rotting seaweed, and old bottles on the beach
were the only information available, I would have no way of knowing if the
walk had been pleasant. Pleasure, as every ancient philosopher understood,
is not a unitary phenomenon psychologically or biologically.

Mitchell Berkun, a fellow graduate student, and I, who assumed the second definition of reward, felt much too smug after we taught rats to strike
a lever so that they could enter a steel wheel where they could run until
fatigued. We concluded that running must be a reward and failed to consider the possibility that our rats were no different from dogs running through
meadows, hawks soaring through the sky, and fish swimming in lakes. The
biology of these animals permitted them to engage in these behaviors. Birds
fly because they can fly. Nonetheless, the puritanically pragmatic conviction
that all effort must be rewarded if it is to produce new knowledge and that
no one in their right mind would do anything unless he or she got something
for it—a version of the contemporary view that all animals are self-interested
because of a biological urge for inclusive fitness—seemed to us irrefutable.

Although scientists still rely on the concept of reward, the belief that a change in stimulation—external or internal—can function as a reward has become accepted. A fundamental principle governing the brain is that neurons respond to change. Changes in illumination or motion automatically activate circuits and provoke attention to the site of change, for that is where information is likely to reside. A reward, therefore, does not have to be something the animal needs, such as food, water, a mate, or relief from pain. Essentially, many events called "rewards" are punctuation marks that, like a white streak in a blue sky, interrupt the stream of experience and, through activation of many brain structures, facilitate the establishment of associations. This is why we remember rare events and movies with unusual photographic effects for the longest time.

It will come as no surprise that a few psychologists, bothered by the functional definition of reward, argued that the definition was circular. Investigators insisted that a reward had to be present if an animal learned a new response, even if they could not specify what it was. If a two-year-old girl alone in her crib talked to herself each night, there had to be reward for her private chatter. Neal Miller recognized this problem and appreciated the utility of Karl Popper's declaration in *Conjectures and Refutations* that the elimination of a bad idea is one route to scientific progress.[19] In an attempt to specify the features of a reward in absolute terms, he borrowed a Freudian notion and declared that all "rewards" had the essential property of reducing the total amount of stimulation an animal experienced. When a visiting student from England asked Miller why he stubbornly defended this single-minded and counterintuitive definition, his reply, spoken in a classic Washington twang, was, "There is only one thing you find in the middle of the road." He did not add, but the students understood, that he meant horse manure. Although no one was sure how to measure "the total amount of stimulation" in most circumstances, this idea could be tested under special conditions.

Fred Sheffield, who had trained with Edwin Guthrie at the University of Washington in Seattle, was the rebel in the department. Guthrie, who did accommodate to human experience, asserted that two events could become associated if they simply occurred close in time. No reward or reduced stimulation was necessary. Guthrie used the phrase "contiguity theory" for this rule. Sheffield's views created a theoretical tension, and any experiment that could evaluate the differential validity of the two positions would be celebrated.

I chose this controversy for my dissertation in the fall of 1953. I had learned about rat sexual behavior from my apprenticeship with Beach and knew that when male rats copulate their penis does not remain in the vaginal canal until an ejaculation occurs. Rather, the male penetrates the female, is reflexively thrown off, waits ten or fifteen seconds, mounts the female again, and, after six or seven repetitions of this sequence, finally ejaculates—an uncommon practice in most mammals. This fact of nature provided a perfect opportunity to test the opposing views of Sheffield and Miller.

It was obvious that a male rat was at a higher, rather than a lower, level of stimulation after his first few penetrations of the female. If Miller was right, no rat should learn to make the correct turn in a maze in order to contact a female receptive for sexual activity if the reward for this effortful response was increased stimulation. My private expectation was that the rat would learn to make the correct turn. Every adolescent girl knows that the longer she puts off her hyper-aroused boyfriend, the more insistent will be his pursuit. And that is what happened. The male rats that were permitted only one or two penetrations and were then separated from the female, or animals that could only mount the female and were denied a penetration, quickly learned where the female was resting. Sheffield had been validated. Nature does not like playing favorites, however, and there was a thread of support for Miller. Across the successive days of testing, the frustrated males waited longer before they made their first approach to the female. Thus, the arousal created by the penetration or the mounting had aversive properties, as Miller would have predicted. Although learning the correct turn in the maze required contiguity between the stimulus features at the choice point in the maze and the salient experience of the brief penetration, the response of approaching the receptive female, which was biologically prepared, could be inhibited to some degree. Boys eventually do stop pursuing girls who never say yes.

The apprenticeship with Frank Beach had its humorous moments. One event remains a flashbulb memory. My first assignment as his research assistant was to find out whether male dogs that had no internal source of male hormone—their testes and adrenal glands had been removed—were capable of an erection. The consensual assumption in 1950 was that an erection was impossible without the presence of male sex hormone. My task, which seemed to be an example of elegant science then, but strikes me as a bit odd today, was to descend to the basement, where the dogs were housed, at the end of the work day, usually after dinner, masturbate the group of male dogs, and measure the diameter of their penile bulb—a structure at the base of the penis that expands with arousal to keep the male locked to the female. I accepted this task, performed the proper fingering of the dogs, and made the measurements with a caliper. To Beach's surprise, all the dogs had erections. I found it disconcerting that after several days of servicing these animals they would bark when they heard my footsteps on the stairs. They were excited by the imminent arrival of their generous friend.

I gave Beach the measurements and forgot about this experience. Twenty years later (I was now at Harvard), Beach telephoned. I remarked that it was good to talk with him, for we had not been in contact for many years. And then, out of the clear blue sky, he asked, "How is your publication list?" I knew at once that he was referring to the dogs, and I replied, with some force, "I do not want to be associated with that work." He told me that he had finally looked at the data, was preparing a paper for a journal, and wanted to know whether I could remember the degree of tumescence the dogs displayed. I replied that I had absolutely no memory and could not help. He pursued the issue by suggesting that he send me photographs of dog penises in different degrees of tumescence to help me answer his question. I insisted that my memory of those evenings had faded and added that if he did submit the paper for publication, I did not want my name listed as an author. He agreed but added, with a laugh, that he might include a footnote that read, "The author thanks Jerome Kagan for his handi-work."

The Inevitable Collapse

The walls of this beautiful palace of behaviorism began to collapse within a decade. The mind can tolerate some inconsistency between its beliefs and the facts. Humans must hold an unquestioned faith in some assumptions, for living as well as for doing science. Each person must commit to a few core premises because there are too many alternatives after morning coffee. Should I garden, go to work, return to sleep, play chess, visit a friend, or talk of Michelangelo. The Swedish novelist Pär Lagerkvist had God reply to a spirit who asked what his purpose was in creating humans: "I only intended humans would never be satisfied with nothing."[20]

Ethical premises serve this function in daily life; theoretical assumptions do so in science. Fortunately, evolution awarded our species a unique talent. We are troubled by semantic or logical inconsistency between what we believe and what we observe (or what others tell us they have observed). We can tolerate a little inconsistency, but an ideology can quickly turn sour when the ugly facts begin to accumulate. That is what happened to the elegant structure of behaviorism, for new evidence had made it vulnerable to attack. An advantage of defending a firm intellectual position is that it motivates a critique that results in a novel perspective. Noam Chomsky, the American linguist, and Jean Piaget, the Swiss epistemologist, with a host of other scholars, gained celebrity by announcing that the emperor had no clothes.[21] Chomsky reminded psychologists of facts that every parent knew. All three-year-olds speak new sentences every day. This should not be possible if the sentences had never been heard and, therefore, had not been rewarded. Piaget's ideas, which had been made comprehensible to American audiences by John Flavell, also required new conceptions.[22] A two-year-old picks up a doll and feeds it imaginary milk with an imaginary bottle. This action, which the child had never seen performed, had to originate in a mind that was continually, and spontaneously, rearranging and creating new mental units without any obvious reward.

One unrecognized mistake in the behaviorists' scheme was the failure to appreciate that there is not always a deterministic relation between a conditioned stimulus and a conditioned response. They thought of this relation as resembling the shattering of a glass that had fallen from a table to the floor. But life systems work differently. Every person infected with flu viruses does not develop a sore throat because the immune system can intervene to prevent the usual symptoms of the flu. A fundamental principle of brain function is that excitatory and inhibitory systems are balanced. If I secrete too much cortisol because of overwork, my brain tells my body to slow cortisol production. The popular nineteenth-century concept of will, now part of the mind's executive functions, was the controller in the tower selecting the actions appropriate for the setting. A boy who has hurt himself and suppresses a cry illustrates the power of "will." We shall see in chapter 6 the dissociation that can occur between bubbly social behavior and a piercing inner tension. Put plainly, living forms are not two-layered systems.

One discovery contributed in a major way to the rejection of orthodox behaviorism. Behaviorists had assumed that any event could be a conditioned stimulus for any reaction. If some events had special salience for a particular species, the animal's biology could trump the power of environmental arrangements and master planning would be impossible. John Garcia performed the execution by showing that rats could not learn an association between a light and a subsequent feeling of illness but that they easily learned an association between a distinct taste and the subsequent, unpleasant sensations.[23] The implication was clear. One could not teach any response to any animal because each animal had biological preferences that, in some cases, could not be abrogated. It would be easy to condition sexual arousal to the perfume worn by a romantic partner, as every manufacturer knows, but probably impossible to do so to the color of the pillow on which the lovers reclined or the sound of the air conditioner in the room. One team of psychologists conditioned a pig to pick up small objects with its mouth and drop them into a bucket. After performing this conditioned response for a few weeks, however, the animal suddenly reverted to its usual practice of burying the small objects. Its biology could not be suppressed indefinitely.[24] Children compare their qualities with those of peers and siblings. It is probably impossible to arrange an environment that would prevent these thoughts from developing. Conditioning is powerful, but its power is limited. The crisp, beautiful assumptions of Pavlov, Miller, and the behaviorists had been wounded, though not fatally, by irrefutable facts, as Ptolemy's argument that the Sun orbited the Earth succumbed to the observations of Galileo Galilei and Tycho Brahe and the brilliant equations of Johannes Kepler and Isaac Newton.

Freud

Psychoanalytic theory, which enjoyed a broad-based popularity in the United States from about 1910 to the late 1960s because it celebrated the power of experience, also came under attack. Sigmund Freud's ideas seemed intuitively correct to large numbers of psychiatrists, psychologists, and citizens, especially in the United States, during the years between the two world wars because history had tweaked the balance between the mental and the biological. Humans have always been, and will always be, vulnerable to bouts of fatigue, apathy, depression, worry, tension, insomnia, and irritability. These complaints have strikingly different causes, including illness, strenuous work, uncertainty over money, job security, health, the loss of a loved one, rejection by a friend, or anxiety, shame, or guilt over desires or acts that violated a personal ethic. The unpleasant feelings are universal because humans anticipate future calamities, wonder what others are thinking about them, and cannot avoid succumbing to some illegitimate temptations. The individual tries to understand the reason for the unpleasant feeling; the local culture supplies the favored interpretations. The most popular interpretations derive their appeal, in part, from nodes of uncertainty in the community, ideas borrowed from other disciplines, or new inventions.

The industrialization of the nineteenth century transformed rural America. Young adults were emigrating from villages to cities, where the accelerating pace of life was accompanied by crime, diminished status, and some guilt over the need to be more competitive and less honest than one wished to be. It is relevant that industrialization, which required energy derived from wood, coal, and kerosene, made everyone more conscious of the concept of energy. When one of the recently discovered laws of thermodynamics stated that all energy was conserved, it was inevitable that someone would apply this scientific principle to human behavior. A neurologist named Charles Beard suggested that each brain, like a saucepan of warm water, possessed a fixed amount of energy, and symptoms would appear if this resource were depleted.[25] Beard invented the word "neurasthenia" in 1869 to describe adults who experienced fatigue, tension, depression, or insomnia because their nervous systems had run out of energy. Lenin was suffering from headaches, insomnia, and fatigue in 1903 and received this diagnosis from a physician who told him he was working too hard.

Neurology was a new medical specialty whose members charged higher fees than most doctors. As a result, wealthier citizens, who more often worked with their minds rather than their muscles, were the most frequent patients in the waiting rooms of this new category of doctor. Beard's diagnosis was flattering, for it implied that the symptoms were a sign of high intelligence and the investment of energy in difficult mental work. A less flattering diagnosis of insanity was given to less well educated, working-class patients whose symptoms were usually criminality, delusions, alcoholism, hallucinations, and severe depression. These pathologies were believed to be the result of constitutional defects rather than excessive mental activity.

Freud brought three original ideas to this historical moment.[26] The first was that early family experiences that frustrated the biological urges for the pleasures of eating, defecation, and genital stimulation, rather than an inherited constitution or conditioned habits, created unconscious states that could influence the later development of personality and neurotic symptoms. The second idea was that too much or too little sexual pleasure was harmful. Many Americans believed that frequent masturbation could lead to insanity. The availability of inexpensive condoms, moreover, made premarital sex less risky, and as a result, women could lower their guard and consider the delights of romance with a relatively new acquaintance. However, they remained vulnerable to anxiety, shame, or guilt for a permissive eroticism.

Sexual frustration could also bring on mental disturbance because some sexual pleasure was required for good health. The ancient notion that the symptoms of female hysteria—extreme anxiety, temporary paralysis, panic attacks—could be caused by sexual frustration remained popular, and physicians were massaging the genitals of their female patients with battery-powered vibrators, or their fingers, until the hapless women had therapeutic orgasms in the doctor's office. Although Galen had used the same therapeutic intervention seventeen centuries earlier, today's doctors would lose their licenses if they chose this form of therapy. Freud's third original suggestion was to replace this and other physical practices with free-associating to a therapist because rescuing anxious ideas from their home in the unconscious and rendering them conscious released the energy that had been used to repress them.

Freud's ideas seemed reasonable to some because he changed the secondary, rather than the primary, features of existing nineteenth-century assumptions. He accepted the belief that each person inherited a fixed amount of energy, which he called libido, but attributed the depletion of energy to the repression of sexual impulses rather than to excessive thought. Freud also acknowledged his society's belief in the importance of early experience, but he made punishment of sexual interest, rather than of lying, disobedience, or incivility, the cause of symptoms. This move shifted the blame from the patients to their parents and supplied an interpretation that was as flattering to the patients as Beard's explanation that an insomniac was thinking too much. The popular explanation of extreme anxiety in a married woman was that she was born with a constitutional flaw that prevented her from regular sexual satisfaction. Many physicians also suspected that, in some cases, the husband was insufficiently sensitive to his wife's erotic needs. These interpretations attributed flaws to the wife, the husband, or both partners. Freud removed the stigma from the couple by blaming the symptoms on the unintentional errors of child-rearing by the wife's parents.

Finally, the suggestion to replace the therapeutic interventions of cold baths, herbs, and electrical stimulation with confessions to a therapist fell on friendly ears because many physicians had become convinced that longer conversations with patients had benevolent effects. The claim that each mind has a limited amount of libidinal energy, family experiences that cause repression of sexual motives lead to symptoms, and confession of the products of introspective analysis alleviates angst were transformations of late-nineteenth-century thought. All three ideas were imaginable and just discrepant enough to be arousing.

Freud's declaration that panic attacks, hysterical paralysis of the legs, and compulsive hand washing were due to repression of sexual thoughts, however, lost some validity after World War II when sexuality became more acceptable and, for some, a domain for achievement. Although the intensity of anxiety or guilt over sexual behavior had become diluted, the frequency of neurotic symptoms had not changed. Attributing the insomnia and nightmares of a Vietnam veteran who had slept with many partners to repression of sexuality became a ludicrous idea.

No one has offered a satisfactory explanation of why so many educated Americans and Europeans during the period 1910–1960 were convinced of the essential truth of Freud's assertions. I confess to being a member of this relatively gullible group as a starry-eyed student in 1950. One part of the answer must involve the chronic uncertainty that hovered over sexuality during that half-century. Desire had been allowed freer access to imagery but not to actions; hence, it seemed reasonable to guess that feelings of tension, which in fact were generated by the many uncertainties of daily life, were due primarily to the restraints imposed on making love whenever one wished. Essentially, Freud's followers thought it reasonable to attribute all uncertainty to sexual restraint.

The dissolution of the barrier between fear and anxiety and the classification of anxiety as a state of "illness" are also relevant. Fear assumed prominence in Christian Europe during the medieval centuries because of the preoccupation with God's wrath. Augustine regarded fear of divine punishment as a blessing because it helped humans behave morally, and John Bunyan, writing almost a thousand years later, reasserted the belief that fear of God permitted one to love the Deity. The contemporary view, thanks to Freud, maintains that fear and anxiety restrict the capacity to love. By arguing that anxiety was not a necessary emotion and could be reduced by emptying one's unconscious of its repressed wishes, Freud implied that everyone could rid themselves of this enemy of happiness.

If life's assignment is to control hedonistic desires, anxiety is an ally and not an alien force. But anxiety is the enemy if one is supposed to gain friends, seduce lovers, and take risks for gains in status and money. If humans are to restrain greed, lust, competitiveness, and aggression, self-control is a prerequisite. But if these are the goals to gain the willful control of self through anticipated anxiety is an impediment. Thus history relegated "will" to the same ash heap of ideas where Newton's ether lies gathering dust. The notion that humans can and should be free of anxiety is one of the distinguishing illusions in Western thought over the past century and one reason why American psychiatrists consider intense anxiety a mental disorder but not intense competitiveness, sexual arousal, or desire for higher status.

I also suspect that the American eroticization of personal freedom awards authority to the argument that liberating the wishes imprisoned in the unconscious would bring health and vitality. A popular psychology textbook published in 1930 declared that the primary goal of development was to emancipate each child from the restrictions imposed by the family. Freudian ideas benefited from the semantic link between the motto on the New Hampshire license plate, "Live free or die," and the rescue of desire from its imprisonment in the unconscious. Freud actually wrote that psychoanalysis "sets the neurotic free from the chains of his sexuality." Freud was acutely aware of his minority status as a Jew in Austrian society and must have hoped that he, too, could be freed from the chains of prejudice that required him to be continually vigilant. He asked Carl Jung to be the first president of the International Psychoanalytic Society, hoping this move would make analytic theory more attractive to a large number of non-Jewish professionals.

Freud's image of mind was as mechanical as that of the behaviorist. He described thoughts and feelings as if they were electrically charged particles that, if diverted from their "natural" target, would be converted into a bodily symptom. This prose made it easier to imagine how a feeling of tension could be transformed into a blinking tic. The explanation shared the concreteness of behaviorists who wrote that the tic was a conditioned response. Behaviorists friendly to Freud suggested that the conditioned stimulus for a blinking tic could have been the sight of a violent or sexual scene that evoked a reflex blink.

One reason that psychoanalytic ideas were less popular among Europeans than Americans when first introduced was that Europe placed greater value on the harmony of the community than on the primacy of the individual. Hence, Europeans were willing to accept some restrictions on personal freedom if the restraint strengthened the social matrix. London, Paris, and Florence were vibrant cities with significant institutions centuries before New York, Boston, and Chicago had paved streets. It is also relevant that European suffering during centuries of bloody wars initiated by men with an exaggerated sense of self had made citizens more skeptical of the assumption that celebration of the unfettered individual was a good idea. Psychoanalytic theory had minimal appeal to physicians or citizens in India, Japan, or China because their attitudes toward sexuality were more permissive, and they, too, believed that freeing each person from his or her obligations to others was not an ideal to pursue. Like John Locke in the eighteenth century, and Karl Marx in the nineteenth, the appeal of Freud's ideas profited from the historical context in which they were introduced. Thus, the attractiveness of the two "theories" that dominated the American conception of human behavior during the first half of the twentieth century was based, in part, on their being pinned to the coattails of deeply held political premises and superficial resemblance to simple physical models of mind mistakenly classified as truths about nature. The credibility of current sociobiological explanations of some psychiatric disorders is helped by a political pressure to rationalize the symptoms as biologically adaptive at other times and in other places so that the poor and uneducated, who more often suffer such symptoms, will be relieved of some blame for their condition and can find relief in new pills rather than in new social arrangements.

Too Much Abstraction

A serious problem with the concepts of behaviorism and psychoanalysis was their extraordinary generality. The terms "drive," "learning," and "reward" (the three legs of the stool that held the structure of behaviorism steady) rarely specified whether the agent was a rat learning to turn right in a T-maze or an adult trying to master the calculus. I remember reading a long theoretical paper on learning in a premier journal in which the author never thought it necessary to mention the animal species observed. This indifference to detail remains strong today. The first sentence in the abstract of a paper published in the December 2004 issue of *Behavioral Neuroscience*—a journal that enjoys high respect—stated: "A learning event can be dissociated into three components: acquisition, storage, and recall."[27] There is no specification of the class of animal, the structure being learned, stored, and recalled, or the method used to measure these events. Freud, too, did not think it worthwhile to distinguish between the libidinal arousal of a nursing infant and a college senior leafing through *Playboy* magazine. A physician writing about illness who did not specify whether the affliction was cancer, arthritis, or diabetes in a mouse, dog, or human would be a target of biting satire. It would be impossible to understand the intended meanings of individuals who spoke only verbs— "lick," "run," "protect," "bite," "taste," "choose," or "give"—and never named the actors or the targets of their actions. Some readers may be surprised to learn that the word "attachment," which was invented by the English psychiatrist John Bowlby to explain why human infants cried when their mother was absent, has been used to explain why rat pups explore a space suffused with a particular odor. This practice assumes that theoretical terms intended for a restricted set of events can, like the joker in a deck of cards, be borrowed and applied to very different phenomena.

This permissive semantic stance attracts scientists who hold strong a priori beliefs, often ethical in content, about the best society, optimal parent-child relationships, and the goals humans should pursue. The concept "positive affect," for example, is popular among psychologists even though erotic scenes, food, and money create distinctly different brain and psychological states and a few adolescents enjoy torturing animals or setting fires. The argument that these five experiences belong to the same natural category strains the bounds of reasonableness. The developmental psychologist Lawrence Kohlberg had decided that the construction of a coherent, semantically consistent set of values that could be defended with a verbal argument represented the "highest stage of morality" and used the answers of children and adolescents to moral dilemmas to defend this position.[28] Because ten-year-olds are not cognitively mature enough to create logically tight arguments, the evidence supported his beliefs. Jean Piaget had decided that the ability to reason correctly about hypothetical events represented the "highest stage of intellectual development" and administered problems to children of different ages to support this bias. Freud used patients' verbal descriptions of their life histories to defend his belief that failure to resolve the oedipal conflict was followed by the development of neurotic symptoms. All three understood that they needed evidence to persuade others of the correctness of the assumptions they had already decided were true. None attempted to refute their intuitions.

Discovery followed by proof of a possible explanation are the yin and yang of science. Ideas that originated in robust evidence usually have a longer life than those arising from thought alone. Charles Darwin had no idea what he would see on the voyage of HMS Beagle; Santiago Ramón y Cajal did not know what shapes would appear under the lens of his microscope; and Edwin Powell Hubble could not anticipate what images would develop on the pictures taken while peering through a telescope at the night sky. The unexpected observations of these scientists led to creative ideas that proved to have a thick thread of validity. Physicists come in two colors. One group tries to find a mathematics that will explain a set of reliable observations. The second group attempts first to imagine the physical events behind the observation. Werner Heisenberg belongs to the first group, Paul Ehrenfest to the second. Psychologists can be assigned to comparable groups. Some try to model, logically or mathematically, the mechanisms behind the learning of associations. A larger group broods on the psychological and biological processes that occur when an association is formed.

The history of all the sciences suggests that the collection of evidence in the service of proving a conjecture is most useful when the synthetic notion originates in prior, trustworthy observations. This strategy can be dangerous in immature sciences, like psychology, that have a meager store of reliable facts. Bruce Alberts, a biologist and a past president of the National Academy of Sciences, wrote that his doctoral research on chromosomes, conceived in a priori mode, failed to find the desired result. As a result, his faculty committee did not approve his thesis. Later, following soul searching, Alberts decided that it was a better strategy to develop a reliable method first and then use it in experiments—a decision that turned out to be wise.

Michel de Montaigne did not discover that moderation was the optimal way to conduct a life; Blaise Pascal did not discover that God existed; Immanuel Kant did not discover that individuals should obey any imperative they want everyone else to follow. These philosophers first decided that these ideas were true and then constructed coherent semantic arguments to support their positions. Investigators who work in a "proving" frame, compared with those who operate in a "discovery" frame, are tempted to use abstract words that maximize the generalizability of their favored construct. The behaviorists wanted to prove that animals and humans learned new associations when a reward followed an action. The headiness of this notion would have been diluted if they had been asked to specify the species, the response, and the reward. The beauty of their theory would have been tarnished if they had been required to list all the exceptions to this principle. Kant would not be celebrated if he had written that the categorical imperative applied to murder but not to stealing. Fewer students would be assigned Montaigne's essays if he had suggested that the doctrine of moderation applied to the drinking of alcohol but not to sexual activity.

I confess to being guilty of this error early in my career. I, too, was certain of the truth of some ideas when I left New Haven to take a faculty position at Ohio State University. I was irrationally opposed to awarding biology any significant influence on development and was convinced that the behaviors, beliefs, and emotions established early in life would persist unless there were consistent attempts to change them. The only premise that turned out to be somewhat more fruitful was the belief that the variation in behavior, mood, and belief among children was caused primarily by the private constructions children created from parental treatments and peer experiences. These symbolic representations, rather than the events as recorded on film, were the effective monitors of development. This notion bubbled up from introspection on daily experience and reading, not laboratory evidence, and I wanted to prove its truth as soon as I unpacked my box of books in Arps Hall on the campus of Ohio State University in the fall of 1954.

Setting a New Foundation

Two types of scientists began to fill the ideological vacuum created by the abandonment of the orthodox versions of behaviorism and psychoanalysis during the 1960s. Both groups were more interested in mental processes than in Pavlov's conditioned habits or Freud's oral, anal, phallic stages, and their ambitions were a bit more modest. The scientists who wanted to uncover universal principles for cognitive processes remained politically dominant in the university. Most psychologists regard 1960, the year that George Miller, Eugene Galanter, and Karl Pribram published *Plans and the Structure of Behavior*, as marking the birth of a cognitive revolution that offered a different answer to the question "Why do we know what we know?"[1] The cognitive scientists accepted the operation of mental rules (as Kant had argued) and rejected Locke's suggestion that experience was mind's only sculptor. The learning and forgetting of words and pictures, usually by college students, were favorite topics. Quality of memory depended on how easily mental units could be associated, and this dimension was attributable to their "degree of similarity." Of course, personal experience determined the similarity between objects or words. Cows and soybeans were more similar for economists, cows and hippopotamuses for biologists, cows and gods for Hindus. Our experience with the effects of different sources of light striking a surface may even contribute to the compelling illusion that a gray circle surrounded by a dark background always appears lighter than the same circle with a white background.[2]

But a central demand of the cognitive scientists was that all humans were prepared to parse the world in particular ways. All cultures create distinct categories for living compared with nonliving objects. And within the former they distinguish between plants and animals, within the latter between natural and manufactured objects. Although there is less agreement on the categories for human psychological functions, I suspect but cannot prove that most societies distinguish public actions from private mental events. Within the former, there should be a tripartite distinction among the behaviors that violate the community's moral standards, those that are necessary for survival, and remaining rituals that fit neither of these categories. Within the category of the mental, there should be a distinction between perceptions/thoughts and feelings/emotions that have bodily sensations as integral components. But there is considerable cultural variation in the ways thoughts and emotions are conceptualized. Western societies make a sharper distinction between these private phenomena than Asian cultures. The former groups have regarded thought as controlling emotion, whereas Eastern cultures treat the two in a balanced relation that varies from occasion to occasion—the yin and yang of Chinese philosophy.

The metaphor for mind as a constructed set of interconnected roads or the wires of a telephone exchange, in which all the components are similar, was replaced with a metaphor of body parts. This image assumes, first, that some parts are more important than others and, second, that the parts have qualitatively distinct functions present at birth. This idea implies the presence of modules with assigned places in the brain. Some locations are devoted to understanding speech, others to perceiving motion, still others to feelings evoked by a foul odor. This view makes it easy to imagine a determinate relation between brain activity and experience.

The intuitively obvious fact that humans have expectations, and are not bulletin boards on which information is pasted, was central to the agenda of the cognitive scientists. But this assumption meant that one had to know a person's history, for the expectations originated in the past. Contemporary readers will find it hard to believe that Hugo Munsterberg, one of Harvard's eminent professors in the early twentieth century, declared that history was the devil to be avoided in psychological explanations.[3] The proper account of Socrates' reluctance to leave the room in which he was imprisoned was a description of the muscle movements that kept him restrained. Munsterberg saw no need to consider Socrates' motives or feelings because they resisted measurement.

The second group, which took Freud as an immediate parent and wanted to understand the variation in beliefs, values, wishes, and emotions, relied more on verbal reports gathered during interviews or, more often, with questionnaires. Their metaphor for mind was an artist who had painted many canvases with the same oils, rather than a stretch of moist sand faithfully registering each footprint. This generative perspective was necessary to explain why a three-year-old said to her mother who had opened a closet containing a dozen tightly packed dresses, "Look, my dresses are friends," why deaf children learning sign language created new signs spontaneously, and why one-third of the utterances of three-year-olds were novel. The task was to figure out the rules minds were using to build novel forms that were neither conditioned responses nor replicas of experience.

I, too, believed that children's beliefs about others, especially their parents, were constructions and that the same objective experiences could produce different beliefs. Examples from three cultures demonstrate my point. In the American colonies, respected, well-educated, seventeenth-century parents beat their children, often harshly, to tame their inherently evil character. Samuel Byrd of Virginia, for example, punished a dependent who had wet his bed by demanding that he drink "a pint of piss."[4] Upper-class English infants were traditionally placed with a wet nurse until weaning and were at home for only a few years before being sent off to boarding school. And in postwar Japan, several well-known men reminisced about their childhoods in a newspaper article. One, the president of an automobile company, wrote about his father, "Once his anger was over he did not nag or complain, but when he was angry I was really afraid of him. His scolding was like thunder. . . . I learned from my father how to live independently, doing everything on my own. He was the greatest model for my life." Another, a physician and novelist whose father was a physician and poet, recalled, "Looking back at my childhood, I can say that my father was, above all, an awesome, frightening, being. He was often enraged. When he became angry, it was with all his physical and spiritual strength. Even when I overheard my father reprimand somebody in the next room, a cold shiver used to run down my spine, not to speak of the times when I was chastised . . . and yet, he was truly a support as I grew up."[5]

These colonial American, English, and Japanese parents did not believe that they were cruel or insensitive, and I suspect that their children did not feel unloved. Rejection, like pleasure, is a symbolic invention of mind, not an inherent property of a social experience. If children interpret harsh parental actions as motivated by a wish to build their character, they do not feel rejected.

The Child's Mind

Studies I began at Ohio State University in 1954 and continued several years later at the Fels Research Institute on the campus of Antioch College in Yellow Springs, Ohio, probed children's constructions of the concepts "male" and "female" and how those concepts penetrated other ideas. People are the most significant objects in children's lives, and they search for effective ways to divide people into unambiguous, internally coherent categories, as a diamond worker looks for the right place to make the first cut in a six-carat stone. The differences in body form, dress, timbre of voice, strength, and behaviors between the sexes are so distinct, children can easily construct a division based on gender.

This research was still not in a discovery mode, for I wanted to prove what I had decided must be true. An artist drew pairs of designs, objects, and animals, no people, with the pictures in each pair differing in size or in signs of varying strength, danger, cleanliness, or gentleness. Six- and seven-year-olds first indicated which picture in each pair was more like their father and, on a later occasion, which one was more like their mother. For example, children shown a big and a small table of the same shape and color usually pointed to the big table as representing the father and the small table as symbolic of the mother. The children's answers suggested that size, strength, danger, dirt, darkness, and angularity were preferentially associated with the father, and their opposites with the mother. Even younger children (three to five years old) believe that physical aggression is more likely in boys than in girls.[6]

My intuition had been confirmed, even though I could not explain why most children called a saw-toothed design "male" and a curved design "female." It is probably not a coincidence that Plato thought that the invisible forms that rendered a food sour had an angular shape, whereas round forms produced sweet tastes. I was forced to assume hypothetical events, none observable, that made it easy for children to associate ideas of potential harm with a saw-toothed design and ideas of safety with a rounded design, and had to add the premise that most children regarded fathers (and males) as more dangerous than mothers (and females). Because it was unlikely that all the children who said that the saw-toothed design was like their father had harsh, punitive, or intimidating fathers, their answers could not be a function of actual interactions with parents but had to be coherent, symbolic constructions created from the bits and pieces of daily experience.

The concept of gender also touched the concept of "school." Because elementary classrooms are usually taught by women, I theorized that young children unconsciously classified schoolwork as a feminine activity. Second- and third-grade children were first taught to associate one nonsense word (dep) with pictures of female objects, a different nonsense word (rov) with pictures of male objects, and a third nonsense word (fas) with gender-neutral objects—a task that took less than twenty minutes. Each child was then shown a new set of pictures illustrating objects found in school, along with neutral objects. Each child was to select one of the nonsense words—"dep," "rov," or "fas"—to name each picture. The anticipated result was affirmed. A majority applied the female word "dep" to the pictures of a blackboard, book, school library, and page of arithmetic. Mary Mullen used the same method to discover that seven-year-old American children regard pictures of natural objects as feminine, especially lakes, birds, plants, trees, and clouds. By contrast, manufactured objects—clocks, houses, telephones, pens, and bottles—are perceived as masculine. This bias must be based, in part, on children's knowledge that females carry, birth, and care for infants. The Pythagoreans regarded the number two as female and three as male because natural events occur more often in pairs than in trios. The strong semantic association between "female" and "nature," established by early childhood, implies that a society's conception of nature can influence its psychological stereotypes for women. If nature is viewed as unpredictable, the community will project this quality on females. When, in the fifteenth century, Catholic Europe categorized sexuality as sin, women were potential witches. Five centuries later, after Freudian ideas rendered sex a natural source of health, a woman's love had become a requisite for vitality. If nature is perceived as protecting life, adolescent girls will assume, unconsciously of course, that killing is a serious violation of their gender. I suspect that the more benevolent view of women that emerged in eighteenth-century Europe was influenced in part by a view of nature as less harsh, more supportive of life, and a source of grace, beauty, and serenity.

In 1957, Charles Osgood and his colleagues at the University of Illinois had published *The Measurement of Meaning*. Though popular at the time, it is rarely read today.[7] Osgood described the results of studies in which adults from various cultures and speaking different languages applied the complementary dimensions of good–bad, strong–weak, and active–passive to names for many familiar objects, animals, and people. People more often assigned "strong" and "active" to masculine objects, such as footballs and fishing gear; conversely, they more often described female objects such as gems and gowns as "weak" and "passive." Several cultures added the contrasts beautiful–ugly and natural–manufactured. In addition to the explicit features that define an object (a slim, six-inch crystal vase for flowers), these extra connotations hover over most encounters, thoughts, and feelings. The brain circuit activated when these judgments occur can be likened to the intersection of Broadway and 42nd Street or the hub city of a major airline.

The gender category even affects the names parents choose for their children. American parents, for example, are more likely to give their daughters first names that have more than one syllable and end in the letters *a*, *e*, or *i*—Sara, Rebecca, Heidi, Elena, or Priscilla—whereas they more often give their sons names that end in a consonant—Daniel, Robert, Thomas, Eric, or Richard. Moreover, when presented with random arrangements of letters that have these male or female features, Americans rate the "male" letter patterns as more active than the "female" ones.[8] Parents are generally unconscious of this bias.

In one study, American college students were asked to rate a large number of first names on each of four personality traits: (1) ethical–caring, (2) fun-loving, (3) successful, and (4) masculine–feminine. Male names were rated as less ethical and less caring but more successful than female names. Androgynous names, such as Dana and Kim, were rated as less masculine if applied to a man but as more masculine if applied to a woman, and uncommon names were rated as less ethical and less successful than common names.[9] Deviance is often judged as less desirable if no other information is available. I recognized as a child that Jerome was an uncommon name in my community and regularly signed my school papers "Jerry."

These facts widened the theoretical space between psychologists who studied humans and those working with animals because the semantic networks for good–bad, male–female, and strong–weak have no corresponding process in any species but our own. This evidence required adding the notion of "representation" to conditioned associations as a fundamental psychological unit. The distinctive property of a representation is an arrangement or pattern of features. A representation of a face, for example, retains the specific spatial relations among the placement of eyes, nose, mouth, and hairline. If the pattern were altered seriously, by placing one eye directly under the other, observers would not regard the features as a face, even though all the features were present. The representation of the concept "mammal" is a pattern of features with variation in the strengths of their relations. Internal fertilization and nursing of the young always occur together, and in a fixed order, whereas fur, a tail, and four feet have weaker relations with one another and with the first two defining features. Early behaviorists were indifferent to pattern because they used simple tones and lights as conditioned stimuli. Yet a contemporary of the early behaviorists, Edward Tolman, contended that a rat exploring a maze learned a representation of the features of the maze, rather than links between the physical features of the maze and motor responses, simply by exploration—a phenomenon he called latent learning.[10] Fortunately, contemporary psychologists acknowledge that the pattern of the conditioned stimulus does affect learning.

Some psychologists argue that the difference between an association and a representation is not as great as it appears. The representation of a face can be viewed as a set of associations among the eyes, nose, and mouth; the representation of a mammal as a set of associations among the concepts "internal fertilization" and "nursing." Although this argument has some merit, most representations are more malleable—that is, more easily linked to others—than associations and far more generative. Some ten-year-olds asked for the first time "How are a tree and a baby alike?" reply after reflection, "They both grow." They were not consciously aware of this fact before being asked. The examiner's question motivates a successful search for the features the two objects share. And from that time forward, trees and infants, which were not part of the same representation before the question, become joined in an expanded representation.

Children, moreover, do not have to be asked a question to detect a feature shared by different representations because minds spontaneously organize and reorganize their representations. When T. S. Eliot first had the thought that eventually led him to write, "I will show you fear in a handful of dust," he linked two representations that had been separate, and those who read that line forged a new representation immediately. Nonetheless, representations, like conditioned associations, are theoretical inventions intended to explain behavior. They are not "things in the brain."

Even though representations differ from conditioned associations, some principles distilled from conditioning animals are useful because thoughts and feelings can function as conditioned stimuli. A child being jeered maliciously by a dozen peers with clenched fists experiences strong feelings along with a rush of thoughts. The harsh jeering can be regarded as the unconditioned stimulus, the uncomfortable feelings as the unconditioned response, and the thoughts as the conditioned stimulus. When the child reflects on this unpleasant experience days later, the thoughts can elicit a muted form of the strong feelings experienced originally. A rat will learn to avoid a harmless food with a distinct taste if administered a drug that created a heightened state of arousal before it tasted the food.[11] No pairing of a light or tone with an unconditioned stimulus is necessary.

Many children experience strong feelings when particular thoughts pierce consciousness. For example, children who are often uncertain about the whereabouts of their parents associate the thought of being abandoned or unloved with the uncomfortable feeling that accompanies being alone in the house. Later, as adults, they are likely to experience a similar feeling if someone inadvertently behaves in a way that evokes the thought that they are unloved. A small number of adults are so hypersensitive to the subtlest sign of rejection that they lose the friends they want so desperately.

Children from poor families who are reminded daily of the economic precipice on which they live associate thoughts about lack of money with uncertainty or shame. Many who were adolescents during the Great Depression of the 1930s carried this association into old age. Ambitious adolescents who strive for a perfect academic record often feel that they do not have enough time to finish their academic assignments. As a result, thoughts of "wasting time" become associated with uncertainty, and as adults, they are susceptible to feelings of tension when idle and not doing something useful. Some become the workaholics who become restless after the first forty-eight hours of a one-week vacation. The childhood thoughts surrounding the absence or loss of a valued resource—love, money, time—can become conditioned stimuli capable of provoking feelings that are interpreted as worry or tension.

The power of a thought to provoke emotion can last a lifetime. Henry Murray, the father of the Thematic Apperception Test (TAT) and a former Harvard professor, was a close friend of the psychiatrist John Bowlby. When Bowlby was visiting Boston, Murray invited him and his wife to dinner in his Cambridge home, along with some friends that included my wife and myself. Bowlby had agreed to Murray's request to narrate his professional career after dinner. After dessert and coffee we retired to the living room, and John, his wife beside him, began his brief memoir by reminding us that he had been a child psychoanalyst in training with Melanie Klein. One of his first patients was a young boy with many fears whom Bowlby was treating with play therapy. The boy was exceptionally anxious during one session and, after making some inquiries, Bowlby discovered that his mother had abandoned the son three days earlier. Bowlby, excited by this discovery, could not wait to tell Klein this important piece of information. His face became noticeably tense as he remembered Klein's reply to his explanation of why the boy had been so anxious. "Dr. Bowlby," she said, "we are not concerned with reality, we are concerned only with the fantasy." As John finished this sentence, the anger that had begun to cover his face earlier now suffused his body. The conditioned association between her indifference to his discovery and the anger it generated had been preserved for more than fifty years.

A coda to this event occurred several years later. A group of child analysts met monthly in the home of a Boston psychiatrist where a guest spoke first and questions followed. As a speaker at one of these evening sessions, I chided the analysts for not accommodating to the new empirical discoveries on children. If psychoanalysts were to regain their former position of prominence in psychiatry and psychology, they must replace their old ideas with concepts based on recent research. When I finished, a woman with a European accent remarked, "Dr. Kagan, you don't understand, we are not concerned with the facts, we are concerned only with the fantasy." My reply was polite, but I remember wishing that Bowlby had been present.

The Inadequacy of Words

One shadow trailing the conclusions of the cognitive scientists was an addiction to words as the primary vehicle of knowledge and a surprising indifference to the structures created by perception of the outside world and events within the body. It is easier to study the strength of the semantic association between "woman" and "apple pie" than the link between the perceptual representation of the face of Julia Child and an apple pie enjoyed the previous Thanksgiving. George Miller who, with Jerome Bruner, had established the Center for Cognitive Studies at Harvard, tried to deal with this problem in a book written with Philip N. Johnson-Laird called *Language and Perception* (1976).[12]

My representations of my elementary school, my mother's smile, and the summit of Mont Blanc on a crystal clear day can be described, albeit inadequately, with words, but they also exist as schemata without words. Because it is hard to measure perceptual structures, they are often ignored. This attitude is understandable because only a limited number of phenomena can be probed during the four or five decades of a scientific career. Biologists could not study bacteria until microscopes had been invented; astronomers could not measure the temperature of the cosmos until they could quantify the radio energy raining down on earth. A parent's love for a child is a significant human experience, but psychologists do not possess sensitive ways to measure the intensity of this emotion accurately.

An important difference between semantic and perceptual representations is that most semantic representations belong to a network. My network for the word "heavy," for example, has branches emanating from nodes for boulders, arcane arguments, serious plays, and dominating colleagues. Each branch is available for exploration, and the setting determines which route the mind follows. But I have no perceptual representation of "heavy," only

representations of objects with that property. Equally important, some semantic terms have antonyms (for example, heavy versus light), and some
belong to a nested hierarchy of semantic concepts. Dogs are pets, pets are
animals, animals are living things. The word "heavy" is a member of the
more abstract category "magnitude." By contrast, each perceptual structure
is particular. It has no opposite and is not part of a hierarchy of perceptual
structures. A three-year-old on a beach staring at the pencil-thin divide between the sky and the sea can have a perceptual representation without any
semantic component and, therefore, no semantic concept of horizon. Infants
younger than eight months have only perceptual knowledge and no semantic
concepts for emotions, numbers, or physical principles. Children who have
no words for colors can tell the difference between red and green and treat
red and pink as perceptually more similar than red and orange.

Experienced therapists have perceptual representations of their patients
that are rich with details of the patient's postures, tempos of speech, timbres
of voice, facial expressions, and modes of dress. By contrast, the representations of patients held by scientists whose knowledge of mental illness comes
primarily from questionnaires, often administered over the telephone, lack
the rich perceptual structures of the clinician. As a result, the two groups do
not always agree on which patients are depressed or anxious. The clinician
will distinguish between reports of depression by an obese adolescent living
in poverty who is failing in school and a thirty-five-year-old successful, attractive, happily married lawyer who is experiencing a prolonged bout of deep
sadness. The epidemiologist, who has not spent hours interacting with hundreds of patients, is likely to conclude that both are suffering from the same
depressive disorder. The two professionals "know" depression in a different
way. I know that a virus can cause AIDS, but a biologist who has studied this
illness for years knows this fact in a deeper way. The millions of adults who
surf Google to learn about events they have not experienced have less understanding than those who have seen, heard, felt, or smelled the events referred
to in the sentences displayed on the monitor.

A serious problem with printed or spoken words is that listeners or readers
often have no idea of the passion or deeper symbolic significance intended
by the author of the sentences. Some people who report on a questionnaire
that they are unhappy do end most days in a sad mood. Others happen to

be suffering from a temporary bout of migraine. A person's health is the best predictor of an American's answer to the question: "Are you a happy person?" Words, like the wrapping of a package, do not reveal all of the content hidden inside the speaker's mind.

The two hemispheres of the brain make differential contributions to perceptual and semantic representations, with the right hemisphere playing a more significant role in perceptual structures—scenes, melodies, body sensations—and the left having a bigger role in the semantic forms of words and sentences. It may be relevant that the pyramidal neurons in the right temporal lobe are closer together—more densely packed—than those in a comparable location of the left hemisphere, whereas the axons of the neurons in the left hemisphere are more heavily myelinated than those on the right. Further, the right hemisphere is preferentially activated by events whose features have relatively lower spatial frequencies (that is, coarser features), like the wide eyes and open mouth of a person surprised by a spider. The left hemisphere is activated more fully by events whose elements have higher spatial frequencies, like a series of very brief eyeblinks. The right hemisphere is thus better than the left in detecting differences in the rhythm and timbre of a person's speech—called prosody—because these features have a relatively low frequency. The left hemisphere is better than the right in detecting the very brief pause between the words "Baghdad" and "was" when I hear a television reporter say, "The city of Baghdad was hit by rockets yesterday."

Although the left hemisphere is more proficient at separating words in the rapid flow of speech, it needs help from the right hemisphere in interpreting the meanings a speaker intended. The different responsibilities of the two hemispheres may have been enhanced in humans because the corpus callosum, a structure that unites the two hemispheres, is relatively thinner in our species than in apes and monkeys (taking into account the larger size of the human brain). This anatomical change should have rendered the two hemispheres more independent. The larger proportion of men over women who are consistently left handed, which implies a relation between the two hemispheres favoring the right side, is influenced, in part, by the secretion of testosterone by the male fetus and a subsequent slowing of the growth of the left hemisphere. These facts may explain why the volume of the corpus callosum that lies to the right of the midline is larger in men than in women.

A diary entry written while I was visiting China with a group of social scientists in December 1973 reads, "There were long lines of children with red neckerchiefs marching from 7 a.m. to dusk; women in blue uniforms sweeping the gutters with brooms of straw; 60-year-old men on bicycles hauling 100-pound loads of cabbages; adolescent girls pulling carts of night soil; older women splashing water from irrigation ditches on fields of rice; and, at all times of day, people so thick no pavement was visible." These sentences do not capture the rich perceptual patina and emotional reactions provoked by those scenes. A small number of adults who suffer from a syndrome characterized by the absence of sensory feedback from the heart and gut to the brain are deprived of the major basis for feelings. Nonetheless, they are able to say that a facial expression is "fearful" and can infer that a hero in a story feels "guilty." These correct semantic judgments are possible even though they lack the supporting sensations that occur in healthy subjects.[13]

The protests against the Vietnam War were fueled by television scenes of weeping Vietnamese and bloody battlefields. Images have a capacity to arouse feelings that words attain only in the prose of unusually gifted writers. There is a good reason why the Pentagon is not allowing journalists to photograph the returning caskets of soldiers killed in the Iraq War. One spring afternoon in 1968, after checking into a hotel in Nashville, I turned on the television set to learn that Martin Luther King, Jr., had been assassinated. The unique feeling formed by the coalescence of surprise, anger, and sadness forced me to leave the room for a walk. Twenty minutes later I found myself in downtown Nashville looking up at a marquee announcing the movie *Bonnie and Clyde*. Several of my students had recommended the film, and needing distraction, I went in and sat down at a moment, toward the end of the movie, when Bonnie and Clyde, trapped in their car, are surrounded by police. I felt faint the moment spatters of blood appeared on their faces. I left my seat and walked quickly to the lobby, where I fell to the ground and remained unconscious for a few minutes. After gaining consciousness, I returned to my hotel room.

I did not realize that this brief experience had established a classically conditioned bodily reaction—called a vasovagal response—to the sight of blood in a context of violence on a movie screen but not to blood in an ecologically natural situation that was due to an injury. For the next two years I had a conditioned fainting reaction whenever I saw blood on a movie or television screen; fortunately, this response extinguished by the third year. I would not have acquired this reaction had I been reading the script of *Bonnie and Clyde*. I had to see the blood on their bodies as they were being fired on at a time when I was psychically distressed by Dr. King's assassination because perceptual schemata are more closely tied to the bodily reactions that create emotions than are words.

One reason for my reluctance to award too much significance to what people say or write is that the meanings of words change over time more readily than perceptual representations of policemen or lemonade. When I was a child, "fuzz" did not refer to a policeman and "cool" was a property of lemonade. The metaphoric relation between fear and dust in T. S. Eliot's line "I will show you fear in a handful of dust" would not be regarded as aesthetically satisfying by medieval monks for whom fear of God was a seminal and benevolent feature of humanity. In "The Death of the Moth," Virginia Woolf wrote,

> Words . . . are the wildest, freest, most irresponsible, most unteachable of all things. . . . Words do not live in dictionaries; they live in the mind. . . . They are highly sensitive, easily made self-conscious. They do not like to have their purity or their impurity discussed. Nor do they like being lifted out on the point of a pen that examines them separately. They hang together, in sentences, in paragraphs, sometimes for whole pages at a time. They hate being useful; they hate making money; they hate being lectured about in public. In short, they hate anything that stamps them with one meaning or confines them to one attitude, for it is their nature to change.[14]

Infants younger than eight or nine months of age have no language and cannot understand the semantic meaning of human emotions and intentions. They possess perceptual representations of smiling faces and parents approaching with a bottle. But these schemata are not to be equated with the semantic concepts "happy" or "intention." I have perceptual schemata for the objects that lie under the hood of my car. But that does not mean that I understand anything about their functions or interrelations. Put plainly, the

meaning of the verb "know" depends on the perceptual and semantic structures linked to an event. A rat, human infant, and college senior may all find a bitter taste aversive, but each agent understands that experience in different ways. Unfortunately, we do not have enough words for the large number of phenomena nature provided. Hence, many words have multiple meanings. Like the members of a small troupe of actors who have to stage all of Shakespeare's plays, some words play many roles. One reason physicists invented the novel words "boson" and "gluon" to describe atomic events was to avoid the ascription of inappropriate properties that might have occurred had they chosen familiar words. The biological term "allele" refers only to the variation in a gene and not to variation in any other biological object. Many psychological words, by contrast, lack this specificity.

Terms like "cooperation," "altruism," "aggression," and "fear" are applied to different species displaying very different behaviors. Hence the sentence "Aggression can be a consequent of fear," which fails to specify species and actions, is so ambiguous as to border on meaninglessness. The recognition that the meanings of words are determined by how they are used within a particular community, which ancient Egyptians and Greeks did not appreciate, represents a profound insight that originated with late Renaissance scholars and found its clearest expression in Ludwig Wittgenstein's writings. Even the meanings of fundamental terms like "alive," "dead," and "family" have changed over the past few millennia. When American psychologists use questionnaire evidence to conclude that "human personality is composed of five factors," the meaning of "personality" is different from, but not necessarily more correct than, the meaning that their subjects understand. Rather than hijack popular words that already have a secure home, psychologists should invent new ones that have an unequivocal meaning, like "basic self-reported traits" or "primary self-descriptions." To rephrase George Orwell, the last thing we should do with words is to surrender to them.

The Assignment to West Point

My stay at Ohio State lasted only six months because the United States was fighting in Korea and my draft board in New Jersey, having learned that my doctorate had been awarded, ordered my induction into the army in March

1955. My wife, daughter of three months, and I returned to New Jersey—they by plane and I by automobile—and I reported to Fort Dix for basic training.

I was about eight years older than the other recruits in my platoon, and a rumor spread that I had been sent from the Office of the Inspector General in Washington, D.C., to evaluate practices at the base. One of the few memories that retains clarity after almost fifty years comes from the night we were transferred, a little before midnight, to the location where the training occurred. As we trudged with our duffel bags across the grass on a pitch-black night I heard a voice behind me yell, "Hey you!" I did not turn around at first, but after a third announcement, I did stop, and a loud voice, about a hundred yards behind me, said, "Yeah, you. Come here." I walked back to an angry sergeant who yelled, "I said duffel bag on the right shoulder. Yours is on the left." He then pointed his flashlight at my face and realized I was much older than the other recruits. After I gave my name and serial number, he asked, "Say, how much schooling do you have?" The hostility against education held by noncommissioned officers at that time was well known. My mind worked fast. If he knew the truth, I would be peeling potatoes for the next eight weeks. I guessed that he had not graduated high school and answered, with a simulated embarrassment, "I had to leave school in the fourth grade." His face softened, he slapped my shoulder gently, and in a nurturant tone, admonished, "Okay, watch yourself."

The second part of this event occurred the next morning. Soon after we were awakened, a sergeant entered the barracks and asked who could type. Although I was not an expert typist, I raised my hand on the assumption that working in an office would be easier than most assignments planned for that day, and I was told to report to the main office within an hour. I felt a surge of terror when the sergeant who had queried me the prior evening entered the room. He did not recognize me as he went to a pile of cards that listed the names and educational backgrounds of the members of his platoon. The fear of being discovered rose to a painful intensity as I watched him slowly finger each card. I was certain he would recognize my name and the falsehood and order a court martial. Fortunately, after leafing through the cards, he left the office.

The remaining eight weeks were uneventful, and I expected to be assigned to Korea. I could not know that the Defense Department had been troubled for several years because about one-third of the first-year students at West Point—the plebes—were leaving the academy at the end of their first year. This high rate of attrition was expensive, and the generals in Washington, wanting to know why, established a research project that relied on three career officers stationed at the academy—a psychiatrist, a psychologist, and a social worker—and they needed a Ph.D. psychologist to do the testing. I must have been one of the few psychologists available for this assignment in the spring of 1955, and my orders were to proceed to West Point to join the research team at the U.S. Army hospital.

Our research soon revealed that most plebes who resigned came from families who could not afford expensive tuition for their sons but believed that an academy education was excellent and tuition-free. The hazing of plebes was so harsh, however, that these eighteen-year-olds decided the psychological cost was too expensive. Plebes whose fathers were career officers rarely left the academy.

Measuring Personality

The social worker or the psychologist, who were career officers, interviewed each plebe. My task was to administer psychological tests, one of which was the Thematic Apperception Test, invented years earlier by Henry Murray and his younger colleague Christiana Morgan. The TAT consisted of a series of photographs. The final item, a blank card, required the subject to imagine a scene and then tell a story to fit that image. Each of the photographs was purposely ambiguous to permit different interpretations. For example, the first photograph in the test was of a young boy with an uncertain facial expression holding a violin. The contents of the stories were presumed to reveal the motives and conflicts of the narrator. Although this test had become popular with both clinicians and investigators, there was insufficient evidence to support the basic assumption behind its use. The psychologist's interpretations of the stories rested on the intuition that each person's salient desires and conflicts, which were complex combinations of images, feelings, and ideas, were present in the semantic descriptions of the pictures. These psychologists failed to acknowledge the broad moat between thought and speech and denied the many times that subjects were unable to find words to communicate their notions of love, ambition, and failure. This was the same error made by the behaviorists who assumed a simple one-to-one relation between a conditioned stimulus and a reaction.

The research of the past fifty years has revealed the flaws in the simple assumption that rationalized use of this procedure. In the late 1950s Gerald Lesser and I hosted a conference at the Fels Research Institute attended by investigators who worked with this test. The proceedings, published in 1961, documented the problems that plagued the interpretations inferred from the stories.[15] One obvious problem was the extraordinary variation in the subjects' verbal fluency. A fluent person told longer stories, and therefore, his or her protocol contained more content. A fishnet with holes two inches in diameter will not retain any fish smaller than that, but that does not mean that those smaller fish do not exist. The lack of a reference to a motive or conflict in a protocol, for example, hostility to authority, does not have a meaning opposite to the one inferred from presence of that content. The fact that a brain site does not show increased activity to a challenge does not mean that it did not participate in the person's reaction because inhibition of the site could have been a component of the reaction.

Another serious flaw in the interpretation of stories to the TAT photographs is the assumption that the content of the narrative reflects the person's preoccupations rather than a cognitive bias to analyze the pictures in detail and, in so doing, detect an ambiguous feature that motivates a particular story. For example, one photograph illustrates a boy near a couch with an indistinct object in the background that most people ignore. When a person does mention this object, it is described as a gun or a knife, and as a result, they tell an aggressive story. Individuals who are prone to detect the details of pictures tell more aggressive stories to this photograph than do others. The aggressive theme reflects not a high level of anger or hostility but a cognitive bias to analyze pictures. A colleague visiting a nursery school years ago was asked to comment on the drawings mounted along the walls. One drawing had all the objects and figures restricted to the bottom 20 percent of the large piece of paper, and he remarked to the teacher that the child who drew this scene must be very constricted and anxious. "No," said the teacher, "She is very short for her age and can't reach any higher."

The arguments in defense of the Thematic Apperception Test had intuitive appeal in the 1950s because psychologists wished to believe that they could measure motives and conflicts. "Wishing it so" is common in all sciences. Seventeenth-century physicians, convinced that illness was caused by toxic elements in the blood, applied leeches to the skin as a popular form of therapy, reasoning that removing the tainted blood would be therapeutic. Modern medicine is not free of this error. A Nobel Prize in medicine was awarded to Egon Moniz in 1949 because he asserted that severing the connections between the frontal lobes and the rest of the brain was an effective cure for psychosis. Psychotics have disturbed thoughts, and the frontal lobes play an important role in thought. Therefore, he argued, if the frontal lobes were prevented from influencing the rest of the brain, the disturbed thoughts would cease. Many schizophrenics had this operation performed for the next twenty years until scientists realized that the surgery did not alleviate the debilitating features of the illness. The Nobel Prize was not revoked.

The Rorschach Ink Blot Test, a sister to the Thematic Apperception Test, was defended with a similar argument. The test consisted of ambiguous inkblots, rather than photographs, that the individual interpreted. Once again, with little evidence, thousands of psychologists accepted the premise that a person who interpreted an ink blot as resembling "tiger's teeth" had more anger than one who said it looked like the "X-ray of a pelvis." The latter response reflected a preoccupation with sex. I remember being criticized by a Yale professor in a graduate seminar because of my interpretation of a Rorschach protocol I had gathered on a client attending a clinic. The woman saw female genitals on several inkblots; convinced that she was trying to shock me with her permissive attitude toward sexuality, I told the class that she wished to present a persona of sexual freedom. "Absolutely not," the professor insisted. "Anyone who sees genitals in ink blots is psychotic."

The unquestioned defense of a universal meaning for an observation is frequent when theory is weak. Consider the early beliefs that a reward has to be present if an animal learns a new habit, tics represent a repressed urge to masturbate, every dream contains a disguised wish, an insecurely attached infant becomes an anxious adolescent, and the current assumption that activation of a woman's amygdala as she looks at an angry face means that her brain is in a state of fear.

The problems linked to the interpretations of these tests became apparent

after I analyzed hundreds of Thematic Apperception and Rorschach protocols in the files of the Fels Research Institute. Although both tests are used less
often today, they remain popular with clinicians who have the responsibility
of diagnosing motives and conflicts. An inadequate method is better than no
method at all, and no one—not scientist, physician, or parent—relinquishes
a ritual, no matter how imperfect, if it helps them meet the requirements of
their role. Clinical psychologists must do something to earn their salary and
retain professional dignity. They are expected to measure motives, emotions,
and conflicts, and they must believe in these methods or find a new job.

One memory from my hundreds of administrations of the TAT to the
plebes remains clear. One tall, quiet adolescent who had been a star quarterback in high school hoped to play quarterback for Army when he became
eligible as a second-year student. As mentioned above, the last item in this
test is a blank card, and the person is asked to imagine a scene and then tell
a story about it. I remember the story he told to the blank card because of
its unusual degree of humility and self-abasement. The plebe imagined an
Army-Navy game in which Army was behind 7–6, was on Navy's five-yard
line, and had time left for only one more play. The Army quarterback selected
the wrong play, and Army lost the game. Peter Dawkins, the young man who
told that story, became an all-American quarterback for Army and a Green
Beret in the Vietnam War, appeared on the cover of *Life* magazine, and was
rumored to be short-listed for armed forces chief of staff when he resigned
his commission to become chief executive officer of Prime America in San
Francisco—not a very self-abasing career.

The Turn in the Path

As the crimson leaves fell in the forests surrounding West Point, I began to
think about my return to Ohio State after discharge from the Army. I was
not eager to return to Columbus. The ambience at the university was not as
intellectually exciting as I had hoped, and faculty lunches were dominated
by discussions of Woody Hayes's successful football team. But the position
was available, and I had told the chairman that I intended to return after
my service. Then reality, always envious of the novelist's freedom to invent
improbabilities, arranged an unexpected telephone call. Lester Sontag, di-

rector of the Fels Research Institute, asked if I would direct a project, recently funded by the National Institutes of Health, that would assess young adults who had been studied at the institute since infancy. I had met Sontag as a graduate student but had declined the position he offered following my doctorate because Frank Beach, whom I trusted, warned me that the geographic and intellectual isolation of Yellow Springs guaranteed that, should I go there, I would never be heard from again. I took his advice in 1954. But this time was different.

I accepted Sontag's invitation to visit the institute and learn more about its mission. The institute was founded in 1929 by a grant from Samuel Fels, founder of the Fels Soap Company. Arthur Morgan, then president of Antioch College, had persuaded Fels, who wanted to support a longitudinal study of typical American children, to place the project in Ohio rather than in Philadelphia, which Fels preferred, because the population in southwest Ohio was more stable and more representative of America than was urban Philadelphia. Morgan's argument worked, and the Fels Research Institute was established as an independent entity on the Antioch campus.

Sontag, the institute's first director, was a physician who knew little psychology and therefore had little faith in questionnaires and interviews. He favored direct observations of children in their homes and in a nursery school run by the institute several times a year for research purposes. Between 1929 and 1957 several hundred families, mainly white, middle-class, and living within forty miles of Yellow Springs, enrolled their infants in a longitudinal study of physical and psychological growth.

Fels's intentions were part of the American zeitgeist. Freud's ideas, which penetrated books and essays, had persuaded citizens and philanthropists that early experience affected children's future personalities and talents. Similar longitudinal studies had been established at about the same time in Denver, Colorado, and at the University of California in Berkeley. Darwin's long voyage to South America was the implicit model behind these projects. If careful observations of nature could lead to the fruitful idea of evolution through natural selection, it was reasonable to expect that equally careful observations of children as they grew would uncover equally original, and more useful, facts.

The history of child psychology in the United States from its origin in the nineteenth century to the late 1970s was characterized by four assumptions. The first swore allegiance to the significance of experience, especially maternal love and effective socialization of good character. The second held that habits, values, and emotions established early would be preserved indefinitely. The third alleged that psychological growth was gradual, and the last declared that "freedom from coercion" was the ideal state every child should attain. When these four premises are condensed into one sentence, their moral connotations become obvious. Each adult's level of talent, character, and success is the product of careful socialization by affectionate parents who awarded their children autonomy. Many members belonging to the recent cohort of investigators are loyal to a canon more characteristic of the natural sciences. They appear to be indifferent to the moral implications of the cognitive abilities of infants and young children and therefore are freer to discover whatever plan nature may be pursuing.

At midcentury, however, American child psychologists had ethical interests and, with their society, had become more conscious of the differences in school performance and psychological health between the children of the poor, especially those from families of color, and those from middle-class, white homes. A deeper understanding of this sad fact might suggest curative interventions. Few psychologists doubted that variation in parental behaviors explained the differences in aggression, conformity, obedience, and school grades that, once established, would be preserved indefinitely. If scientists could discover the early experiences that produced the variation, they could tell parents what to do to create optimal profiles. My peers detected no flaw in this argument, which assumed that the first feelings and habits had priority over later ones—a doctrine called infant determinism. We ignored the many exceptions to this rule in other domains. The quality of a honeymoon does not predict the stability or vitality of a marriage. The brain structures that emerged later in evolution are larger than those that emerged earlier; for example, the convoluted cortex is larger than the medulla.

I took the overnight train from New York's Pennsylvania Station to Xenia, Ohio, and spent several days reading typed reports gathered over the previous two decades by observers who had watched the children in their homes and in the Fels nursery school. About two to three hundred pages of typed material described each child from infancy to early adolescence. In addition, each child had been administered the Thematic Apperception and Rorschach procedures, as well as intelligence tests, on many occasions. The assignment was clear. The prose records and test protocols had to be quantified, and the adults, now in their third decade, had to be willing to come to the institute to be evaluated. I had to decide what concepts to extract from the prose material, what to measure in the adults, put the two sets of information together, and see if there was any reasonable relation between them. Any robust relation that made theoretical sense would be celebrated. If nothing of interest were discovered, however, no one would believe that conclusion and the effort would be ignored. The promises and risks were perfectly balanced. Sontag did not tell me that two psychologists, a few years older than I, had turned down this assignment because of its ambiguity.

I had no right to be optimistic about this venture. The prose reports were written in everyday language by different observers. Had I obsessively analyzed the flaws in this information, I, too, might have rejected Sontag's offer. I probably would have done so if the same invitation occurred today. But it was 1957, I was twenty-eight years old, ambitious, ingenuous, and reluctant to return to Ohio State. So I denied the problems and with high hopes told Sontag I would join the staff. Frank Beach gave me the same advice he had offered three years earlier, but this time heart overpowered mind. Had Alfred Wallace been able to predict the painful illnesses and the loss of his specimens at sea during his first trip to the Amazon, he would not have made the trip and probably would not have taken the later excursion to Southeast Asia that led to the same evolutionary hypothesis Darwin had arrived at during the voyage of the *Beagle*. The young like risk and are optimistic. Children who wake on Christmas morning to find a pile of hay on the porch assume their parents bought them the pony they had asked for.

On a cold January afternoon in 1957 my family and I arrived in Yellow Springs and moved into an old but lovely house owned by the college to begin a project that became a seminal influence on my future work. But I could not have known that then. I had to solve two problems: how to put numbers on the unwieldy prose summaries and what information to gather on the adults. Some discussion of how I arrived at answers to these questions illustrates how hard it is to escape the prejudices of one's training and the opinions of colleagues.

What to Quantify?

The verbal descriptions of each child's behavior were clear, but the settings were not identical. Some had siblings, some did not; some lived in big houses, some in small ones. Further, the many observers often focused on different actions. Some found aggression salient, whereas others emphasized obedience. I could not count the number of written references to any particular behavior and had to invent more abstract categories, and then rate how well diverse behaviors defining a psychological concept fit a particular child for a given stage of development. This strategy, which remains popular in psychology, is used by clinicians to arrive at a psychiatric diagnosis.

It was not at all clear which concepts would be fruitful. John Bowlby and his colleague Mary Ainsworth would have quantified security of attachment; Mary Rothbart would have chosen reactivity; and Nancy Eisenberg would have evaluated emotional regulation.[16] None of these ideas was popular in 1957. My history, formal and informal, had taught me that passivity to challenge, dependency on others, conformity to adult requests, and achievement, affiliative, sexual, and hostile motives were theoretically powerful ideas. Each of these notions had evaluative connotations; society regarded aggression, dependency, and passivity as undesirable qualities that could generate anxiety.

Years later, Joanna Erikson, Erik Erikson's daughter-in-law, gave me the copy of *Birth to Maturity*—the 1962 book that summarized the Fels project— on which her father-in-law had written marginal comments.[17] One sentence in the book read "Anxiety over anticipated loss of parental love and nurturance is an unusually strong and important force in the socialization of the child." Erikson had circled the word "anxiety" in the text and wrote in the margin, "One of the most subjective states imaginable."

The plans for a summer holiday can be guided by concrete images of beaches, mountains, or museums or abstract concepts like "fun," "relaxation," or "intellectually stimulating." Some scientists planning a study focus their thoughts on concrete phenomena; others begin with abstract concepts. The social scientists who prefer the latter strategy often select concepts that have connotations to semantic networks for good and bad, assume that these concepts refer to real things, and search for ways to measure the exemplars of these ideas. Intelligence, attachment, regulation, and executive control are examples. Some economists fail to realize that the statement "Behaviors that do not serve self-interest are irrational" is not a description of nature but an ethical proposition.

I do not remember the degree of confidence I had in the concepts selected and suspect I was more certain than I should have been. Because the numbers to be assigned to each child had to be independent of those given the adult information, someone else had to evaluate the early prose reports. Howard Moss, who had just received a doctorate from Ohio State, agreed to come to Yellow Springs to be a collaborator.

I interviewed each adult for several hours because I needed to know facts that could not be obtained by observing the subjects in their usual settings. I rejected questionnaires because of the smug assumption that I was clever enough to get information a person might not reveal on a questionnaire. But I needed other forms of evidence. Once again, the methods popular at the time were used as a guide. Mechanical tachistoscopes allowed pictures to be shown at very fast speeds, and psychologists asked subjects to describe what they saw. The logic in this procedure resembled the one behind the Thematic Apperception Test. I assumed that if a picture was ambiguous because it was visible for a tenth of a second, the verbal descriptions might reveal something about the individual's motives and conflicts. An artist drew pictures of ambiguous scenes—an adult on his knees in a supplicant posture, two men fighting, a couple lying on a beach—to evoke thoughts of dependency, aggression, and sexuality. I hoped that each subject's interpretations would provide objective support for similar concepts Moss was rating from the childhood material and I was judging from the interview replies.

What We Found

After Moss had rated the prose material and I had interviewed and tested the adults, we examined the independent sources of information and thought we had gleaned four facts and one enticing clue. First, with one exception to be noted, the behavioral variation during the first three years bore no relation to the psychological variation in adulthood. However, a reasonably good prediction of adult motives, concerns, and behaviors could be made from the behaviors displayed after school entrance, between six and ten years of age. Third, a behavior that was inconsistent with the American sex role standards of the first half of the twentieth century eventually disappeared. The two most obvious examples were the decrease in aggressive behavior in girls and dependent behavior in boys as each approached adolescence.

The fourth fact was the single exception to the lack of preservation from the first three years to adulthood. A small group of children had been rated as passive to challenges; they avoided strangers, were reluctant to engage in risky behavior, and retreated in unfamiliar situations. Today I would have called this quality "inhibition to unfamiliarity." The small group of one- to three-year-olds with this profile became subdued adults who found it hard to make friends and find sexual partners, reported strong feelings of tension before examinations and challenges, and required a great deal of emotional support from their family. Howard Moss and I toyed with the possibility that this cluster might have biological roots. We wrote in *Birth to Maturity* that this trait might have a constitutional component, meaning a temperamental bias, and urged further study of this possibility. I had no idea that forty years later, after several intervening projects, I would return to this theme to affirm that early intuition with a group of Boston children.

It was fortunate that John and Beatrice Lacey, who had joined the Fels staff years earlier and ran the psychophysiology department, were collaborators. The most surprising finding, but one neither the Laceys, Moss, nor I understood, was that the adults who been rated as passive to challenge during the first three years had minimally variable heart rates. The Laceys, who had been exploring the correlates of heart rate variability, had discovered that when college students are looking at pictures their heart rates become lower and more variable, but when they are solving cognitive problems, their heart rates rise and the variability of their heart rate decreases.[18] They concluded that when a person is doing mental work the brain tries to shut out distracting external stimulation. The decrease in heart rate variability is a sign of that process.

The fact that the dependent, introverted adults who had been passive children showed a minimally variable heart rate suggested that they were creating a psychological barrier between themselves and the world. Most of the time a single, unexpected result on a small sample is an artifact that will never be replicated. It is a mistake. This is especially true in the social sciences. Hence, reviewers are appropriately vigilant when they evaluate manuscripts because their role is to protect the community from spurious nonfacts. If on arriving at his laboratory Alexander Fleming had interpreted the death of his streptococcus colony as an artifact of leaking water or a breeze through an open window, someone else would have discovered penicillin. We thought that an important insight, evading us at the moment, was hidden in the relation between heart rate variability and this personality trait. I have forgotten most of the facts that emerged from thousands of hours of data analyses, but I never forgot that result, and as we shall see, it probably was not spurious.

The ability to sense when, and when not, to take an observation seriously is an art form, for there are no rules that permit this distinction. One handy guide is to attend to the relation if the measures have different sources and ignore it when they have the same origin. Heart rate variability is very different from answers in an interview or in prose descriptions of behavior. A second rule is to trust a result if there is an initial explanation with some reasonableness. The Laceys did have an initial account. Although it may not be the explanation they would use today, it did render the evidence understandable.

One result deserves mention, for it contains a suggestion to students embarking on a research career. In addition to the brief presentations of pictures, an artist drew a number of simple figures in different poses, wearing different clothes, and displaying varying facial expressions. The adults were asked to sort the figures into as many groups as they wished. Our a priori hunch, which turned out to be wrong, was that the groups selected would reveal the person's preoccupations. This premise is essentially the same as the one behind the use of the TAT and Rorschach tests, but it had the advantage of avoiding words. If a subject grouped all the attractive females, I would have inferred an ascendant concern with sexuality. But if he grouped all the men with angry faces, I would have inferred a preoccupation with hostility or fear of authority. I now appreciate the flaw in this idea, but it seemed reasonable in 1957 because personality theory, still Freudian in flavor, regarded a conflict between opposing wishes as the primary basis for neurotic symptoms. The concept of conflict between motives played the same role then that anxiety does today.

The contents of the adult groupings bore no relation to any of the childhood or adult information. In a mood of deep disappointment and frustration, I examined each protocol while simultaneously looking at the figures each subject selected. One evening, close to midnight, after several weeks of tedious study, I saw that some subjects consistently used small details in the figures—the presence of a hat, shoes, or belt—as the basis for their categories. Others relied on the inferred thoughts or motives of the figures. I realized that this procedure measured not conflict but the degree to which the subject attended to subtle perceptual details in the figures. And the subjects who attended to the details always took longer to make their groupings. The primary difference among the adults was how long they studied the figures before they selected a few to place together. The concept of reflection-impulsivity was born that evening and led, in time, to the construction of the Matching Familiar Figures Test for children, which evaluates the tendency to reflect on alternative solutions in a setting in which the child believes that a cognitive ability is being tested. This test does not measure a bias for a reflective or an impulsive strategy when one is buying clothes, writing a manuscript, or reacting to a personal insult.

I would not have arrived at the notion of reflection–impulsivity if I had not recorded the latency to each grouping. Investigators should record as many variables as they can, even those that at the time seem only marginally relevant. Years later, in my research on temperament, my assistants recorded each child's eye color, height, weight, and allergic symptoms. That evidence permitted us to discover a relation between an infant's temperamental bias and some of these physical features. Children who had a high-reactive temperament as infants were more likely than those who had been low-reactive to have a tall, thin body build, a narrow face, and blue eyes, and both they and their first-degree relatives were more likely to suffer from hay fever. These facts imply that the physiology that accompanies a temperamental bias of high reactivity renders a child vulnerable to a host of other biological properties. This experience taught me to trust evidence as if it were a slag heap with a pearl of extreme beauty hidden within it. The task is to find it.

I failed to question a practice that I would criticize years later. I accepted the validity of anxiety and conflict, searched for procedures that would reflect their presence, and convinced myself that the methods chosen were sensitive. I did not first explore the varied influences on the subjects' groupings. Had I done so, I would have learned that a reflective or impulsive style influenced the categories selected, and I would not have used that procedure. Fifteenth-century Europeans, who were certain there were witches, used trusted methods of examination to determine if a rumor that someone was a witch was correct. Some contemporary psychologists assume that a larger-than-average eye-blink reflex to a brief burst of loud sound while the person is looking at a picture of a rattlesnake reflects anxiety or defensiveness. The advocates of this idea did not first explore all the conditions that could produce a large eye blink to a loud sound. Had they done so they would have learned that engaging in complex thoughts, tension in facial muscles, and excitability of cerebellar neurons can produce large eye blinks, and they might not have initiated studies based on the assumption that a larger-than-average reflex is a sign of anxiety.

I noted in chapter 1 that the adult belief that one had suffered parental rejection during childhood is a private construction that is not easily inferred from watching parents and children interact. Several adults in the Fels study who experienced very harsh treatment, according to the prose descriptions of their socialization, told me during the interview that they were glad their parents had been strict. They were certain that this experience allowed them to build a strong character. All were happy with their jobs and in their marriages.

A few families in the Fels sample who anticipated the "hippie" rebellion of the late 1960s lived frugally in small houses in a forested area called Glen Helen. The staff member who visited regularly to observe each family always called to make an appointment so the parents would know when she would be arriving. When the visitor arrived at one girl's home, knocked on the door, and was invited in she was surprised to see the father having intercourse with the mother while the girl, three years old, was sitting on the father's back rocking and smiling. She excused herself and quickly returned to the institute. We had a staff meeting that afternoon to discuss the seriousness of this class of experience. All of us were convinced that regular exposure to parental sexuality would damage the girl's psyche permanently. We decided not to intervene with the family's habits but to watch the girl's development carefully. Twenty-five years later, when I was now at Harvard, the girl we worried about came to my office and we talked for several hours. She had graduated from college with an excellent record, was training for a professional degree, was happily engaged, and struck me as a very well adjusted woman. Jung's reply to a journalist who had asked why Freud placed such an emphasis on the psychic dangers of sex was that Freud was a "city boy" who, having missed frequent exposure to the mating and birthing of animals, failed to appreciate the naturalness of sexuality.

This project, like a buoy between the harbor and the open sea, sat midway between loyalty to a strategy of hypothesis and proof compared with one of discovery. I had to commit to some a priori concepts so that Howard Moss could rate the prose reports and I could conduct the interviews and construct the tests. But neither Howard nor I knew what we would find. We had no specific outcomes we wanted to prove. We were open to any message nature might whisper, as long as it whispered something.

The Constant Dilemma

The balance between commitment to a favored idea and accommodation to observations creates a tension in every science. This difference in approaching nature can be seen in the opposing views of Plato and Aristotle. Plato was certain that the true nature of an object was not in what was observed, which was imperfect, but in the beautiful, permanent geometric forms that were its invisible essences. Aristotle, by contrast, put his trust in observations, rather than quiet reflection, to reveal nature's secrets. Niels Bohr and Albert Einstein are a more recent contrast. Bohr assumed that the mathematics of quantum theory was correct and tried to imagine the reality that corresponded to the equations. Einstein started with facts and tried to find a mathematics that would explain the experimental evidence. Because Plato's stance is parsimonious and promises a tidier understanding it has more beauty, but unfortunately, it is often wrong. Aristotle's strategy is burdened with tedious detail and ambiguity and therefore is less beautiful, but it is more often correct. By correct, I mean that it corresponds to reality. A. J. Leggett, a physicist at the University of Illinois, observed that we should not confuse the meaning of truth with the evidence gathered.[19] Although this sentence will strike many nonphysicists as confusing, Leggett meant that logically consistent formal systems that predict observations, like the mathematics of quantum mechanics, might not describe the true nature of reality if scientists had access to that state.

The concepts "stress" and "stressor" have aesthetic appeal because they imply that a broad class of diverse events has a similar effect on the human body. Yet the ugly facts challenge the beauty of this notion because the stresses of solving arithmetic problems in a laboratory, anticipating an impending job interview, surviving the loss of a spouse, experiencing an earthquake, and being unemployed for three years have distinctly different consequences for the immune system. A single concept of "stress" is therefore not a useful idea. Nature stubbornly refuses to reveal its secrets until scientists become just as compulsive and specify who, what, when, and where.

Scientists struggle continually against the restraints that observations impose on high-flying theory. Evolutionary biologists used to believe that mutation was the only cause of a new feature that might result eventually in a new species. Later discoveries forced them to add genetic recombination and the addition or removal of a methyl group from a DNA sequence. Other mechanisms leading to speciation will undoubtedly be discovered in the future. Nature dislikes being understood too completely and takes pleasure from muttering "wrong" whenever a scientist believes that he or she has stumbled on a broad truth. George von Bekesy, who won the 1961 Nobel Prize for his elegant studies of the role of the basilar membrane in hearing, noted in his Nobel address that Leonardo da Vinci was his hero because the Renaissance artist wished to learn from nature rather than outdo it.

Understanding requires a mysterious marriage of fact and imagination. Because facts do not speak, observations without some conception that organizes them into a meaningful idea have little value. But a synthetic imagination that ignores facts usually, but not always, yields a false account. Because the mind can generate a number of explanations for most events, evidence is needed to prune this number to one of reasonable size. We celebrate Isaac Newton for the stunning intellectual insight of the inverse square law, which states that the gravitational attraction between two heavenly bodies is positively related to their masses but inversely related to the distance between them. Yet Newton could not have arrived at that extraordinary idea if hundreds of observers had not recorded the changing locations of the stars and planets over hundreds of years. Because the generation of a profound inference is more difficult than writing down observations, most agree with Bertrand Russell that abstract conceptions are the triumphs of science. However, this celebration of theory over facts is as flawed as is the decision to award more significance to temperature than to humidity when snow falls or greater power to genes than to experience in explaining a fear of spiders.

Physicists, chemists, and biologists have a strong faith in their inferences because powerful methods allow them to eliminate many incorrect explanations. The concept of dark matter required amplifiers that could measure radio energy coming from distant sources. Because psychologists do not enjoy the advantage of new methods introduced regularly into the laboratory, they less often discover novel facts and rely more heavily on a priori ideas. Those interested in human personality and psychopathology, for example, usually use interviews and questionnaires to measure emotions and conflicts because more sensitive methods do not yet exist. The Freudian concepts of hysteria and obsession were based on the verbal statements of patients. Modern personality theorists use informants' checkmarks on questionnaires to infer personality types, such as emotional or conscientious. The basic form of evidence has not changed much over the past hundred years. What has changed are the labels: from hysteric to emotional and from obsessive to conscientious. Until different methods that produce new evidence are invented and tried, the field of personality will idle in place, renaming the same phenomena over and over again.

The Trial

The publicity generated by the Fels project, even before publication of *Birth to Maturity*, in 1962, was probably why I became a third collaborator on a textbook in child psychology. Paul Mussen, who was teaching at the University of California in Berkeley, and John Conger, who was at the University of Colorado, had written the first edition of a text called *Child Development and Personality* in 1956. The book was successful because it was the first to make personality development a central focus and one of the first to adopt a chronological approach to development rather than make psychological functions the titles of the chapters. Mussen and Conger wanted to lighten their workload for the second edition and invited me to join them as a third author. The succeeding editions of the text were adopted by many instructors, and as a result, this book later became involved in a plagiarism case.

A conglomerate that owned a textbook company decided to hire freelance writers to copy successful textbooks in different academic areas and ask a well-known scholar to be the official author to award respectability to the book. The academician's responsibility was to read the manuscript and correct the writers' account. Mussen, Conger, and I were unaware that our textbook had been selected as a target for this treatment. One afternoon a new text in child psychology arrived in the morning mail. As I leafed through the book, I realized that it had copied our organization almost perfectly but had changed the vocabulary. It seemed obvious that this book had plagiarized ours, even though the words had been altered. I called my colleagues; they called the executives at Harper and Row, our publisher, and all agreed we had a good case. The attorney for Harper and Row sued the conglomerate and the academic author, who was a faculty member at a major university. They, in turn, countersued, accusing us of libel, and the case was heard by a judge in a federal court in New York City. The night before I was to testify, the three of us, with our lawyer, were discussing over dinner the mistakes a lawyer can make with a witness. John Lankenau, our attorney, remarked that a good lawyer never asks a question for which he does not know the answer.

I was on the witness stand the next morning when their lawyer—whose name was Mr. Burger (the same name given the opponent lawyer in the Perry Mason television series)—asked me whether the new textbook was theoretically different from our book. I remembered the dinner conversation and knew that Burger had no idea what the term "theory" meant. I paused and in a professorial tone asked, "Mr. Burger, do you know what a theory is?" He remained quiet for about twenty seconds, and then, smiling, I gave a brief lecture on the meaning of theory. I saw, in my peripheral vision, a smile on the judge's face.

We won the case, but I felt sullied by the experience. We were the victims of a crime, but I felt ashamed of being a participant in a legal proceeding. I suspect victims of rape experience a more intense form of this emotion if they wonder whether their behavior in any way invited the attack. Simply being a participant in an ethically tainted event—even if one did nothing—generates an uncomfortable feeling. Some soldiers who only witness atrocities, as occurred in Vietnam or Baghdad, experience a similar feeling that, in rare instances, can lead to post-traumatic stress disorder.

An event that followed the plagiarism trial was a sign of the changes occurring in the American ethos. The academic psychologist who put his name on a book he did not write was asked to leave the university, but another university hired him knowing the facts of the case. I interpret that decision as a sign of the moral confusion that began to seep into the American mood after World War II. A committee of full professors at Harvard Medical School was asked, in the 1980s, to investigate the case of a young scientist who had fabricated his results. After due deliberation, the committee noted in its published report that competitive pressures in a laboratory can contribute to such a serious breach of scientific standards. By attributing causal power to "conditions in the laboratory," the committee was suggesting that a sane, intelligent adult with twenty years of education should not be held completely responsible for abandoning an ethical rule he not only understood but had the willpower to prevent. It is no wonder that some delinquents tell a judge that the scenes they saw on television were responsible for the crimes they committed. Writers capture this moral uncertainty in novels that portray characters who rarely feel shame over their actions. "The Greatest Man in the World," a satiric short story by James Thurber, describes an uncivil young man, Jack "Pal" Smurch, who is the first aviator to fly across the Atlantic, becoming a national hero. The American president, who is obligated to meet and congratulate him, enters Smurch's room on the twentieth floor of a New York hotel, but our hero remains seated, smoking a cigarette and ignoring the president. The tension in the room is high when Smurch rises to stand before an open window. The president nods to a Secret Service agent, who pushes Smurch out the window.

The traits of civility, honesty, loyalty, and humility that were rewarded with signs of success in the nineteenth century are being replaced with shameless self-promotion. Shame requires an individual to care about others' opinions of what they do or what they are. This emotion, which almost every four-year-old is capable of experiencing, can become a relic when a majority in a society became indifferent to the thoughts of strangers. If an executive of a Japanese company behaved as did the chief executive of Enron, he would have immediately resigned. Adam Smith, who would not have understood the American posture, was certain that unbridled self-aggrandizement and brazen dishonesty could never permeate a society because all humans care about the opinions of others. Smith was wrong. It is possible for historical events to create a social ambience in which many, fortunately not all, care little about the evaluations of those who are not close friends, relatives, or authority figures who can give or withhold rewards. Americans do care whether "others" can help, love, harm, or frustrate them, but they are less concerned with the ethical evaluations of their actions. That privilege belongs only to the individual.

Birth to Maturity, a Study in Psychological Development won that year's Hofheimer Prize of the American Psychiatric Society. Surprised by the award, Moss and I reasoned that it was given because the community wished to believe in the preservation of personality traits from childhood to adulthood but no one had provided evidence sufficiently persuasive of that idea. Our conclusion that aggressive ten-year-old boys were more likely than other boys to become angry men who lose their temper easily and that dependent ten-year-old girls were more likely to be adults who required family support represented the first time anyone had used relatively objective data to find a relation, albeit modest, between a feature of childhood and one in adulthood. We were applauded because we had discovered what many wanted to believe.

The early 1960s, before the Vietnam crisis and the rise in civil unrest, was a time when interest in human development was burgeoning. Americans were optimistic, motivated to perfect their society, and convinced that attaining this idealistic goal required a deeper understanding of children. Psychology departments without extensive programs in human development now began to hire faculty with those interests. The subsequent research of that new cohort marked an extraordinary period of growth in developmental psychology.

THREE

Flirting with Biology

The mothers of children born after World War II and entering the work-force in greater numbers needed surrogate care for their young children. This new form of rearing, discrepant from the tradition of their mothers and grandmothers, evoked uncertainty because of the verity that infants needed the loving care only a biological mother could provide. Anything less placed an infant at an unknown level of risk for some later bleak outcome. This be-lief, which was less common in Europe, permeated Sunday sermons in colo-nial America three hundred years earlier and was the central theme in Erik Erikson's influential book *Childhood and Society* (1963), which listed intu-itively attractive stages of development with a primary goal for each phase.[1] The task for infants was to learn to trust others, and the biological mother was the first and preferred target of this trust. This declaration, presumably based on science, had a clear moral imperative. A mother who abandoned this responsibility by delegating care to another woman should understand that she was rendering her child vulnerable to a life of cynicism, anxiety, and far less happiness than the child was entitled to enjoy. Half a dozen years later the British psychiatrist John Bowlby published the first volume of his influ-ential trilogy on attachment.[2] Although Bowlby used different evidence and slightly different arguments, the deep meaning was the same as Erikson had intended. All infants should establish a secure attachment with a primary caretaker during the first year. If they failed this natural assignment because the mother was unavailable or insensitive, the same dark consequences that followed from lack of trust would stain a future that could have been beautiful. Nineteenth-century commentators did worry about a mother's love for her infant, but they were apparently indifferent to the significance of the infant's affection.

Jean Piaget's ideas on cognitive development were a second reason for the interest in children. These ideas were not initially popular, either in Europe or in the United States, because Piaget was interested in the growth of logic and reasoning rather than in emotions, morality, and friendships, and he was indifferent to the influence of caretakers. Piaget's child was a lone agent manipulating an inanimate environment. Finally, the Soviet launch of a space vehicle, which in the United States provoked a wringing of hands over the disheartening quality of science education in American schools, catalyzed concern with the growth of intellectual talents.

Each of these forces—working mothers, Sputnik, and the writings of Erikson, Bowlby, and Piaget—came together, like the components of a perfect storm, to generate a broadly based curiosity about young children, and private philanthropies and the federal government were ready to provide ample funds for research on children. Universities responded by establishing, or expanding, their faculty in human development. Harvard University had a developmental program in the Graduate School of Education, directed by the anthropologist John Whiting, who, with his wife, Beatrice Whiting, studied cultural influences on development, a topic not high on the list of concerns of most anthropologists.[3] The anthropologists at midcentury had been persuaded that the unique structure of each culture precluded the discovery of universal properties across societies. The Whitings, trained at Yale, were searching for behavior universals rather than the growth of cognitive functions or the development of individual children.

The Move to Harvard

The Harvard psychology department persuaded the dean to appoint a professor in human development. The search for this new appointment was under way when Howard Moss and I were finishing the analysis of the Fels data, and David McClelland, chairman of Harvard's psychology department, had read one of our early papers. McClelland was studying the motives for achievement and affiliation inferred from stories told about the photographs of the Thematic Apperception Test. Moss and I had found a modest relation between the frequency of stories containing achievement content and both childhood concern with academic accomplishment and the adolescent's academic record. I suspect this is one reason why I was invited to visit Harvard for the fall term of 1961.

My responsibilities were light. I gave a few lectures in Robert White's undergraduate course and met the faculty while finishing the manuscript of *Birth to Maturity.* The lectures must have been well received, because several months after returning to Yellow Springs I was invited to join the psychology department to create a program in development. Readers will be surprised to learn that I was not eager to accept the invitation. My family had become attached to the quiet gentleness of Yellow Springs. I often walked the tree-lined mile to lunch at home, there were no committee meetings to attend or papers to grade, and I was free to do research, uninterrupted, for as many hours as I chose in a community of liberal, minimally arrogant faculty. It was Eden-like, and my wife and I wondered why we should give up this rustic nirvana to live in a gritty, noisy, crowded city with the extra scientific demands of university life. I asked for more time to make a decision. More than a year passed, and I remained ambivalent. Finally, McClelland, who had grown impatient, told me that the department could wait no longer and that an answer was required by the summer of 1963. When I told McClelland we would be vacationing in New England that summer, he suggested that we stop by his summer home in northwest Connecticut on our return and give him our answer.

The fateful afternoon arrived. Although we had only a few hours to go before reaching McClelland's house, we remained uncertain and decided to stop, have a glass of wine, and make up our minds then and there. We parked the car in an isolated forested area with a very old picnic table scarred with names enclosed in crude hearts and, on the left side of the table, the four capital letters "FELS." If I had been a deeply religious person, I would have interpreted this improbable event as a message from a metaphysical force telling me to remain in Yellow Springs. But I wanted to taste the Harvard environment and resolved the remaining ambivalence by arguing privately that if we did not like Cambridge, we could always return to Yellow Springs. I told McClelland I would come to Harvard, and a year later, in the late summer of 1964, we drove from Yellow Springs to a rented home in Lexington, Massachusetts, with my wife and daughter nursing a sad mood for most of the fourteen-hour journey.

Probing the Infant's First Year

The interests of psychologists in 1964 were considerably different from the preoccupations present only fifteen years earlier. The technical papers in leading journals revealed a waning interest in behaviorism and prophesied the current attraction to biology in articles on the biochemical bases of memory, critical periods in development, pleasure centers in the rat brain, the genetics of Down syndrome, and the biological competences of newborns. The renewed interest in infants raises the issue of how to conceptualize this creature.

The human infant, like billowy summer clouds, invites different perceptions. Montaigne, who saw sixteenth-century infants suckling goats, regarded this life form as an animal. Locke perceived a pristine block of marble ready to be sculpted. Freud's infant was avaricious, while Erikson and Bowlby, wearing rose-colored glasses, portrayed an innocent, gentle, helpless creature looking for care and affection. Each description was an intuition that felt right because of the historical moment in which it was introduced.

By the 1960s the infant was being described as "knowing" some of the rules that permitted an understanding of the world, and the new cohort of developmental psychologists wanted to study the infant's mind. However, perception, inference, and memory are not obvious in the play or conditioned responses of infants and a novel method was needed. Robert Fantz, a scientist at Case Western Reserve University in Cleveland, Ohio, answered this need with a relatively simple procedure that promised to reveal the principles that governed the infant's attention.[4] The psychologist shows infants different stimuli and notes which ones are stared at for a longer time. Application of this method affirmed what many parents had noticed informally. Infants pay attention to unexpected events that alter their sensory field, as well as unfamiliar ones that differ a little from those experienced in the past. When an unexpected or unfamiliar event appears, infants turn from what they were watching or doing to gaze at the novelty.

Clever use of this procedure allowed psychologists to say something important about the infant mind. Robert Fantz, along with others, discovered that young infants looked longer at moving than at still objects, at objects with contour, like black and white bull's eyes, than at homogeneously gray squares, at curved compared with straight lines, at red compared with blue circles, at symmetrical compared with asymmetrical designs, at the top rather than the bottom of stimuli with internal elements, at faces compared with nonfaces, and at upright compared with inverted faces. Monkeys showed some of these same biases. My enthusiasm was captured by the heady implications of these discoveries and I spent more than forty years probing the cognitive processes of infants.

I had applied to the National Institutes of Health for a research grant during the final months at Fels, and the approval of this request allowed me to begin a project soon after arriving at Harvard. I wanted to use Fantz's methodology to explore both universals and variation in behaviors related to attentiveness. This investigation was in a discovery frame. The only a priori assumption was that longer periods of staring reflected greater attentiveness and attentiveness was proportional to an event's novelty. I learned later that this assumption was flawed because the relation between duration of attention and the unfamiliarity of an event is not linear.

I had not forgotten about the heart-rate deceleration in the Lacey laboratory. Before I left Fels, Michael Lewis, a young psychologist who had joined the Fels staff, and I presented infants with interesting visual events, and when we saw the polygraph pen recording the infant's heart rate move down a few centimeters, we became as excited as schoolboys who had discovered an unopened box of candy. Readers might smile at the imbalance between this simple observation and the intensity of our exuberance. Scientists who believe they are the first to observe a regularity in nature are like the first climbers to reach an untouched summit or bird watchers who are the first to see a species in a geographical area that is not their usual habitat. Nobel Prize–winning physicist I. I. Rabi once wrote "Each seeks God in his own way" to describe how he felt when he first observed the spin of a sodium atom.[5] Scientists vary in their image of this beautiful but rare moment. Nature, in my version, is a lovely mansion filled with precious gems locked in a row of steel safes that a beautiful woman opens for inspection at irregular intervals. The lucky observer is present when one of the safes is opened.

Many psychologists would have regarded this project as philistine in its theoretical austerity. We coded duration of attention, frequency of smiling and vocalizing, and magnitude of heart-rate change to various visual events, hoping to detect meaningful patterns as these responses changed with growth. I did not assume we were studying intelligence, emotional regulation, or a host of other popular abstract concepts. I was trying to accommodate to nature. Aristotle and Francis Bacon would have been pleased.

I have only a partial understanding of my suspicion of a priori concepts. Unlike Bekesy, it was not because of Leonardo da Vinci. One distant source was the prejudice I had experienced as a youth, which had convinced me that holding false ideas was an all-too-common human fallibility. Another originated during the year I worked at the Clifford Beers Child Development Clinic in New Haven. I remember muttering to myself on many evenings as I trudged home for dinner that if the children I was interviewing, who were failing in school or charged with delinquency, had not held wildly incorrect beliefs about themselves they would have been saved a great deal of psychic agony. The third reason, more inchoate, was the intuition that thought bends nature's message to fit the mind's odd-shaped cupboard. Even Max Born, one of the founders of quantum mechanics, insisted that thought alone, without experimental facts, was unlikely to discover what was true. Four lines from a poem by Seamus Heaney captured my greater faith in what I saw, heard, and touched than in words.

Keep your eye clear
As the bleb of the icicle
Trust the feel of what nubbed treasures
Your hands have known.[6]

The biographies and autobiographies of many natural scientists, including Robert Boyle, Charles Darwin, Louis Pasteur, and Hans Krebs, taught me the wisdom of being prepared for surprises and suspicious of dogma that blinds investigators from detecting an unsuspected but significant fact. I have always used a few lines from Darwin as a personal mantra: "I have steadily endeavored to keep my mind free so as to give up any hypothesis, however much beloved . . . as soon as facts are seen to be opposed to it. . . . I can't remember a single first formed hypothesis which had not after a time to be given up or greatly modified. This has naturally led me to distrust greatly deductive reasoning in the mixed sciences."[7]

Psychology is a young discipline, and immature fields advance more quickly by relying on inferences from observations, many unexpected, than by trying to prove deductions from a priori conceptions. Abstract words with ambiguous referents fail to note the specificities in nature's products. The unique shape and location of the old maple tree in my backyard are missing from its classification as a tree. Words are like black-and-white photographs of Oregon's Crater Lake taken under a blue sky and bright sun that fail to capture the sensory patina as one looks down on the deep purple water from the mountain rim. I trusted nature to be honest, as long as I promised not to put words in nature's mouth. I am more certain of that belief today than I was in 1965 when we began our longitudinal study of the first year.

Nature was generous. The most important, and unexpected, fact was that the duration of attention to four different masks of a human face (one had a regular arrangement of features, one an irregular pattern with eyes, nose, and mouth rearranged, one had only eyes, and the fourth had no facial features) was long at four months, decreased across the first year, and then, surprisingly, increased after the first birthday. The decreased attention after four months was understandable because, with growth, infants can relate the masks to their cognitive representations of human faces. Because infants look only as long as they need to assimilate the stimulus to their schematic knowledge, they should look for a shorter time following experience with faces in their environments. This logic demanded that the twenty-seven-month-olds should have assimilated the masks more quickly than the thirteen-month-olds and looked minimally. But attention was longer in the second year than at seven months.

A tentative explanation was that brain maturation introduced a new cognitive ability, which I called "the activation of hypotheses." Older infants activate schemata that represent how faces should appear, and perhaps the events that created their unusual form, and continue to attend to the face while this cognitive work is ongoing. The increase in attention to unfamiliar events toward the end of the first year, which is now an established fact, implies a maturational change in brain organization and a parallel change in the ability to relate the representations acquired in the past to the present moment. This ability is called working memory. We now know that one component of the maturation involves the establishment of connections between structures in the temporal lobe and the prefrontal cortex. This idea also explained why the ability to remember where an adult hid a toy usually appears at about eight months of age. The more mature brain enables eight-month-olds to hold in a working memory circuit the schema of the object they saw moments earlier that is now lying under a cover. As a result, they reach correctly.

This new talent could also explain why infants cry to strangers and to temporary separation from a caretaker. One-year-olds can relate the departure of the mother from a laboratory room to their earlier representation of her presence, hold both representations in a working memory circuit, and as a result are provoked into a state of uncertainty that can lead to a cry of distress. The decision to conduct this study in a discovery mode led to a fruitful result and a new interpretation of object permanence and separation fear, two phenomena psychologists had previously regarded as unrelated.

A few years later Nathan Fox and Sally Weiskopf affirmed this conclusion by repeatedly administering twelve problems requiring working memory to eight infants across the period from five to fourteen months of age. The results were beautiful. The robustness of working memory improved most between seven and ten months in each of the eight infants. The evidence from more than a hundred studies in different laboratories points to the same conclusion. Sometime between six and ten months infants begin to "think" for the first time because brain sites that were unconnected in the young brain have become connected. The more mature brain permits the infant to find the representations relevant to a current experience and to keep the two schemata active until they can be combined. If they cannot, the infant turns away.

The frequency of smiling, babbling, and change in heart rate, however, did not show the developmental pattern displayed by attentiveness. The magnitude of heart-rate change decreased steadily from four to twenty-seven months, and vocalization and smiling failed to increase after the first year.

Thus, babbling, smiling, and heart rate, which are also signs of an attentive state, invited a conclusion different from the one suggested by time spent looking. The separate growth functions for looking, smiling, vocalizing, and heart rate forced me to title the chapters in my book *Change and Continuity in Infancy* (1971) with names of the measures instead of terms like "attention," "intelligence," and "cognitive development."[8]

The lack of coherence among behaviors that psychologists believe reflect one process is all too common. Infants interacting with a friendly adult suddenly hear the adult voice change in quality. This unexpected event produces greater cessation of movement—a common sign of surprise—at seven than at nine months. However, the likelihood of gazing up at the adult is lower at seven than at nine months, and greatest at twelve months.[9] I suspect that looking up at the adult, but not the brief cessation of movement, reflects the activation of hypotheses. Thus, two behaviors that intuition treats as equivalent signs of surprise have different meanings.

About fifteen years later, Steven Reznick found that fourteen-month-old infants first exposed to different examples of the same category (for example, a series of dogs with different shapes and colors) and then shown an object from a new category (a doll, for example) showed no increase in attention. However, many infants vocalized, smiled, or pointed at the new object, indicating that they recognized it had different features. The paper summarizing these results (1983) cited the physicist-philosopher Percy Bridgman: "There is no sharp dividing line between the instrument of knowledge and the object of knowledge."[10] Bridgman meant that the meaning and validity of every conclusion is inextricably bound to the evidence that is its foundation. Biologists trying to decide whether two species are closely related in their evolutionary history arrive at different estimates if some rely on similarities in anatomy and others use similarity in DNA segments. Disagreement is frequent in psychology because investigators often use the same concept to describe very different kinds of evidence. The concept "conscientious," for example, is used to describe both adults' answers on a questionnaire and their observed behaviors. The concept "aggressive" is applied to both a rat biting an intruder animal and to an adolescent demanding money from a peer in exchange for protection. The concept "attachment" is invoked to describe both an infant rat that remains in an area containing the smell associated with a female rat that "abused" the rat pup and a crying one-year-old child who is easily quieted by a mother's caresses. This semantic permissiveness is obstructing progress. The Dow Jones average, the unemployment rate, inflation, the difference in income between the top and bottom 25 percent of the population, consumer confidence, and the federal debt as a percent of the gross national product yield different conclusions regarding the health of the American economy. That is why economists look at all six items.

The Power of Discrepancy

This project generated one other important but less novel idea. Infants looked longer at the face with regular features when they were four months old but looked longer at the face with irregularly placed features when they were twelve months old. Attention was prolonged by events that were a little discrepant from their acquired knowledge of faces. Familiar events that are understood immediately, as well as events that bear no relation to the infant's knowledge, even though they are perceptually discriminable, are studied minimally. The longest bouts of attention occur toward events that share elements with the infant's knowledge. Infants who detect a difference between a familiar and an unfamiliar event may not show prolonged attention to the less familiar event if it does not engage any existing schema. Put plainly, the interest of infants, like that of adults, is usually recruited by events that differ only a little from what is familiar and therefore are understandable with some effort. It is not a coincidence that thirty years of research on the brain reveals that discrepant and unexpected events are among the most reliable causes of activity in neuronal circuits. When this robust fact is better understood, psychologists will possess a deep insight into the functioning of the brain and its heir, the mind.

Claude Shannon, the father of information theory, formalized the idea that humans are most likely to be alerted by events that are unexpected.[11] This powerful yet simple principle applies to every aspect of psychological activity. It might even explain why humans are more alerted by a concave surface—an indentation in a car door—than by a convex one—an elongated rear light on a car—for the convex shape is more frequently seen in daily experience. Noses and hills are more common than dents in a saucepan or holes in a lawn. During every waking moment the mind-brain of mice as well as humans expects a particular envelope of events to occur. If that expectation is disconfirmed, a state of alert attention follows, and the next state in the cascade depends on whether the event is familiar or unfamiliar and is or is not potentially dangerous. Examples of the four possibilities produced by crossing familiarity with danger are: a bulb in a lamp fails, the smell of smoke from a nearby room is detected, a stranger wearing a red eye patch enters the room, and a novel pain in the groin pierces consciousness.

We received few requests for this paper because it contained the unpopular message that no certain inference could be drawn from a change in duration of attention to an event, whether increased staring or looking away. Nonetheless, psychologists continue to make bold inferences about what infants do or do not know from changes in attention alone. The psychologists who claim that infants can "add," or know that a ball cannot pass through a solid barrier, assume a linear relation between duration of attention and degree of difference between an event and the infant's expectations built from experience. Because the relation is curvilinear, scientists cannot infer that an infant who did not look longer at a pink ball after seeing a red one failed to detect the difference between the two balls. Infants can discriminate between a pair of circles and a pair of squares, each enclosed in a larger circle, but surprisingly they do not look longer at the squares after being familiarized with the circles because they assimilate the pair of squares enclosed in a circle to their schema for a human face. Infants who have been familiarized on a sphere devote prolonged attention to a cylinder but not to an irregular piece of Styrofoam—which is far more distinctive—because they do not try to relate the Styrofoam object to their knowledge.

The Problem with Looking Time

Increased attention to an event, moreover, need not imply that the infant "knows" anything about the meaning of the event or its origin. I will turn toward the window if I hear a loud, unfamiliar sound, but after ten seconds of quiet staring at the outside scene I might have no better understanding of its nature or origin. Young infants who are first familiarized with a face displaying a broad smile will stare at the subsequent presentation of a face with clenched jaws because of the physical differences in the features of the two faces and not because they know anything about joy or anger. A pair of psychologists claimed that fifteen-month-olds can infer the private thoughts of an adult examiner because the infants showed prolonged staring when the woman, facing two distinct boxes, reached into the box that, from her perspective, should not have contained a toy.[12] But staring in the service of surprise is not equivalent to inferring another's beliefs. I would stare at a pedestrian hopping across a busy street without necessarily inferring any of the pedestrian's intentions. Put plainly, staring at a target need not reflect any deeper knowledge about the target, except that it was alerting because of its physical qualities or because it was unexpected. The staring only means that the person is in a momentary state of surprise. One-year-old infants shown the letters "TRUE" for sixty seconds and then presented with the letters "FALSE" would devote prolonged attention to the second stimulus, but no one suggests that this behavior means that they understand anything about the concepts "true" and "false." The same conclusion applies to brain measurements. Infants just eight weeks old show a distinct neuronal response when, following a series of "ba" sounds with a duration of one-fifth of a second, they hear a "ba" sound that is one-tenth of a second longer. The human brain from birth forward is exquisitely sensitive to change, any change, but this reliable reaction does not permit only one obvious conclusion regarding what the mind understands.

The history of psychology is littered with the broken hopes of those who mistakenly assumed that a single measure permitted a confident conclusion about a psychological process. When I was a student, the behaviorists believed that how quickly a hungry rat ran down an alley toward a food reward was an index of the strength of the animal's conditioned habit. Others assumed that increased sweating of finger or palm—called the galvanic skin reflex—measured fear or arousal.

When I was at the Fels Institute, I asked school-age children to describe a series of pictures. Seconds after seeing each picture, they were asked to draw on a blank piece of paper the picture they had just described. Some children failed to draw salient objects they had mentioned; others drew objects they had not described. Twenty years later Ken Livingston, a Harvard graduate student, demonstrated that estimates of a child's understanding of the concept "animal" depended on the procedure used to obtain the estimate.

To each guess about the meaning of a single measurement, nature's usual reply is "Sorry, wrong" because its meaning depends on the agent (animal, infant, child, adult), the details of the setting, and its function at the moment. The meaning of a single measure is as ambiguous as that of a verb lacking a noun or object. Put plainly, there is not one example in the history of the social sciences in which a particular measure had a single, unambiguous meaning—not one! Although people laugh at a joke, they also occasionally laugh as they describe their anger at an injustice. Differences in duration of attention to one of two events are ambiguous because duration of attention is determined by more than the infant's expectation. Thus, the bold conclusions regarding what infants "know" based only on how long they look at an event will probably have to be retracted in the future. The meaning of the verb "know" cannot be separated from the evidence used to infer its presence. Most languages honor forms of knowing with different words. In English, for example, the terms "educated," "clever," "experienced," and "wise" imply distinct forms of understanding of a domain like "the economics of the marketplace."

Finding Optimal Novelty

Infants are alerted by events that are slightly discrepant from their schemata. Adults show the keenest interest in ideas that are slightly discrepant from their existing knowledge. The celebrated writers and artists of any era are able to anticipate themes that are not yet, but are about to become, nodes of uncertainty in their society. The mood of alienation running through T. S. Eliot's *The Wasteland* was enhanced among Europeans after World War I, and as a result, the poem brought Eliot celebrity, even though it sold fewer than three hundred copies in the first six months after its publication. Its cynicism has become so prevalent during the past few decades, however, that the poem has lost some of its initial power. John Donne's poems, written in the early seventeenth century, were also replete with skepticism. His readers, however, were not prepared for his dark descriptions and his works were criticized by many, including Dr. Samuel Johnson, who called them "full of disgusting hyperbole." Two centuries later, partly owing to Eliot's advocacy, Donne's writing enjoyed a renascence.

In a lecture to undergraduates in 1964, I suggested that the popular play and then movie *Tea and Sympathy* was applauded because Americans were psychologically ready for a story about the wife of a private school headmaster who, in a mood of nurture, seduces an adolescent boy attending the school to help him overcome his extreme timidity with girls. I added that American society might be psychologically ready for a play about incest between a father and daughter in about twenty years, and one of them might begin writing such a script. It turned out that in 1984—exactly twenty years later—a major television network aired a one-hour drama, *Something about Amelia*, in which a middle-class father living in a quiet suburb has an incestuous relationship with his adolescent daughter. A few years later, the French filmmaker Louis Malle made *Murmurs of the Heart*, which portrayed an incestuous relationship between a mother and son. Vladimir Nabokov's *Lolita*, first published in Paris in 1955, was banned in France the following year, and when the novel was published in the United States in 1958, the *New York Times*'s reviewer found the book repulsive. Forty-three years later *Lolita* became a Hollywood movie for the second time. A similar sequence had occurred thirty years earlier when many publishers rejected James Joyce's *Ulysses* as obscene. The poet Czeslaw Milosz recognized that the celebrity or indifference awarded a work of art depends on the relation between the art and the community mind. The artist who wants acceptance cannot "run too far ahead . . . of the reader."[13] Over time the mind-heart, like a butterfly flitting from flower to flower, finds a fresh novelty that recruits attention to a theme it can understand with effort and in that process becomes emotionally aroused. That is one reason why the form of psychotherapy that works best changes every twenty to twenty-five years.

The curative power of psychoanalytic techniques began to wane when the therapists' secrets became public knowledge. The same fate may be in store for today's favorite psychotherapeutic regimens. Humans have the unfortunate habit of mistaking originality for wisdom because novelty is alerting and, if understandable, creates an intuition of truth. A popular form of psychotherapy called cognitive behavioral therapy is effective with many patients suffering from one of the anxiety disorders. A critical feature of the treatment requires patients to confront the target of their anxiety so that they can recognize that the anticipated dangers do not occur. This treatment differs radically from the older dynamic therapies, derived from psychoanalysis and requiring patients to probe their childhoods, and is effective without the help of drugs. This novel approach leads patients to expect remission of their symptoms, and the enthusiasm of therapists motivates patients to conquer their problem in order to avoid disappointing the person who has worked so hard to help them. It remains a possibility that twenty-five years from now, when the rituals of this therapy have lost their novelty, and therapists have lost some of their current enthusiasm, this intervention, too, will lose its effectiveness. I hope I am wrong.

Because unexpected or unfamiliar events are arousing, they are usually remembered for the longest time. Roger Brown, a colleague at Harvard, called these recollections "flash bulb memories" because the details remain so clear. Many Americans who watched television on September 11, 2001, will have flashbulb memories. Many older Americans remember exactly where they were and what they were doing when they first heard that John F. Kennedy had been assassinated. I was sitting at my desk at the Fels Institute analyzing data. My earliest memory is entering the hospital with my father when I was four years old to visit my mother and newborn brother. Children were not allowed to visit patients, and my father had hidden me inside his bulky coat. The earliest memory with a fear component occurred a year later when I was at a resort hotel with my father, who took me away for a weekend of recovery from a tonsillectomy. I cried in pain when a bee stung me as I walked toward a lake where my father planned to rent a ro boat. After we got in the boat and my father had rowed to the middle of the lake, he told me to sit still while he dove into the water to enjoy a brief swim. He did not anticipate the strong breeze that rose suddenly and pushed the boat several hundred yards away into a bank of tall grass. I grew frightened and yelled that I was going to jump into the water. My father wisely gestured to a man on the shore, near the tall grass, who swam to the boat to rescue me. I have never forgotten the details of that experience.

These and similar robust facts challenge the popular notion that most children repress the first occasion of sexual molestation by an adult. If the unexpected exploitation evoked a strong emotion of fear or shame, it was probably not forgotten. If, however, it was not particularly arousing or if the emotion dissipated because the exploitation continued for months or a few years, it could have been forgotten. Repetition can dull emotion and tuck the accompanying memories in a locked closet. That is why adults can remember the details of their first day at school or college but not the many harrowing preparations for the examinations that filled their school years.

Although the renascence of spirituality in the United States and Europe has several causes, one small factor is the public's growing ennui with new scientific facts. Most scientific discoveries do not arouse the excitement they did a half-century ago. Before World War II, when there was no World Wide Web, there were far fewer scientists, and new discoveries were less frequent, each revelation had a greater potential to generate a moment of wonder. The day after most newspapers told the world that British astrophysicist Arthur Eddington's research team had discovered that light from the stars appeared to bend as it brushed the sun, affirming a prediction of relativity, Albert Einstein became a world hero. It is much harder to imagine a current discovery in any scientific domain that would have equally dramatic consequences because the density of stunning new facts has increased over the past fifty years. We are barraged with novelties, from pictures of Mars's surface to cloned dogs. Because the appeal of a fresh fact is correlated with its capacity to generate a tiny jolt of emotion, the current plenitude of scientific declarations guarantees that, except for scientists in a particular field, most new facts do not provoke a great deal of emotion in most people. The space missions of NASA have become routine, and it is unlikely that more than a tiny proportion of the public knows the names of those who were on the last flight to the space station. One reason for the current attractiveness of spirituality is that, because its source in intuition is so radically different from the densely factual, rational nature of science, it generates a feeling that people interpret as a sign of truth and leads to a vitality that reassures those disheartened by a materialism that challenges each person's free will and the anomie of contemporary life.

Features or Relations

Our research on infants also motivated brooding on the importance of the context in which an event occurs. Every event can be described, or conceptualized, by noting its special features, on one hand, or by noting the relations into which it enters—its links to the past, usual settings, or functional consequences—on the other. A pencil can be described as a long, thin piece of wood wrapped around a shaft of graphite or as an object usually found on tables or desks that people pick up in order to write. A child's definition of a hole as a thing one digs or a cookie as an object one eats does not describe the inherent features of these objects.

Consider, as a better illustration, an eight-month-old infant playing alone on the floor of a living room who, on seeing a man with a beard and eyeglasses approach, stares and, a few seconds later, cries. An observer can focus either on the physical features of the adult as the cause of the infant's distressed state, usually called "fear" and a bias more characteristic of Western scholars, or on the fact that an unfamiliar person was approaching an infant who was not close to a parent, a bias more characteristic of Eastern scholars. The second view emphasizes the relation between the event that caused the cry and the infant's knowledge, as well as the fact that the infant was not near a target of attachment.

The typical approach of Western scientists, which favors a determinate relation between an incentive and a subsequent psychological state with stable features across settings, motivates a search for other events that produce the same essential state. For example, many American and European scientists attribute "fear" to a rat that freezes to a tone that signals electric shock and to a mouse reluctant to enter a brightly lit unfamiliar area. By contrast, a focus on the fact that the adult approaching the infant was unfamiliar invites a search for other examples of reactions to unfamiliarity and, perhaps, a grouping of the crying infant with behaviors animals display in any setting that is unfamiliar. Under these conditions, the infant's cry to a stranger might be categorized with a rat exploring an unfamiliar cage or a mouse biting an unfamiliar intruder. A photograph of a face with an angry expression can be treated as an incentive for "fear" because of its physical features or as an unexpected event that surprised a person lying in a scanner. Many psychologists and neuroscientists favor the former view, even though photos of angry faces, as well as desirable events that are unexpected or infrequent, for example, an attractive nude, produce very similar patterns of activation in the amygdala and other brain sites. Erotic scenes produce a larger waveform in the electroencephalogram than pictures of tables, chairs, or apples because most adults do not expect a psychologist to show them sexy pictures in a laboratory set-ting. The brain's first question to every intrusion is: Was this event expected or unexpected? Less than two-tenths of a second later it evaluates the specific meaning of the event and may generate an emotion.

When a child answers an adult's question the interrogator's first task is to figure out what question the child was answering. One of my students, Eliza-beth Nolan, once brought me a paper from a neurology journal describing a procedure physicians were using to determine whether a five-year-old had delayed brain maturation. The neurologist would tell the child to close her eyes and seconds later tell him whether he had touched her in one place or in two places. The doctor would then touch her face and arm simulta-neously and ask the child to reply. Some five-year-olds would report that they were touched on the face and ignore the stimulation of the arm. Be-cause older children typically reported stimulation of both sites, neurologists concluded that these children were "biologically delayed." I was convinced that the young children gave the less mature answer because they did not expect to be touched in two places and therefore mentioned only the face, even though they perceived the second touch. So I told Elizabeth to find some five-year-olds and to tell them initially that she might touch them in two places. That simple statement worked. All the five-year-olds acknowl-edged being touched in two places. They were not delayed, just answering a question that the neurologist had not appreciated.

These facts point to the utility of treating events in a relational frame. My perceptions and representations of the spaces in which I live are composed of objects, like books, lamps, and tables, the spatial relations among them, and the contexts in which they are found. I have representations of the color, size, and printed title of one of my books and the place where that book rests in my study, in the library of my building, and in the office of a colleague. These are three distinct representations of the same book, and each evokes different thoughts. A lion can be described as a large, dangerous mammal, one of many species found in Africa, or a caged attraction at zoos. Change the context, and the psychological meaning of the object is altered.

Cultures differ in the relative attractiveness of these alternative ways to conceptualize nature. Chinese and Japanese have a preference for the rela-tions that objects, animals, and people enter into, whereas Americans and

Europeans pay more attention to the isolated features of the same events. If asked, "What do you do?" I am apt to reply, "I study children." A Japanese psychologist is more likely to say, "I am on the faculty of the University of Tokyo." Asian parents are likely to remind their children of their relationships to kin, whereas Americans emphasize the child's traits and talents. Hence when Chinese-Americans who were not fully acculturated to American society were asked to recall the emotional experiences of their childhood, they often included others in their verbal remembrances. Indigenous Americans are more likely to describe their actions and feelings stripped of the presence of parents, siblings, or friends. Had I been asked to recall my salient childhood experiences, I would have described the time I was stung by a bee in sentences that focused on my feelings of pain and fear. A Chinese-American would more likely have emphasized that he was walking with his father on a dirt path toward a lake.

The assumption that the individual, and not family, friends, or community, is the primary social object has penetrated the American mind so deeply that few people consider an alternative answer to the question "What do you want from life?" Most informants reply that they want to be happy, healthy, or successful or to gain one of many outcomes that enhances self. It is rare for Americans to say they would like their town to prosper or their mother to enjoy a long, healthy life. The notion that any other person or group should have priority over self strikes most Americans as irrational or even bizarre. A poll of 3,160 adults from around the world (40 percent from the United States and Canada) revealed that one of every two respondents said that their health was the most important factor in the happiness they expected in the coming year. Only one in ten nominated social and community activities.[14] Students may memorize John Donne's line "Do not ask for whom the bell tolls, it tolls for thee," but its message remains insulated from an ethic that places self first.

The conception of self as an isolated agent whose needs usually have priority is not universal. Eastern cultures in particular have treated social relationships as an intimate component of each person's identity. This is one reason why the seventeenth-century philosopher G. W. Leibniz admired the greater civility of Chinese society compared to his own. During a visit to an exhibition of the paintings of younger artists in a Tokyo museum, I noted that a large proportion of canvases symbolized the contrast between *tatemae*—the psychological face a person displays to nonintimates—and *honne*—the posture assumed with intimates. For example, two birds in a painting of four flying cranes had exposed feet, whereas the feet of the other two were invisible. Another artist painted one adult facing forward and another turned around. Few Western artists would paint such scenes because the psychological contrast between tatemae and honne, which assumes that each person has two identities, each defined by the nature of the social setting, is a foreign concept. Some rural villages in northern China forbid a woman from engaging in sexual behavior in the home in which she was raised because the "place" in which the act occurs influences its moral status.

Chinese college students presented with the words "peach–tree–pineapple" and asked to pick the two most similar words, choose "peach" and "tree" because peaches grow on trees. American students, by contrast, are more likely to pair "peach" with "pineapple" because both are fruits.[15] More than twenty-five years ago I constructed a test for American school-age children that measured the preference for a relational or a categorical bias. Each child saw drawings of three familiar objects on a page and had to select the two that were most similar (for example, a man, a pot, and a woman). Younger children paired the objects that were related to each other (for example, the woman and the pot); the older children more often selected the two drawings that belonged to the same category because they shared features (the man and the woman), even though they were capable of a relational concept if told to find several ways to group the pairs of pictures.

Some emotional terms used by residents on the isolated atoll of Ifaluk in the Western Caroline Islands of Micronesia distinguish between feelings provoked by humans compared with those provoked by nature or situations.[16] For example, Ifalukians use one term for the anger produced by the behavior of another—a rude act—and a different word for the anger generated by a storm that interrupts an important activity. Many Americans would use the same word—"angry"—for both situations because the person's feeling tone is similar in both situations.

Some current psychiatric categories for mental illness implicitly acknowledge the context in which the symptom occurs. Patients with social phobia are distressed by interactions with strangers. Patients with panic disorder are threatened by sudden inexplicable changes in heart rate and breathing. But other categories, unfortunately, are indifferent to context. "General anxiety disorder," "depression," and "psychopathic" ignore the settings in which the symptoms were developed or are displayed. A homicide committed by a man who was insulted in a bar after having had five beers is often an impulsive reaction to a sudden rise in anger; a homicide that was part of a premeditated robbery is not. Psychiatrists would possess a more fruitful set of categories if they always acknowledged the contexts in which the patients spent their childhoods and in which they were currently living. Simply living in urban Copenhagen rather than in rural Denmark increases the risk of developing schizophrenia among people who have a family member with this illness.[17]

A child with older siblings who lives with one parent is at increased risk for a number of psychiatric symptoms because this combination is more common among economically stressed families. A depressed mood is more prevalent among the poor, who live with frequent frustration and loss, than among the middle class. A depressed single mother with four children who grew up in poverty and lives on public assistance in a two-room apartment in a large city might belong to a diagnostic category different from a woman with the same symptoms who grew up in a privileged home and lives with a loving husband in a middle-class suburb. The first has a more realistic basis for her mood than the second. There is a linear relation between reports of anxiety or depression and such physical complaints as backache, headache, and heartburn.[18] But both depression and physical complaints are more common among adults with a low income who did not attend college. Most American psychiatrists who attend only to the reports of anxiety or depression write as if all their patients possessed the same biological vulnerability to these emotions. It is more fruitful, I believe, to view anxiety or depression as components of different clusters in which a compromised social-class position—which is a chronic context—is a primary feature of one cluster. Compromised lung function due to working in a coal mine has an origin and prevention strategy different from the same disability due to a genetic vulnerability. Rather than report that 20 percent of Americans develop an anxiety disorder over a lifetime, psychiatrists should report the prevalence of anxiety (and mood) disorders separately for different class and ethnic groups.

A person's social class is defined not by any absolute set of features but by the relative differences in property, literacy, and type of work between one individual and another. In dirt-poor villages, where everyone lives in mud huts without electricity or sanitary facilities, those who own a quarter-acre of land or can read have "higher" status than those without either feature, and their children perform better on tests of intellectual ability. The anger felt by citizens from underdeveloped nations toward Europeans and Americans is exacerbated by their awareness of the stark differences between their circumstances and those of richer societies. Many leaders of poor countries could sleep more deeply if their youth had no knowledge of the material advantages of the West. It is the relative difference between people, groups, or nations, not absolute characteristics, that fuels envy and war.

The biological concept of inclusive fitness is always dependent on the animal's ecology because the setting determines whether a particular set of genes renders one group of animals more fit than another. Even the activity of a gene depends on its place in the body, whether brain or liver, and its consequences, for anatomy or physiology, depend on all the other genes in the person's genome. The creation of an infant's organs during pregnancy must be described in terms of relations among parts. The path of each migrating neuron, for example, like a child in a crowd trying to find a parent, is determined by the cells and molecules it encounters on its journey. The most fruitful model for development, anatomical or psychological, is a village of collaborating agents with different features. The Chinese, bless them, had it right. Although the Earth is a distinct object with a circumference and mass, life on Earth depended on its relation to the Moon and Sun.

Genetically identical mice placed in exactly the same apparatus and subjected to the same procedures do not always behave similarly in different laboratories. Although molecular biologists have found that humans and fruit flies have many of the same genes, they understand that the differences between a child and a fly are due to the arrangements and interrelations of those genes rather than to the number of shared genes. Elizabeth Browning's sonnets and a college student's poems contain the same twenty-six letters. Truth and beauty are found in patterns, not in their separate elements.

Although Charles Darwin and Alfred Wallace independently invented the mechanism of natural selection in evolution — and both were Englishmen — Darwin was celebrated as a genius whereas Wallace's name lies in the shadows of the public mind. A reasonable explanation of this asymmetry involves the community's attitudes toward each man's pattern of traits. Because Darwin was financially secure, his efforts seemed "purer" than those of Wallace, whose expeditions to South America and Malaysia were motivated, in part, by a need for the money he might make by bringing exotic specimens back to England. Second, Darwin remained loyal to a materialist interpretation of life and, therefore, fit the approved prototype of the objective, unsentimental scientist. Wallace, who argued for a spiritual force in nature, alienated the British scientific establishment by introducing an inconsistent element into the biologists' worldview. Even though both men arrived at the insight of natural selection, Darwin eclipsed Wallace because Darwin's pattern of characteristics was a better "fit" for the social context in which the two men lived.

Most concepts in neuroscience emphasize the anatomical and physiological features of particular brain sites rather than the conditions that activate the site. The former perspective favors localization of functions and such conclusions as "the dorsolateral prefrontal cortex mediates working memory." In a relational frame, however, the emphasis will be placed on the circuits activated by all tasks requiring working memory. Under these latter conditions, the dorsolateral prefrontal cortex would be grouped with the other brain structures activated when a person, or animal, is holding information in a working memory circuit.

Current claims about the amygdala provide an especially clear example of this difference in perspective. Neuroscientists who believe that increased amygdalar activity to a face with an angry expression produces a state of fear imply that this emotion is localized in this structure, even though, as noted earlier, the amygdala can be activated by many events that have no relation to fear. Pictures of nudes, couples in romantic embraces, and people with sad postures and facial expressions can evoke as much amygdalar activity as scenes of mutilated bodies, snakes, or angry faces when the images are unexpected.[19] The unexpected appearance of food activates the amygdala of rats, and one-year-old monkeys whose amygdalae had been removed in infancy showed signs of fear to other monkeys.[20] Reflection on all the evidence reveals that the primary cause of amygdalar activation is an unexpected event, whether a snake or a friend not seen for many years. A more fruitful under-

standing of this structure is obtained by focusing on the conditions that activate it rather than on the emotions it provokes.

A preference for one object or event over another is usually a function
of the relation between the object and the category to which it is assigned.
Stated differently, every human judgment, whether of a feeling, person, or
event, is colored by what the agent chooses as a comparison. This rule applies with equal force to the ranking of pleasures, pains, objects of beauty,
and targets of anger. If asked to rate, on a seven-point scale, my differential
preference at breakfast for muffins or scrambled eggs, I would give muffins
a six and the eggs a two—a difference of four. But if asked to rate the same
two objects with reference to all the foods I eat, muffins would receive a four
and eggs a two—a difference of just two. My preference for muffins over eggs
was diminished when the category expanded. Human resentments honor the
same principle. If asked to rate the intensity of my anger toward all those
who are alive, Osama bin Laden would receive a seven and Robert Mugabi
a four. But if the category were enlarged to include those alive and dead, bin
Laden would get a five and Mugabi a four because Hitler and Stalin would
receive sevens. This mental strategy implies that the smaller the comparison
group the greater the difference in hostility between members of a group with
different values. Perhaps that is why the hatreds between different religious
and ethnic groups who live in a small region are more intense than the hostility among groups living in large, more diverse societies. Before television,
radio, and the Internet working-class American youth compared their circumstances with the more privileged in their community and felt some level
of deprivation. Today's youth, who see refugees in Sudan, butchered victims
in Rwanda, and starving children in so many parts of the world, feel more
privileged when they compare themselves with these less fortunate groups.

The main point is that each object, person, event, or action is a member
of more than one category and all human judgment is colored by the category selected. The Sun is a delicious source of warmth when the category is
"seasons of the year" but a malevolent force when the category is "cancer."
Optimists have a habit of selecting a desirable category; pessimists choose an
undesirable one; realists, who see both sides, are usually ambivalent.

When scientists routinely acknowledge both the features of an animal or
a person together with their history and the settings in which they are act-

ing, a mouse that bit an intruder entering its territory will not be grouped with the boys who killed their classmates at Columbine High School. And an adolescent from an affluent suburb who stole a friend's bicycle will not be put in the same category with a boy living in an urban ghetto who, with three friends, robbed a grocery store. Traditional Chinese law distinguishes between stealing from a close relative and stealing from a stranger because the social relationship between one person and another dictates the propriety of a behavior. Western law, which is indifferent to the relation of the criminal to the victim and is concerned only with the decontextualized act of stealing, fails to honor this distinction. The lesson to be learned from biology and history is to view every observation as an event in a context. Hans Krebs, a biologist who discovered an important physiological cycle, was asked why he, and not an equally brilliant chemist working on the same problem, uncovered this significant fact. His answer was that the chemist conceptualized the reaction as it occurred in a test-tube, whereas he imagined it as a dynamic process in a living person.

Coherence of Conditions

Advances in both science and information technology are creating an intellectual climate in which the notion of "coherence" is competing with, and may eventually replace, the current perspective, which awards prominence to causal relations between a singular condition and an equally particular outcome—heat a pot of water and it boils. The new but still nascent view is apparent in phenomena that require the collaboration of many independent conditions. A New England hurricane in October and an April blizzard in Georgia require the merging of several forces no one of which is sufficient to cause the event. Scientists are now demonstrating what they had believed but had been unable to prove; namely, that a psychological symptom, such as depression or a panic attack, requires both a genetic vulnerability and a set of life conditions. Either one alone is insufficient to produce the disabling state. For example, intense feelings of depression occur in children when early parental abuse, lack of social support, and a genetic vulnerability that affects the amount of serotonin in the brain are combined.[21] In this and other examples there is no single cause. A coherence of several factors is necessary to produce a particular phenomenon.

Let us suppose that each of three independent conditions (early abuse, minimal social support during late childhood, and a particular genome) has four possible psychological outcomes and, further, that serious depression accompanied by a suicide attempt is a rare but possible outcome for each condition. The probability that an adolescent exposed to all three conditions will develop this profile is very low, and only one or two of every hundred children encountering these conditions will become depressed and suicidal during the adolescent years. Depression, chronic delinquency, hyperactivity, or panic attacks, like a Georgia blizzard in April, require an improbable blending of relevant conditions joined at the proper times. Few psychological profiles have the causal properties of a window shattered by a baseball.

Coherence of Information

The extraordinary growth of information technology, represented by radio, cell phones, television, and the global Internet, which most of the world's eight and a half billion inhabitants will exploit by 2050, has made coherence of communications a salient issue. The meaning of coherence when it refers to information is different from its meaning in the context of causal conditions. The coherence of sentences, stories, pictures, or films is defined by the magnitude of the correlation among its components within a culture. The higher the correlation, the greater the coherence. The sentence "The dog ran to its owner entering the house" has greater coherence than "The dog galloped to his friend jumping into the house" because, in English, the transitional probabilities are higher for "ran" than for "galloped" following the word "dog," for "owner" rather than "friend" after "the dog ran," and for "entering" rather than "jumping" following "ran to its owner." The higher the transitional probabilities between successive words in a sentence, the greater the coherence. Similarly, a scene illustrating half a dozen adolescent boys standing on a street corner near a grocery store has greater coherence for Americans and Europeans than six boys standing near an isolated barn in a meadow or six cows standing on a street corner. The coherence of a sentence or scene always varies with the past experiences of the reader or listener. Sentences and scenes that are coherent for Americans would be less coherent for rural Indonesians presented with the same information.

It is important to appreciate that meaning coherence applies to sentences or scenes and applies less well to fleeting sensations, thoughts, or images. Many thoughts and feelings cannot be expressed in language or illustrated in pictures. Words cannot describe faithfully the combination of feelings and ideas that flood consciousness the moment one wakes from a nightmare or sees a magnificent sunrise on a crystal-clear morning. Hence, many thoughts escape the judgments of true or false, right or wrong, which can be applied to the symbolic information in sentences and pictures.

Perhaps the most provocative implication of the ascendance of meaning coherence is that the primary features of matter—size, mass, location in space, and electrical charge—are inappropriate for symbolic communication. The information exchanged among a dozen participants from as many countries during a conference call cannot be described with the materialistic vocabulary of physics. The assumption that, at its root, the world consists only of matter seized the Western mind after new machines and sources of energy were introduced. But now that we have become accustomed to the gifts of electric lights, airplane travel, and hip replacements we are aroused by watching people scurrying to their destinations holding cell phones and talking to partners miles away. This new technology, added to radio, television, and the Internet, will generate a new vocabulary that will compete with, but not replace, the materialistic metaphors speakers will use at the end of this young century.

Concern with the coherence of information also requires accommodation to the variation among human groups—their language, ethnicity, religion, and values—rather than a uniform biology across humanity or shared with animals. Because a story need not have the same psychological effect on all readers, there can be no universal cause-and-effect relation between a series of sentences (or scenes) and a particular state in a recipient. A plate falling from a table to a concrete floor produces a sound in every setting.

Scholars working in the natural sciences will, of course, continue to discover new facts that will make work easier, travel faster, and life healthier. Yet the traditional canon of deterministic causal relations between one natural event and another, which has been a model for legislatures, novelists, and educators, will compete with a model in which coherence becomes a second, but not exclusive, criterion for judging truth. For example, when the Soviet Union beat the United States into space by sending up the first unmanned vehicle in 1957, Americans became concerned with the quality of science and mathematics education in the schools. The National Science Foundation spent many millions of dollars to develop new curricula in these subjects. Unfortunately this massive effort did not have the desired results because the authorities assumed a simple one-to-one relation between a better curriculum and student achievement and ignored the role of the teacher, the school setting, and the prior preparation of the students.

The current debate between creationists and biologists, which has become a regular feature on the nightly news, points to the emotional consequences of disturbing meaning coherence. The creationists argue that a biological account of the remarkable properties of the human eye, hand, and heart is less coherent than the biblical explanation. The scientist's silence when asked, "What existed before the highly condensed ball of energy that exploded in the Big Bang?" is inconsistent with the principle of causality that requires a prior condition for every event. This claim is not to be interpreted as an endorsement of the creationists' position. I believe, without reservation, in the biological evolution of our species and a material origin of the universe unaided by the intervention of a supernatural force. But the current inability to provide a semantically coherent explanation of these mysteries is one reason the creationist position has become attractive to many Americans. Many well-educated adults who are not particularly religious and accept, without reservation, the tenets and facts of modern science are unwilling to reject completely the possibility that a supernatural force — intelligent design — made some contribution, albeit small, to life on earth. Faith in that assumption, though bereft of objective evidence, renders their understanding of the world more coherent. Only a hundred years earlier many Americans found equally coherent the social Darwinian argument that the poor school performance of the children of illiterate European immigrants was due to genetic taint.

The human moral sense enhances the salience of meaning coherence. Human biology demands that we apply the concepts "good," "bad," "right," and "wrong" to events. Humans feel uncomfortable in a world in which no human action or natural event can be classified, absolutely, as "good" or "bad." Most American college students are certain that the practice of circumcision of adolescent girls by a small number of cultural groups is morally abhorrent, even though many mothers in these cultures are sure it is proper because it renders their daughters more attractive to prospective suitors. The argument for female circumcision has coherence for these parents. Even the U.S. Supreme Court acknowledged the legitimacy of local values when it ruled in 1973 that pornography could not be defined absolutely and that each community had to decide what films it found offensive.

The continued popularity of movies like *Gone with the Wind, Casablanca,* and *The Wizard of Oz* imply that most Americans enjoy affirmation of the moral implications in these stories: selfishness is punished eventually; true lovers forego self-interest for their beloved; and everyone can attain the celebrated virtues of wisdom, empathy, and bravery. These films have coherence for Americans even though the facts they present are not in close correspondence with the evidence.

The establishment of the League of Nations after World War I and the United Nations after World War II served the optimistic hope that it was possible one day to have one community sharing the same values regarding family, sex, aggression, and the same assumptions about nature and our place in it. This hope has been shattered by ethnic cleansing in Rwanda and the former Yugoslavia, suicide bombings in the Middle East, and demands for sovereignty by ethnic minorities throughout the world, including the Scots, Tamil Tigers, and Kurds. Separateness, not commonality, has become a fact because local coherence is defeating the beautiful idea of a community of eight billion brothers and sisters. From television and radio most contemporary adolescents have learned about the serious value conflicts between Israelis and Palestinians, Basques and Spaniards, Bosnians and Serbs, Hutus and Tutsis, Republican and Unionist Irish, and evangelical Protestants in Georgia and agnostics in New York and, unlike their great-grandparents, accept the sad fact that a permanently peaceful world is impossible.

The resistance among many Americans to the legalization of gay marriage grows out of the semantic incoherence, and resulting mental confusion, produced by changing the meaning of a word whose definition has remained relatively stable for thousands of years. "Marriage" between two men or two women is as semantically incoherent for these citizens as statements describing ethnic cleansing among ants or the claim of quantum theory that time can go forward or backward. The argument for evolution, rather than the biblical account, in mid-nineteenth-century England created a threat to coherence. Most citizens were proud of their membership in the category "English," and England was a Christian country. If evolutionary ideas were correct, Christian doctrine had to be incorrect, and that state of affairs would compromise the potency of the category "English."

Words are an important vehicle of understanding; hence, changing the meanings of terms that refer to the fundamental phenomena of daily life will be resisted. Scientific discoveries, engineering advances, and historical events have combined to make the coherence of symbolic information a new model for writers, legislators, and institutions by the only species that cares about both ideas.

Although a tolerant attitude toward each group's ideology is necessary in a diverse society, it deprives each person of the moral smugness that accompanies the conviction that self's values are more true, or more moral, than those of another. An increased awareness of the world's cultures, made possible by information technology, combined with an explicit imperative to acknowledge the legitimacy of each person's premises, make it harder to sustain the illusion of self-importance that follows loyalty to one's beliefs. Surprisingly, the demand for ideological tolerance sits cheek to jowl with a growing, and often intimidating, tyranny of political correctness that punishes anyone who suggests that some individuals might be compromised by their genes, physical limitations, past experiences, or social position. However, those who overcame an acknowledged limitation often end up happier than those who received charitable communications, implying that they are perfectly fine and that the source of their problems lay with the prejudices of others. This defense often leads to a corrosive anger if life turns out to be less generous than they were told or to a feeling of helplessness if their coping reactions fail.

The unpredictability and moral ambiguity of contemporary life have created a mood among our celebrated writers that reflects the uncertainty felt by their readers. Few poets, novelists, or philosophers writing before 1900 depicted the human condition as a collection of solitary sailors in tiny boats without a compass rowing desperately on an infinitely large sea unaware of storms brewing thousands of miles away that might thwart the course each thought he was charting. A loyal, willful Odysseus who, despite multiple adversities, found his way back to faithful Penelope waiting patiently in Ithaka is being chased from the stage by the hapless, confused tramps in Samuel Beckett's *Waiting for Godot*.

FOUR

Accepting Biology and History

The flirtation with biology that began with our study of the infant became a commitment after my sabbatical year on Lake Atitlán in northwest Guatemala. But the sabbatical would have been spent somewhere else had I not been a member of a group of consultants to a research institute in Guatemala City. The purpose of the visit was to evaluate a research proposal designed to determine whether malnutrition was an important contributor to intellectual development. The rationale for the proposal originated in American politics.

The Potency of Class

One of the most robust facts in the social sciences is that poor American children, often born to parents with less than twelve years of formal education, have greater difficulty mastering school skills than those born to college-educated families. The powerful effect of social class on academic achievement is not restricted to the United States. Most of Warsaw was destroyed by Allied bombs during World War II, and after the war, Poland was dominated by the Soviet Union. Minimizing class distinctions was thus a political imperative when Warsaw was rebuilt, and well and poorly educated families lived in the same large apartment houses while their children played in the same yards and attended the same schools. Although the experiences outside each apartment were similar for all children, those born to parents with a college education had higher IQ scores and attained better grades than those from families with less education.[1] The same relation was found in France: school-age children born to French parents with little education but adopted as infants by middle-class French families had higher IQs than their brothers or sisters who remained at home with their biological parents.[2] The best predictor of academic failure, delinquency, and psychiatric illness in adolescents born on the island of Kauai, in the Hawaiian chain, was, once again, the social class of the parents.[3]

The National Institutes of Health had conducted a study, many years earlier, designed to illuminate the conditions that led to cerebral palsy. Thousands of infants from many American cities were assessed at birth and followed for many years. Some infants were born with a biological insult brought on by prematurity, toxemia in the pregnant mother, anoxia of the newborn during delivery, or a host of other compromising conditions. But the best predictor of the IQ scores of four- and seven-year-olds who were studied was the level of their parents' education, rather than any biological condition, with the exception of a tiny proportion born with serious cerebral insult.[4] The family's social class had precedence over a number of biologically compromising conditions. I was in a breech position before my birth and was delivered by a pair of forceps that damaged the cornea of my left eye, rendering me monocular for life. My head, minutes after delivery, was abnormally large because superficial blood vessels were hemorrhaging, and the attending physician told my father I might not survive. I was a brain-damaged newborn, but my parents' encouragement of intellectual development won the competition with this biological insult.

One December afternoon in 1973 I was in a Shanghai hotel with a group of American social scientists, including William Kessen, Urie Bronfenbrenner, Bettye Caldwell, Eleanor Maccoby, George Miller, Marian Radke-Yarrow, Harold Stevenson, and Martin Whyte, who were visiting the People's Republic of China as part of a scholarly exchange. We met with a Chinese psychologist to find out what he taught his students. Mao Tse-tung was still head of the country and the Red Guard a potent force. The psychologist told us that he taught his students that social class was the cause of all psychological variation. No other force, biological or experiential, was relevant. Eleanor Maccoby challenged this claim by noting that because the People's Republic was eliminating all class distinctions, he would have nothing to teach when that victory was achieved. There was a long silence until Hseih Chi-kang, our escort and a high-ranking member of the Communist Party, rescued the embarrassed faculty member by reminding Maccoby that a society can only approach classlessness; it never reaches it.

Enough! The social class of a child's family is a proxy for a complex set of experiences that includes quality of prenatal care, childhood illnesses, parental treatment and behaviors, values communicated, schools attended, role models encountered, and, of course, peers and neighborhood temptations. Variation in social class represents an ecology of growth that predicts variation in physical and psychological health, longevity, intellectual talents, vocational achievement, frequency of sleepless nights, and the likelihood of self-mutilation. As early as the first birthday, infants in middle-class families are more attentive to discrepant events than are children in economically stressed homes. And by six or seven years the experiences that distinguish poor from more affluent homes separate children as clearly as a mountain range separates an original group of monkeys into two species. If one team of expert psychologists had access to the filmed records of a thousand children over the first two years of development but no other information, and a second team knew only the social class of each child's family, and both teams had to predict the personalities, motives, cognitive skills, values, and anxieties of these children at age twenty-one, the second team would be correct more often than the first.

The differences between the plants and animals on the island of Tasmania and those in Australia required many, many generations to develop. Class of rearing can separate groups of children within one generation. Many children born to impoverished, illiterate European immigrants who came to the United States at the turn of the twentieth century became doctors, lawyers, professors, scientists, and playwrights within one generation. The uncle who wanted me to study law was a member of this group. This is why Americans have been, and remain, social Darwinian in their explanation of the variation in privilege. There will always be some who, through a run of bad luck, live with disadvantage. However, perseverance and moderate talent are supposed to allow most to improve their class position—Abraham Lincoln, Andrew Carnegie, and Bill Clinton are three examples. Alexis de Tocqueville was impressed with the lack of class snobbery that was so prevalent in Europe when he toured parts of the Republic in 1831–1832.

The school performance of poor American children has always lagged behind that of the middle class, but this fact became a more acute concern, and source of occasional guilt, after the Civil Rights protests of the 1960s. A social fact that had existed since before the Declaration of Independence could no longer be ignored. Although nineteenth-century Americans attributed the class differences to parental rearing practices, the politically correct rhetoric of the 1970s was hostile to this explanation because it was regarded as racist. "Do not blame the victim" became the politically correct mantra. It was necessary, therefore, to find a cause that placed less blame on the rearing practices of poor parents. One candidate was the food that children ate.

Experiments with mice and rats suggested that animals raised on a diet containing inadequate protein failed to develop the motor and cognitive competences of well-fed animals. Because middle-class children ate more steak, eggs, and fish than poor children, it was easy, and politically desirable, to argue that lack of protein was an important cause of the larger number of high-school dropouts among the poor. Parents' failure to read to their children and to encourage them to finish their homework assignments, which implied a moral failing, was replaced with a financial inability to feed children a proper diet. If scientists could prove this idea true, Americans could solve a frustrating problem by ensuring that poor children received the right diet. There would be no need to rebuild neighborhoods, create jobs, provide better schools, or raise teachers' salaries. All the nation had to do was provide poor children with more hamburgers, and that was easy.

The Guatemala Project

The staff at the National Institute of Child Health and Human Development began to look for a locale to prove this pleasing idea. Guatemala was a logical choice. This small Central American nation was within six hours by plane from Washington, D.C., and a respected research institute there was studying the effects of nutrition and supplying protein supplements to poor families. Families in the eastern part of the country, known as *mestizos*, were of mixed Spanish and Mayan ancestry, spoke Spanish, and lived in small villages with a relatively high prevalence of malnutrition. Families north and west of the capital, Guatemala City, were of Mayan heritage and did not speak Spanish. Since it was harder to travel to the northwestern locales than to the east, the staff selected six mestizo villages for the study.

All individuals in three villages would receive a dietary supplement for several years. Every man, woman (pregnant or not), and child who wished to walk a few minutes to the village center would receive a bowl of food containing protein. What to do in the three control villages that did not receive the protein supplement was debated. Because the experience of interacting regularly with professional visitors from Guatemala City might have a positive effect on villagers' psychological growth, the staff decided that the three control villages should be given something. It would have been unethical to hand out water, so residents received soda sweetened with sugar, which had calories but no protein, when they came to the village center. This decision seemed wise because it was assumed that protein was what permitted proper brain growth and intellectual development.

I joined a large group of American scientists in Guatemala City to listen to the research plan, knowing that we would later advise the government as to whether they should support the project. On the first morning, the director of the institute (Instituto de Nutrición de Centro America y Panama, or INCAP) called on staff members to present parts of the research plan. One presentation will evoke a smile. A central issue was how to assess the child's usual level of nutrition during the year. The young woman who presented the solution INCAP had chosen said that they had tried two methods. The oral method required the visitor to the home to ask the mother what foods the child had eaten the previous day. The visual method required the visitor to write down the foods she saw in the home. She reported that she and her colleagues had evaluated the day-to-day consistency in the results of the two methods—called reliability—and had concluded that the oral method was superior because it yielded more consistent results across visits. At this point, one of the consultants raised his hand to say that he did not understand why the oral method was better. The young woman replied, without blushing, that asking the mothers what their children ate was more reliable because they usually said, "I don't know." The institute received the grant.

On this trip I met Robert Klein, an American Ph.D. from the University of Minnesota, who had joined the staff of INCAP and would be in charge of the psychological aspects of the research. We liked each other immediately and that week began a friendship that endures to this day. I accepted Bob's invitation to help with the development of psychological procedures because of the beauty of the country and an interest in the development of these children. After several visits to the villages in the east, Bob took me to Lake Atitlán in northwestern Guatemala. The scenery's stunning beauty and the unchanged life of the Indian villages that lined the cobalt-blue lake moved me deeply.

San Marcos

The possibility of learning more about the development of children who had no contact with American ideas and artifacts was appealing. I had studied American children for about twenty years and was eager to learn about psychological growth in this more isolated setting. I asked Bob if I could spend my sabbatical year working in one of the villages on the lake. He thought it was feasible, and with financial support from the Foundation for Child Development in New York City, I spent 1971–1972 studying life in San Marcos, population eight hundred. I chose this small village because it was one of the poorest on the lake and had no contact with tourists. There was a small school that few children attended but no electricity, regular postal delivery, or resident priest. Here, I thought, I would learn something significant about development. The meaning of a vivid dream the night before my departure was clear. I was an adult visiting the office of my childhood pediatrician. The office was crowded, as it usually was, and I told the receptionist that I would wait. After several hours a nurse, holding the hand of an old Mayan Indian woman, approached me and said, "I think she will be able to help you with your problem."

I was open to surprises and had no strong a priori prejudices as the work began. My family and I lived in Panajachel, the major tourist town on the lake, but each morning I took a small motor boat across the lake to the small dock at San Marcos, a run of about forty-five minutes. Helping me were Lisa Shulman, a recent graduate of Radcliffe College who lived in San Marcos, and a San Marcos adult who spoke both Spanish and the Mayan dialect of

Cacquichel, who examined the children in the dialect and translated their replies to us in Spanish.

In a rented hut we administered a variety of cognitive tests to the children of San Marcos. The rest of the time I visited families to see what was happening in the home environments and wrote up each day's observations after returning to Panajachel in the evening. A few months of observation persuaded me that the slower psychological development of the infants, which was obvious, was abrogated once the children were old enough to leave their huts. The villagers believed that infants were vulnerable during the first year and had to be protected from the stares of strangers and men fresh with perspiration from the day's work. The infants, swaddled in old rags, were placed in a hammock in the rear of the hut where no one but family members could see them, except when the mothers nursed their infants while sitting near the single opening to the adobe home. The one-year-olds were pale, unresponsive, and would have been classified as retarded by American psychologists. The few test procedures I was allowed to administer affirmed their slower cognitive growth and lack of emotional expressivity. But the six-year-olds scurrying about the village trails were lively and full of vitality, and their performances on our tests were reasonably competent. Because these six-year-olds had experienced the same depriving environments when they were infants, the obvious inference was that the psychological retardation of the one-year-olds was temporary and that the cognitive growth of children was malleable. A first year spent with minimal variety of experience did not doom a child, even though most American infants do not live under these conditions.

I felt that this insight was important and was eager to inform my colleagues of the optimistic conclusion that early deprivation of variety need not sentence a child to permanent retardation. But I was ingenuous and failed to appreciate the American zeitgeist during the 1970s. William Kessen, a Yale developmental psychologist, began his review of two of my books in the December 10, 1978, issue of the *New York Times Book Review* this way: "More than any other people and more than at any other time, educated Americans in the twentieth century have believed in the continuity of human development. For us, Wordsworth's child-as-father-of-the-man is at once principle and fact; what happens to children early in their lives defines their lives. Early experience is seen as crucial (even implausibly social exchanges in the first hours of life); the family is assigned first responsibility for the mental health of children; personality is assumed to be early formed and relatively unchanging; and most unfortunately, if the child is not performing well at home and in school by the age of 6, it may be too late for remedy."[5]

One of the benevolent consequences of the Civil Rights protests was congressional allocation of funds for programs intended to help the development of poor children. David Weikart was running an extensive program in Ypsilanti, Michigan, and Head Start centers were being established. The rationale for these efforts assumed that infants would become permanently retarded if they did not receive adequate stimulation. My American colleagues did not want government and private foundations to learn that early retardation need not be permanent for they feared that funding for these programs would stop. I felt this concern was exaggerated and was not prepared for the criticism Bob Klein and I received when we published our results in a journal sent to members of the American Psychological Association.

One of the first papers I read on my return from Guatemala, which came from Harry Harlow's laboratory at the University of Wisconsin, arrived at a similar conclusion.[6] Harlow and his students had supported those who believed in infant determinism by demonstrating, years earlier, that infant monkeys taken from their mothers and raised with a wire surrogate who supplied only food developed bizarre behaviors that seemed, on the surface, to be permanent. This discovery, described in every textbook, was an important basis for insisting on the significance of early experiences on later development. But the recent paper described what happened when the monkeys who had experienced the deprivation were placed with infant monkeys. The interactions between the infants, who did not threaten or dominate the older animals, were therapeutic, and the deprived monkeys began to develop relatively normal profiles. This was exactly the conclusion we had reached on Lake Atitlán. Klein and I regarded the paper by Harlow as supporting our position.

I reported the results of our work at a meeting of the American Association for the Advancement of Science. Margaret Mead rose after the talk to ask why I was telling this audience an obvious fact. All anthropologists, she insisted in an irritated voice, were aware of our claim. I checked my anger and replied politely, "Professor Mead, psychologists are not as smart as anthropologists."

I confess to a deep sadness over the criticisms of our paper by colleagues I respected and whose admiration I sought. I rationalized the disappointment by rehearsing silently that if our conclusions were seriously flawed, the *American Psychologist* would not have published them. At least one reviewer must have regarded our views as worth dissemination. This experience thickened my skin a bit, for I believed what Klein and I had written. Fortunately, I continued to receive grant support, other university faculty remained friendly, and my students seemed, at least on the surface, to be on my side.

A visit to David Rigler, a child psychologist working in Los Angeles in June 1973, also supported my new view. The Los Angeles police had found a girl, about thirteen years old, whose mother had restricted her to the basement of the home. The state had assigned the girl—named Genie—to Rigler and his wife until a permanent home could be found, and I was eager to see how much progress Genie had made after about a year with the Riglers. Mute when discovered, Genie could now speak, though her conversations with me resembled that of a four-year-old. But she was now toilet trained and each morning dressed herself, had breakfast, and went to the street to board a bus that took her to a special educational class. Genie was obviously not a normal thirteen-year-old, yet in less than a year, she had made remarkable progress.

Sometimes childhood rejection is transformed into a strength. If a child or adolescent can survive feelings of exclusion, either through effective rationalizations or the winning of compensatory prizes, the later anticipation of criticism provokes minimal uncertainty. Many years ago, two psychologists at the University of California in Berkeley compared mathematicians and architects who had been nominated by their peers as extremely creative with members of the same profession who were successful but judged less creative. A major difference between the two groups was that the creative professionals had experienced peer rejection during adolescence because of physical stigmata, less talent at peer-valued skills, or membership in a minority group. The chronic rejection permitted these creative professionals to develop an indifference to peer opinion that made it easier to entertain ideas they knew would be unpopular.[7]

Frank Sulloway has made a similar argument for the effects of ordinal position in his book *Born to Rebel* (1996).[8] Sulloway, a historian of science, found that revolutionary scientific ideas that violated the beliefs of the educated public, as well as members of the discipline, were usually opposed by firstborns but supported by later-borns. More later-borns than firstborns endorsed both Darwin's hypothesis of natural selection and Freud's ideas on neurosis during the first decade following the publication of their seminal works. Later-borns feel less privileged than firstborns in the family and as a result are less concerned with pleasing their parents. This indifference to parental opinion is transferred later to authority figures in society. It is no accident that both Darwin and Wallace were later-born.

One More Try

Robert Klein and I made another attempt to defend our position. We returned to Lake Atitlán, this time with a hypothesis. John Flavell, a psychologist at Stanford University, had published several important papers suggesting that a significant cognitive competence that developed in childhood was learning what strategies to use when faced with a cognitive challenge, especially one involving memory.[9] Flavell called these mental tricks metamemory, and they included rehearsing what one has heard and classifying information into categories that could be remembered more easily. There was a lawful growth in metamemory abilities in American children, and we wanted to see if the San Marcos children showed similar growth.

Fortunately, Barbara Rogoff, a graduate student at the time, and Gordon Finley, who had been a graduate student, were interested in working at the lake. Barbara decided to do her thesis research in San Pedro, a village a couple of miles from San Marcos that had a good school, electricity, a better-educated population, and a church with a resident priest. This town was a perfect comparison for San Marcos. The physical ecology and ethnic backgrounds of the two towns were identical, but their values, practices, and degree of contact with the world outside Lake Atitlán were different. So, with their help, Klein and I compared the performances of children and adolescents who lived in San Marcos, San Pedro, and Cambridge, Massachusetts.

The children in all three settings improved in their metamemory skills with each year of development. But the setting determined how early the children reached what we regarded as maximal competence. The Cambridge children did so by seven or eight years of age; the San Pedro children by ten or eleven years, the San Marcos children by thirteen or fourteen years. Most San Marcos children were six years behind those living in Cambridge, but their level of competence on problems that were artificial and unrelated to their daily lives approached those of American children by adolescence. No San Marcos child had to remember the order of placement—right side up or upside down—of twelve identical dolls. The enhanced ability of the unschooled San Marcos children to remember more units of information as they grew implied that the improvement in metamemory skills was a natural consequence of growth; it did not have to be taught.

Because the eight-year-olds from Cambridge were so different from the eight-year-olds in San Marcos, some who criticized our earlier paper interpreted the new data as an apology for our earlier claim, based on weaker evidence, that the early deprivation of the San Marcos infants had no consequences. Our view was that the early deprivation was irrelevant; it was the lack of schooling and the absence of any need to learn the skills we assessed that produced the cultural differences. The data, however, can be viewed from either perspective. Klein and I regarded the evidence as implicating the importance of schooling; others regarded it as support for the importance of early stimulation. Both conclusions have some merit.

Martha Sellers, a Guatemalan who had worked with Bob Klein and had become a graduate student at Harvard, pursued this problem in her thesis research in an isolated village in Costa Rica. Martha wanted to see if the children in the village would invent cognitive strategies spontaneously and perform as well as those who were taught metamemory skills directly. She explicitly taught one group of children the cognitive strategies needed for good performance on a set of problems. A second group of children, who did not receive direct instruction, had to figure out how to solve the problems on their own. After several weeks of working with each child, Martha evaluated all the children on a new set of problems. Both groups did equally well on a majority of the problems, but at Christmastime, children from the untutored group brought her Christmas presents. When she asked why they had brought her gifts, they replied that they wanted to thank her for helping them learn how to think.

The Guatemalan observations produced two important changes in my ideas. I began to question more seriously my earlier commitment to the permanent power of early experience and to think more systematically about the role of maturation on the age of attainment of universal milestones, as long as conditions were not excessively harsh. This latter notion, which was not original, culminated thirty years later in a book I wrote with Norbert Hershkowitz on the constraints brain maturation imposed on psychological development.[10] Almost twenty years had passed since my indoctrination in behaviorism and psychoanalytic theory, and I was beginning to unshackle myself from the prejudices against biology held by both theoretical positions.

It took almost twenty-five years of brooding over observations in the laboratory, Mayan huts, and American homes, as well as reflection on writing in anthropology, philosophy, and history, to release me from the dogma I had been taught at Yale. The ideas indoctrinated during graduate training can limit the conceptions the mature investigator entertains. I used to begin the first meeting of my graduate seminar by telling the dozen or so students that much of what I had been taught at Yale turned out to be mistaken, so they should remain skeptical of everything I said over the next four months.

History

I also became more respectful of the significance of history and culture. Alex Inkeles, a sociologist in the Department of Social Relations at Harvard, took me to lunch soon after my arrival in Cambridge and in a gentle, almost fatherly tone chided me for assuming that events within the family were the most significant determinants of a child's future view of self and society. I was ignoring the force of history, he insisted. I understood the words; today I understand the deeper meaning he intended. I began to read more regularly in history and came to recognize the wisdom of his judgment that afternoon.

All individuals live in a small space fenced by their historical moment and the associated beliefs of their community. Imagine what the world would be like if mechanical transportation, electricity, books, guns, and chlorination of water supplies had not been invented. It is difficult to escape the boundaries of the enclosure history built because each time-culture warp provides a limited number of ways to make a livelihood, creates a few salient uncertainties, and offers a folk theory that explains how life's challenges are to be met and why only some are successful in carrying out life's assignments.

Changes in the relative salience of the family, community, social institutions, and the individual are among the most significant products of history. Our species spent most of its early history in small, roaming groups to which loyalty was given in exchange for protection, ethical guides, and identity. The establishment of fixed communities following the domestication of plants and animals led eventually to civilizations in which religious, educational, and judicial institutions assumed the functions of the small group. The authority of these institutions reached their apogee in the West during the two millennia between the ancient societies of Egypt, Greece, and Rome and the Renaissance. And then, slowly at first and accelerating with industrialization, the individual emerged as the primary social unit. The person, not his or her family, group, or community, became the object to protect and the source of moral justification. The meanings of words bent to accommodate to this change. The modern term "economics," which emphasizes individual competitiveness, derives from the Latin *oeconomica*, which means family life. Although the contemporary world is divided on this issue, it seems to be moving, inexorably, toward a celebration of the isolated agent pursuing personal needs, mistrusting authority, and acting as both judge and executioner.

The current web of conditions shapes each person's beliefs, the values to which loyalty is given, nodes of worry, and the behaviors that fill most hours of the day. Some cultures are characterized by worry over the judgments of dead ancestors who might bring illness as a punishment for a transgression. Most Americans worry about personal failure—on school tasks when young, in one's vocation when older. But the emotion that follows failure depends on the interpretation imposed; shame if due to inadequate talent, anger if the product of prejudice, and guilt if the result of insufficient effort. The conviction that humans have inalienable rights and societies must try to equalize access to power and treat all with dignity are new ideas in the history of our species. Adolescents in Kosovo and Baghdad have witnessed cruelties that will make many of them skeptics for the rest of their lives. Samuel Beckett exploited his adolescent memory of the anarchy that tore through Ireland in the early decades of the twentieth century when he had one of the tramps in *Waiting for Godot* say, "This is becoming really insignificant," and had the other reply, "Not enough."

All humans experience some level of worry over one or more possible events. Their culture supplies the unwanted targets, whether God's wrath for not praying daily for the health of relatives or meeting strangers at a cocktail party. A small number experience a level of uncertainty so intense that it interferes with life's responsibilities. Cultures invent different explanations for this deviance. Our society has recently altered the weights assigned to childhood experiences and the exigencies of daily life and awarded more power to inherited biological vulnerabilities.

The private explanation of one's life circumstances may be one of the most significant changes wrought by history. Landless peasants in seventeenth-century England usually remained in the village in which they were born, saw their family almost every day, established close relations with neighbors, and believed that their harsh life was the result of forces over which they had little control. Landless laborers in a factory in contemporary Manchester may have moved to the city a year before to obtain their jobs and may know few neighbors, but unlike the seventeenth-century peasants, they blame themselves for their poverty because newspapers and television tell them that England is dedicated to giving every citizen the opportunity for an adequate education and the success that is supposed to follow. As a result, poverty evokes a sharper feeling of shame and self-reproach today than it did three hundred years ago. Seventeenth-century Europeans coping with economic uncertainty could protect ego from self-reproach by placing the blame on heartless kings, God's will, or the prejudices of the elite. These explanations usually lead to anger. It is harder to exploit this rationalization today because people are told that anyone willing to remain in school and persevere should be able to rise to a more privileged position. As a result, shame and guilt have become more common reactions to the recognition of compromised status. Shame and guilt are more corrosive of vitality than anger.

Mayan Indian men living in the highlands of Guatemala work their maize fields for most of the year, travel to the coast for a few months to work on plantations for extra money, and feel oppressed by the non-Mayan majority who run the country. Their ancestors, who built the temples at Tikal, had a loftier sense of their dignity until they were defeated by the Spaniards. A century from now most will be boarding crowded buses to commute to jobs in small factories.

About a year after my return from Guatemala I visited two of my graduate students, Charles Super and Sara Harkness, who were doing their thesis research in a small village in northwest Kenya. The contrast between this African village and San Marcos was striking, even though both groups lived in isolated agricultural settings. The adults of Leldayet displayed vitality, dignity, and pride, compared with the passivity, fear, suspicion, and shame of the residents of San Marcos. One reason for these differences is that the Leldayet adults did not regard themselves as an oppressed group, whereas the Mayans of San Marcos felt inferior to the residents with power in Guatemala City. Historical events, not the experiences of early childhood, led one group to feel pride, the other shame. Communities, like siblings, compare themselves with others. History selects the targets of comparison and the interpretations of difference.

The social and political differences between the North and the South in early-nineteenth-century America were due, in part, to the prior economies of these regions. The average household in New England during the seventeenth and eighteenth centuries could survive on a small landholding on which the family grew grains and cared for chickens, pigs, and cows. As a result, seventy or eighty households could live in a relatively small area and were able to band together to build a school and a church and establish a community. By contrast, economic survival in the South relied on tobacco as the main crop. Because raising tobacco required four hundred to eight hundred acres, each household was isolated from neighbors and it was more difficult to unite eighty families to build a school, church, and community. Moreover, had businessmen in Richmond, Virginia, or Charleston, South Carolina, rather than Boston, decided in 1810 to exploit the recent invention of the power loom and build factories producing cotton cloth, the landscape of American politics and educational institutions might have been seriously different. Virginia or South Carolina, rather than Massachusetts, would have been the cultural center of the young nation.

African pastoralists whose livelihood was dependent on cattle were mobile, whereas those who relied on agriculture settled in one place. The pastoralists, who took their property with them, were more independent and pragmatic. The agriculturists, whose survival was contingent on the weather and whose vitality depended on not being a target of a neighbor's gossip, were more fatalistic and superstitious.

The expansion of technology and education in the late nineteenth and twentieth centuries produced a large population of Americans and Europeans who carried their vocational skills with them. Carpenters, masons, doctors, dentists, accountants, scientists, and lawyers, are, like the pastoralists, pragmatic, individualistic, and independent. As the nineteenth century ended psychologists like G. Stanley Hall were railing against the excessive civility of adolescent boys and urging an easier access to the anger needed in the competitive American economy. I wonder what Hall would write today if he could read about the gangs that terrorize urban neighborhoods. Thus, the extreme individualism and low threshold for hostility that characterize Americans are due, in part, to the economic and social changes that rendered each worker an entrepreneur willing to move from Pennsylvania to California to secure a better position. History has brought to the brink of extinction farm families working their fifty acres and owners of small grocery stores, who, like the African agriculturalists, were tied to a place.

The West's attraction to laws that apply to an act rather than to an action in a context—stealing compared with stealing from a relative—may have been influenced by the commercial economy of Europe in which strangers living in different places entered into contracts. These conditions required laws that punished the breaking of contracts whether with kin or strangers. This impersonal approach to violations of community norms is less relevant in small, agricultural villages where most adults know one another. Under the latter conditions, the elders of a village, like parents in a family, can take into account the particularities of the plaintiff and defendant and adjust penalties to fit these specific details.

Most parents have an implicit conception of the psychological properties necessary for adaptation to their community and try to prepare their children for the challenges they will have to face two decades hence. Thus, parental socialization contributes to the adult profile, but the foundation for the rearing strategies is the culture in which the families live. Americans are perfectly capable of fatalism, superstition, trusting cooperation, or the continuous suppression of anger. But the roll of the dice that birthed them in Denver rather than Dhaka pulled the thread labeled individualism from a hat holding a variety of life itineraries.

Karl Marx came close to this insight when he suggested that the economy of a society influenced the psychology of its members, but he erred in assuming that the major division was between employer and employed. Marx failed to recognize that loyalty to one's family, tribe, religion, region, and ethnic group trumps loyalty to one's vocational role and social class. Each person is first a Muslim, Hindu, Catholic, Baptist, Jew, Hutu, Hispanic, African-American, or Chinese and, secondarily, a janitor in a large apartment complex or the owner of the building.

There is a tension between those who insist there are permanently true statements about nature and those who argue that nature is continually changing and therefore there can be no permanently true statements. The second view has to have some validity, for there was no Earth twenty billion years ago and therefore no true beliefs about life on our planet. Of course, some states of nature change very slowly, others more quickly. It is easy to be persuaded, however, that some descriptions of nature must represent permanent knowledge. But because human societies change more rapidly over history it is much harder to make the same confident assertion. The current belief that parental punitiveness toward children is psychologically harmful is historically contingent and was less true five hundred years ago than it may be today. We yearn for absolutely true knowledge about human nature, but the best history can produce is beliefs that last a few lifetimes.

The Emergence of Human Uniqueness

The success of the strategy adopted in the study of the first year, which affirmed the power of maturation, suggested the wisdom of a similar design for the second year of development. By observing small groups of children many times, at home and in the laboratory, I hoped to gain a deeper understanding of the properties that emerged during this developmental phase. Most psychologists knew that language, reciprocal play with peers, and an awareness of prohibited actions appeared during the second year. Regular observations of children might reveal the times when each quality emerged and permit the construction of fruitful theory. Roger Brown's study of three young children beginning to speak—the famous Adam, Eve, and Sarah—was the model.[11] Brown's imaginative analyses, summarized in *A First Language* (1973), revealed the times of emergence of various grammatical elements.

For example, the plural appeared before the past tense, the past tense before the participle, and the participle before the passive. One could not ask for a lovelier demonstration of an open-minded approach to language acquisition. It seemed wise to imitate this design and hope for equally dramatic insights. Imitation is the highest form of flattery.

We evaluated language and symbolic abilities, memory for the locations of objects, inference, and quality of play with an unfamiliar child. Once again, nature was in a cooperative mood. The behaviors displayed during the second year, typically between seventeen and twenty-four months, suggested the ability to infer the feelings and intentions of others, the first awareness of right and wrong actions, and an initial consciousness of self's intentions, actions, and power to effect changes in their environment.

Two observations suggested that two-year-olds could infer the thoughts of another and understood the difference between right and wrong actions. Each mother-child pair entered a playroom with toys on the carpet. Half of the toys were new and without flaws; the others had been compromised in some way—a handkerchief had been stained, a wheel had been removed from a toy car, a doll was missing an arm. Every child noticed the flaws by the time they were eighteen months old and would bring a flawed toy to the mother and indicate, in speech or facial expression, that they understood something was wrong. Some children said "yukky" or "boo-boo"; some displayed a face of disgust, even though they had never seen these toys before and had not broken them. The recognition that a truck with a missing wheel violates an ideal form means that the children possessed a concept of undesirable outcomes produced by prohibited actions, probably because they had been chastised for breaking something at home and had generalized to the broader concept of prohibited behaviors.

The second critical observation occurred when the examiner, sitting by the child, acted out three brief play sequences with toys. She picked up a female doll and toy pot, said that the mother was making dinner, and placed imaginary food on a plate. After displaying two other acts, she said, "Okay, now it's your turn to play," and returned to the couch to talk with the mother. The examiner did not say, "Do what I did"; she allowed the child to infer that the adult intended that he or she meet that obligation.

The thirteen- and fourteen-month-olds showed no sign of any emotion;

they either returned to their play or made some attempt to imitate what they had seen. But as children approached the middle of the second year, they cried within a few seconds of the examiner's simple declaration, "Now it is your turn to play." They did not cry because the examiner had interrupted their play; we tested that possibility. Thus, the adult's display of the three acts had to be the cause of the children's distress. One reasonable interpretation is that the children inferred that they ought to imitate the acts observed. But because it was difficult to remember all three acts, the children were unable to do what they believed they ought to do and, as a result, cried. This interpretation requires attributing two competences to the two-year-olds: an inferred obligation to imitate the examiner's behaviors and a feeling of distress because self is aware of its inability to do so. When psychologists say that a person has a conscience, they mean that the person knows which acts should and should not be performed and that he or she is vulnerable to feeling uncertain, ashamed, or guilty if he or she cannot meet the presumed standard.

When Randy Gellerman made the same observations with immigrant Vietnamese children living in California, and Mary Maxwell Katz with children living on isolated atolls in the Pacific, I was ready to conclude that the first phases of self-awareness and a moral sense emerge in all children during the second year. I recognized that I was simply affirming Plato, Kant, and a number of other philosophers, but this claim was based on empirical evidence with children. The emergence of the concepts of right, wrong, good, and bad are as inevitable as speech, laughter, and chasing a friend once the brain has reached a certain level of maturation. A key competence in the second year is the ability to infer the thoughts and feelings of another. Michael Tomasello, a keen observer of children and apes, calls this ability "shared intentionality."[12] Young children also infer the possible "causes" of an event. Two-year-olds, but not one-year-olds, infer that a familiar object with a flaw— for example, part of the handle of a mug is missing—must have been acted on in some way. Hence, they still call it a cup.[13] The automatic habit of adding to each perception of an event a guess as to its origin, which is probably unique to humans, means that different reactions to the same event can be due to varied inferences regarding its source. I learned years later that the neurons of the third layer of the cerebral cortex, which supply the fibers of the corpus callosum that unite the two hemispheres, show a burst of growth in the second year. This fact implies that more efficient transfer of information between the right and left hemispheres might be one prerequisite for this psychological advance.

Guessing Other Minds

A seminal talent that emerges by the second birthday, which is necessary for a moral sense, is the ability to infer what another may be thinking or feeling. The two-year-olds who pick up a piece of Styrofoam lying next to a cup and a doll when an examiner says, "Give me the zoob," infer that the request for a "zoob" must mean that the adult wants the only object on the table for which they have no name. This talent is critical for children learning new words when they hear others speak.

I was surprised by a report in *Science* of a border collie that had been trained by its owners over many years to retrieve any one of a large number of objects the owners would call for, such as "Fetch the plate." When psychologists from the Max Planck Institute in Leipzig learned about this amazing dog, they went to the owners' home and administered the same problem we presented to our children. They placed a number of objects familiar to the dog, along with one unfamiliar object, in a room, told the dog to fetch, and then spoke a word the dog had never heard. Surprisingly, the collie brought back the unfamiliar object, just as our children picked up the Styrofoam form.[14] This remarkable fact invites one of three interpretations. On one hand, we can award dogs, or at least this dog, the capacity to infer human intentions. Because chimpanzees lack this ability and chimps evolved more recently than dogs with a larger and more convoluted brain, it strains credibility to conclude that dogs can infer human intentions, even though I recognize that most dog owners are certain this is true.

A second interpretation is that neither this dog nor two-year-olds infer adult intentions. Both the unfamiliar object and the unfamiliar word evoked a state of "surprise," and the similarity in feeling mediated the behavior. A third explanation, and the one I favor, is that the two phenomena, although superficially similar, are mediated by different mechanisms. The dog retrieved the unfamiliar object because a state of "surprise" was generated on hearing the adult say an unfamiliar word and, seconds later, on seeing the unfamiliar object. This is the second explanation described above. Two-year-olds, however, do infer that the adult intends to name the novel object. There are many instances in nature in which a behavior displayed by two species appears similar but the psychological states in each species are distinct. A wolf urinating near a tree in a forest intends to mark his territory; a hiker does so because he or she is miles from a bathroom.

It took more than a year of poring over all the evidence to appreciate that the appearance of words that referred to self—words like "I," "my," "mine"—and to the child's feelings was the best predictor of the month when dramatic improvements in performance on our cognitive tests appeared. The emergence of an awareness that self could initiate and suppress actions, be evaluated by others, and experience feelings functioned as an organizer.

Consciousness

This suggestion invites an analysis of "consciousness," which in most writings refers to all targets of awareness—sensations, ideas, control, and properties of the self. When the origins of a word lie in the community, it is usually not scientifically useful because its referents are too broad. The awareness of cold fingers on a January morning is not identical, in either physiological foundation or psychological state, to the awareness that one is losing the ability to remember the names of friends. The differences between the psychological and biological states activated by the roar of a jet engine on takeoff, compared with imagining the day's responsibilities on awakening, are equally distinctive. It is surprising, therefore, that some neuroscientists continue to look for the unique circuit in the brain that is the foundation of "consciousness," for the search implies that there is only one state. Both Francis Bacon and Thomas Jefferson recognized the error of assuming a phenomenon in nature simply because the community had a word. The absence of a single word for consciousness in the vocabulary of the ancient Greeks might mean that they recognized that no single term could capture the multiple phenomena that the English word lumps together. Scientists should probe the varied forms of consciousness as they study the different forms of anxiety, memory, and motor skill.

The word "consciousness" refers to a family of phenomena that emerges from distinct brain processes because, like a state of "need," there is no consciousness without a target and different targets create varying states. One target of consciousness refers to sensations, like the sweet taste of chocolate, the soft touch of velvet, the heady aroma of perfume, and sensations that originate within heart, gut, and muscle. We might call this phenomenon "sensory awareness"; the biologist Gerald Edelman calls it "primary consciousness."[15]

When the target is reflection on sensation, thought, or action, a different consciousness, which we might call cognitive awareness, is present. Cognitive awareness can occur without a sensory stimulus; individuals can be aware of the flow, as well as the logic and coherence, of a train of ideas. A cognitive awareness of "being annoyed" could be produced by sensations as different as a jackhammer, a faucet dripping in a hotel room, the smell of cigar smoke in a waiting room, or anticipating a boring afternoon meeting. The sensory awareness of three sharp knocks on the door of one's bedroom elicits different emotions depending on whether the knocks occur at 9 a.m. in a New England bed and breakfast or at 3 a.m. in a Moscow hotel. A patient close to a state of coma can have sensory awareness without cognitive awareness.

When the target is the awareness of the ability to choose a particular behavior or to control one's actions and emotions a third form of consciousness is actualized. Nineteenth-century writers called this phenomenon "free will." B. F. Skinner's book *Beyond Freedom and Dignity* (1971) stirred considerable public controversy because it challenged the intuitively compelling belief that humans can choose freely among alternatives.[16] Soon after publication of the book Skinner and I were members of a panel discussing his ideas at a public meeting in Washington, D.C. The audience, troubled by Skinner's message, peppered him with critical questions. When it was my turn to speak I asked the audience why Skinner's ideas upset them and reminded them that their sons and daughters were living in communal groups in unheated Vermont houses exchanging sex partners. These behaviors seemed to be chosen freely, for they had been not rewarded during childhood. These social facts, I pointed out, seemed to invalidate Skinner's claim that all human behavior was the product of conditioned habits. As we left the platform Skinner whispered to me, "I never cared much for philosophy, but your remarks were interesting."

Last, when the target refers to self's symbolic properties—traits, talents, social categories—a phenomenon we might call "awareness of self's features" emerges. The sentences "She stubbed her toe on the stone," "She thought about the stone on the brick walk," "She picked up the stone rather than the shell," and "She regarded her personality as 'cold as a stone' " capture the four types.

These four forms of consciousness probably did not evolve at the same time. Chimpanzees might have a sensory awareness of the taste of particular foods and of patterns of light and shadow on the forest floor, but it is unlikely that they possess the other three forms of consciousness. It is also relevant that the four types of consciousness do not emerge at the same time in development. Sensory awareness is absent at birth but seems to be present long before the second birthday. Cognitive awareness emerges by two or three years of age. Almost all two-year-olds who look in a mirror and see a spot of rouge on their nose touch their nose, suggesting that they concluded that the image in the mirror refers to them.[17] But most children are unaware of their ability to control their actions or emotions until they are three or four, and most do not become conscious of the several symbolic categories to which they belong until they are five or six. Further, knowing that one is Catholic, a cellist, and a husband requires the integrity of the left hemisphere; knowing that the reflection in the mirror belongs to self requires the integrity of the right hemisphere.

There is honest disagreement whether these four classes of consciousness share enough features to warrant treating this phenomenon as unitary or whether it is theoretically more fruitful to treat the four classes as qualitatively different processes. Color, shape, and motion recruit activity in different parts of the brain. The neurons initially activated on seeing the skyward movement of a red balloon are not the ones activated by a spot of light. That fact invites a distinction among kinds of visual experience. Discoveries in neuroscience support the argument for varied forms of consciousness. The vigilant state of attention that follows an unexpected event, like the screech of a bus, is mediated, in part, by one neurotransmitter, whereas the longer-lasting state of alertness that accompanies the memorization of verbs is mediated more completely by a different molecule. And the state of a person playing the piano is mediated more completely by still another chemistry. Individuals may say that they feel "alert" under all three conditions, but I suspect they could differentiate between the state that accompanies the screech of a bus and the feeling that accompanies memorizing Russian verbs. Because the forms of consciousness described above rest on distinct neurochemistries and brain circuits associated with different psychological targets, it is reasonable to maintain that there is not one consciousness but many consciousnesses. There is no single place in the brain where self-awareness resides.

Why should the first forms of speech, a moral sense, and self-consciousness appear during the second year? The close correspondence in time suggests that a new brain organization permitted these properties to emerge. One aspect of the new organization is the degree of connectivity between the two hemispheres. A thick cable of fibers called the corpus callosum unites the right and left hemispheres. Scenes, sounds, and bodily sensations are more fully represented in the right hemisphere; syllables, words, and sentences are more fully represented in the left. Rapid and efficient communication between the right and left hemispheres should be accompanied by an integration of both kinds of information. A child who knows what cows look like and has heard his mother say, "Look at the cow," while leafing through a picture book, should, on seeing a cow in a new book, combine the perceptual and the semantic information and announce, "Look mama, a cow." The two-year-old boy who has heard, hundreds of times, "Don't spill the milk on the table" will be able to combine the semantic command with the feeling of uncertainty experienced in the past when a parent chastised him for that action. As a result he is more careful with the cup of milk. Finally, the girl who has heard her name thousands of times over the first two years should be able to combine that semantic knowledge with her conscious feeling of desire for a cookie and say, "Mary cookie." It cannot be a coincidence that the neurons in the third layer of the cortex, which comprise the cable connecting the two hemispheres, show a dramatic burst of growth early in the second year. When these fibers begin to thin after sixty years of age adults realize, with embarrassment, how hard it is to remember the name of a familiar face. Thus the qualities that distinguish humans from apes cannot appear until the brain has reached a particular stage of growth.

It was apparent by 1981, the year my book *The Second Year: The Emer-*

gence of Self-Awareness was published, that my research was drifting from the central interests of my colleagues in developmental psychology.[18] A domain within a discipline is not unlike a hurricane, for the elements close to the eye possess more power than the wind and water on the periphery, and in addition, the location of the eye changes with time.

I recall a dream in 1982 that symbolized my feeling of distance from the eye of psychology. While walking alone on a beach I saw a large group of adults renovating an old house. I approached and asked if I could help. The leader pointed to an antique cherry chest in serious need of repair and told me to work on it. After many years of solitary effort, in which I did not look at the others, I had restored the chest's original beauty. When I turned around the house was gone.

Research on conditioned responses in animals was "in the eye" in 1950, and I was close to that position when Mitchell Berkun and I conditioned rats to strike a lever to run in a wheel and when I trained male rats to make the correct turn in a T-maze to gain the reward of a receptive female.

But I had moved to the periphery when I measured the child's symbolic constructions of parents, genders, and schoolrooms because few psychologists cared about this issue. Most developmental psychologists wanted to know what actually happened to children, as recorded on film, rather than their idiosyncratic constructions, because they believed that the sharp parental criticism, not the child's interpretation, shaped the child's future.

I recall an interview with a sixteen-year-old girl who had been locked in a bedroom with her younger sister for her first three years by a psychotic mother. The girls had been fed every two or three days by an older adolescent sister but had no other social contacts. When the police learned of this horrible condition, they removed the girls and placed them in a middle-class family when they were approximately two and a half and three and a half years old. Both girls were mute, asocial, and, of course, seriously retarded when I interviewed them a few weeks after their release. But two years later, before leaving Yellow Springs for Cambridge, both had made considerable progress. I returned a decade later—they were living with the same adopted family—to interview them. When I asked the older girl to guess why her mother had locked her in the room, her face softened and she replied, with empathy, that her mother had many children to care for and she and her sister would have been less of a burden if they were isolated in a part of the house. She seemed to be saying that she had forgiven her mother.

If children believe that a harsh parental punishment serves a parent's affectionate wish for "a better" child, the punishment can have benevolent consequences. If this were not true, most children in seventeenth-century Puritan New England homes would have suffered from insomnia, anxiety, or depression, and a John Adams would have been impossible. Astronomers Tycho Brahe and Johannes Kepler would not have had the same thoughts had they been standing together on the same hill the moment the Sun was rising because of the different assumptions they brought to that scene.

The results of the study of the second year provoked a deeper interest in human morality—its development, underlying mechanisms, and the common features found across societies. Biologists are fond of writing that nothing in biology can be understood without acknowledging the force of evolution. Nothing about human thought, feeling, and behavior can be understood without acknowledging that humans evaluate events, others, and themselves on a good-bad continuum and try to acquire the personal features they judge as praiseworthy. It may be worthwhile, therefore, to summarize my current understanding of this slippery idea.

Human Morality

The routine evaluation of experience as good or bad distinguishes *Homo sapiens* from every other animal. There is not the slimmest shred of evidence to suggest that the most precocious chimpanzee applies notions of good and bad to its actions or those of others. All children agree that hitting another for no good reason is bad but are puzzled if asked whether "eating potatoes is bad." That evaluative language is selectively applied to particular thoughts, feelings, and actions that, on some occasions, provoke anxiety, shame, guilt, or pride, implies a special set of representations that psychologists call moral standards. It is understood that membership in this class can be temporary. Citizens of modern Egypt no longer feel obliged to worship a Sun god; citizens of Salem, Massachusetts, no longer worry about possession by the devil.

Even though the English philosopher G. E. Moore insisted that the meanings of "good" and "bad" were given intuitively and therefore could not be defined objectively, most philosophers and citizens were unhappy with such permissiveness, and philosophers have tried, for millennia, to defend definitions that were rationally rigorous or referred to events in the world.[1] However, there is no consensus on the meanings of "good" and "bad," or on the adjective "moral," or whether these terms should be applied to a person, judgment, action, feeling, intention, or the consequences for another of a freely willed behavior. A "good" behavior can be accompanied by a "bad" intention or an unwanted consequence, and a "bad" act by a good intention or benevolent consequence. Although Medea, the mother in the Greek tragedy, killed her children out of anger, the mother in *Beloved*, Toni Morrison's powerful novel about slavery, killed her child in the service of love. The act and its consequences for both children were the same, but the intentions were different and most Americans would regard the former slave's act as more moral. The meaning of the adjective "moral," like "heavy," depends on the noun it describes.

Further, each referent for "moral" has multiple features whose priority must be ranked. If feelings are the primary feature of "moral," should priority be awarded to self's pleasure or the state of another? If intentions, should a desire to be kind to kin take precedence over the wish to be truthful or to enhance a friend's esteem? If actions, should aggression, dishonesty, coercion, or sexual exploitation be the most abhorrent? And if consequences are the criteria, should primacy be given to another's dignity, health, serenity, economic security, or freedom from coercion? Further, whose welfare is most important—self, spouse, child, kin, anyone at risk, the local community, or the maximal number of living persons? Most Western philosophers have defended a definition that made aggression, exploitation, stealing, dishonesty, and arbitrary coercion "bad" because they disrupted the harmony of a society. Eight of the Ten Commandments are absolute prohibitions on behavior, and imposing restraint on these acts was "good."

Some commentators have advocated a more active empathy for the less privileged and laws that increase the proportion of the economically disadvantaged with access to better colleges and more desirable jobs. Accommodation to this value conflicts with a meritocratic imperative that relies on talent and achievement as the primary criteria when deciding who shall have the opportunity for self-enhancement. It is not obvious that "fairness" has a weaker moral claim than "acquired skill." The argument against the former ethic maintains that, if ability is not given priority, America's economic health will suffer in the highly competitive global marketplace that emerged over the past half-century. And yet, an economically competitive society with one-fourth of its citizens feeling alienated is likely to be burdened with levels of crime, substance abuse, and depression that tear the fabric of the entire community.

On one hand, the number of behaviors that all humans, across time and culture, would classify as "bad," and capable of generating shame or guilt if committed, is small; on the other hand, few people are immune to shame or guilt following some thought, feeling, intention, or action. Thus, the question "What is moral?" resembles "What is beautiful?" as Wittgenstein recognized. Although humans cannot agree on the acts, thoughts, or emotions that are morally binding, almost everyone feels that they ought to suppress some behaviors and root out some intentions and feelings.

Eighteenth-century European scholars, influenced by a new respect for nature, individualism, and science, argued that each person's private feelings of pleasure or displeasure, rather than the authority of religious texts, should be the primary basis for deciding what was good or bad. The problem with loyalty to this criterion, in societies consisting of unrelated strangers differing in privilege, is that it permits the exploitation of those with less power by those with more. This serious flaw set the occasion for Kant's invention of the categorical imperative, which stated that a moral standard was binding on anyone who wished that restraint to apply to everyone. This powerful idea, which is present in the book of Leviticus in the Old Testament, accomplished three goals simultaneously. It permitted morality to rest on each person's free, but reflective, choice, refuted the pessimism of Thomas Hobbes, and, most important, allowed a rational defense of a small set of standards that included the control of aggression, dishonesty, disloyalty, and the stealing of private property. Humans, however, are so skilled at disguising their true intentions that Kant's creative notion failed to solve the social problems he tried to resolve. A Palestinian suicide bomber, like an eleventh-century Christian knight on a crusade, might be willing to defend the morality of killing if it served a spiritual aim. Remember that Abraham was prepared to kill his beloved son Isaac because God ordered him to do so. If, under some conditions, murder can be a moral act, it is difficult to construct a moral code in which some acts are always amoral.

In desperation, nineteenth-century philosophers retreated to a pragmatic criterion in which the consequences of an action determined whether it was "good" or "bad." The agent's actions or intentions were of secondary importance. This clever argument resembles the demand by twentieth-century minority groups for equality of outcome rather than opportunity. The pragmatic utilitarians argued that the best outcome was one in which the largest number of individuals was made happier. It is easier for a legislature than for a person to rely on this principle. More important, the outcome of an agent's action is unpredictable. A strict interpretation of the utilitarian view denies any moral accolades to a man who jumps in the sea to save a child who is drowning and, as a consequence, kills both the child and himself.

Some contemporary scholars equate morality with judgments of hypothetical situations and ask informants, "Is it morally acceptable for a bystander who sees a train approaching five people standing on the track to pull a switch that would divert the train and save the five persons but, in so doing, kill one person standing at the point of diversion?" The cognitive judgment as to which act is more moral and which less is interesting, but we should not confuse this restricted meaning of morality with an agent's behavior or intention in a real rather than hypothetical situation. I suspect that the cognitive judgments of moral dilemmas given by hardened criminals would be similar to those of law-abiding grandmothers. A small number of philosophers who performed a semantic dissection of the concept "moral" concluded that a logical defense of any ethical standard was impossible and therefore that human morality was a myth.[2] This claim resembles the attempt of a few eighteenth-century philosophers who used equally clever arguments to deny that the paper on which I am writing this sentence exists.

Surprisingly, a few scientists have begun to use brain activity as a referent for a moral feeling or judgment. Psychopaths who are shown an aggressive picture while their brain activity in an area called the orbitofrontal prefrontal cortex is measured display less activation than law-abiding citizens. The conclusion that this area is the biological basis for morality awards a unique meaning to the concept "moral." Most adults with damage to, or a compromise of, the orbitofrontal prefrontal cortex never commit a serious crime, whereas most who lie, cheat, and steal have perfectly intact brains.

My ideas on morality and its development took many years to mature. The first attempt appeared in 1984 in *The Nature of the Child*.[3] Several years later, a conference on morality at Harvard, supported by the MacArthur Foundation consortium on development, debated six issues:

1. Should the referents for moral be actions, judgments, intentions, feelings, or persons?
2. Do most individuals conform to community norms on behavior because of reason or feeling?
3. Are there any moral standards that are universal across all societies?
4. Are children biologically prepared to develop a moral sense?
5. Is the distinction between conventional standards, which change with time, and moral standards, which do not, useful?
6. Is any scientific evidence relevant to philosophers brooding on morality?

Sharon Lamb and I edited the conference papers and discussions in a book titled *The Emergence of Morality in Young Children* (1987).[4]

Although there was no consensus on the first three questions, there was general agreement that children were biologically prepared to appreciate the difference between right and wrong by the time they reached age three. Richard Shweder and Eliot Turiel engaged in a lively debate on the utility of the distinction between conventional and moral standards. Violation of a conventional standard is rarely accompanied by guilt because individuals understand its arbitrariness. Six-year-olds realize that wearing a hat at the dinner table and eating chicken with one's fingers are conventional standards, but asked whether it is all right for a particular teacher to permit children to hit others, reply, "No, it is not okay." If the adult should ask, "Why not?" children say, "Because that is like making other people unhappy; it can hurt them that way; it hurts other people; hurting is not good."[5] Most older children believe that unprovoked harming of another, deceiving a friend, or failure to care for a sick relative are always wrong, even if an authority claimed that these behaviors were permissible, and violation of any one of those standards would probably create guilt.

History, of course, can convert a conventional standard to a moral one. Most white Americans in 1900 regarded the suppression of insulting racial comments as a conventional standard. Large numbers of Americans today regard the suppression of bigotry as morally binding. The reverse can occur, too. Although a majority of nineteenth-century Americans regarded a wife's adulterous affair as a violation of a moral standard, this behavior has become conventional for many contemporary adults. The diluted ethical value of manual work in the People's Republic of China following Mao's death reveals how quickly the change from moral to conventional can occur.

Harvard developmental psychologist Lawrence Kohlberg had died before the conference took place, but his claim that children pass through fixed stages of moral development, as measured by their verbal judgments, permeated the discussions.[6] Eliot Turiel, who had been a student of Kohlberg's, argued that the most mature judgments defended personal freedom and justice as the highest obligations. Richard Shweder disagreed, suggesting that Western societies had fewer moral and more conventional standards because the celebration of freedom was correlated with a preference for conventional values.

Carol Gilligan, a former faculty colleague of Kohlberg's, had criticized him for adopting a masculine perspective in the celebration of the moral primacy of justice and personal freedom, the two ideals of the New England Transcendentalists who, during the decades before the Civil War, argued that the individual, not the society, was the sacred object to perfect.[7] Had Kohlberg been a woman, Gilligan implied, love, loyalty, and nurture, especially for those in need, would have enjoyed an equally prominent position in the moral tapestry. The obligation to love one's children, she argued, is not a less mature moral obligation than the imperative to defend each person's liberty.

Lawrence Blum, one of the philosophers at the meeting (W. V. Quine was the other) reminded the group of what the Chinese have always understood — namely, that every obligation is tied to a social context. There is always an actor, an action, and a situation, and the balance among them determines the morality of an action or intention. Hence, science might be able to help the philosopher.

My last attempt to systematize this heady theme was presented at the Nebraska Symposium for Motivation in April 2003. I argued that individuals fortunate enough to be free of worry over survival and chronic pain, hunger, and disease would be continually concerned with their virtue. Animal families have unique profiles of biologically prepared abilities and concerns. Migrating geese monitor the angle of sunlight; salmon sense the olfactory qualities of streams. Gazelles are vigilant for lions lying in the grass; baboons watch for dominance by another. Humans spend most of their waking hours trying to find, or create, evidence that affirms that they rightfully belong to the category "good person" and to avoid, or at least minimize, acquiring features inconsistent with that classification. The authors of the tree of knowledge allegory in Genesis were insightful when they made an angry God punish Adam and Eve, and their progeny, by ensuring that they, but no other animal, had the ability to know when they have done wrong. A view of human morality as biologically inevitable was less prevalent among eighteenth-century Europeans. Eugène Delacroix, the celebrated French painter, wrote in his journal that conscience would assume a different meaning if the universe had not been created by God.[8]

The concepts "good" and "bad" even penetrate the self-descriptions on personality questionnaires. When Americans and Australians rated themselves on more than seventeen hundred psychological qualities, four traits emerged as salient. The adjectives that defined these four seminal traits were all undesirable and, by implication, bad. They were: (1) quarrelsome and spiteful; (2) impulsive and undisciplined; (3) withdrawn and untalkative; and (4) hypersensitive and emotional.[9] It is not a coincidence that more than half of the rules that all cultures share are ethical obligations, such as "know oneself" and "practice moderation."

Moral Development

The first stage in the development of a moral agent, usually observed before the first birthday, assumes the form of the selected suppression of actions that the family is socializing and exploits the child's vulnerability to discrepant experiences. A mother who has just seen her fourteen-month-old spill milk on the tablecloth says in a voice louder and a face sterner than usual, "Don't do that." That unexpected event creates a state of uncertainty that is assimilated to the child's schematic representation of other unpleasant experiences, such as pain, hunger, and cold. The child quickly learns that spilling food is followed by uncertainty and inhibits these actions. It may be impossible to raise a child without interrupting some actions that are potentially harmful or violate a family standard.

The child's representations of prohibited actions, always tied to a context, are associated with the parents' reactions and a subsequent unpleasant feeling of uncertainty. These linked elements become conditioned incentives for uncertainty when the child is in a situation that resembles the one where discipline had occurred. This first stage of moral development resembles the state of a puppy that whines when it has to go outside to urinate.

The second phase, usually observed by the second birthday after self-awareness is present, is marked by the ability to anticipate facial expressions or bodily postures in others that are signs of disapproval of an act that had not been punished before. The child now possesses schematic concepts for prohibited actions, which include representations of behaviors never committed. Most three-year-olds will hesitate, or not comply at all, if a parent asks them to violate a family norm. A child who had never poured cranberry juice on a clean tablecloth and therefore could not have been punished for it, usually refuses to perform that act when asked because he or she possesses a concept of prohibited actions. The mother of a three-year-old in one of our studies reported that her son asked, "Is it okay to say 'God damn it'?" It cannot be a coincidence that the same time the child becomes aware of what behaviors are prohibited he or she also begins to use words like "good," "bad," "dirty," and "nice."[10]

A state of empathy with a person or animal in obvious distress, which requires the ability to infer the thoughts and actions of another, is also observed late in the second year. Two-year-olds have experienced the unpleasant state that follows criticism, aggression, or teasing and are able to infer those states in others. This ability motivates them to restrain behaviors that might harm another. This restraint will be acquired even if the child has never been aggressive and asocial actions were never punished. That is one reason why children refuse to attempt tasks they believe are too difficult to perform successfully. Remember, many children cried when the examiner modeled three actions with toys and told them to play because they sensed their inability to perform those actions. Parents from diverse cultures recognize that, by the third birthday, most children are aware of many prohibited behaviors. The Utku Eskimo of Hudson Bay name this awareness *ihuma*, or "reason"; the Fijians name it *vakayalo*, or "a sense of what is proper."[11] It is likely that the early emergence of an appreciation of which acts are wrong was adaptive for our species. The birth of the next child in cultures without birth-control strategies usually occurs about two years after the prior birth. All two-year-olds are jealous of the attention given the new infant and have the strength and opportunity to harm their sibling. But the frequency of such acts is so rare that each occurrence makes the headlines of the local newspaper because the two-year-old now knows that aggressive behavior is wrong.

I remember an afternoon when two three-year-old boys in our laboratory were sitting side by side on a couch with their mothers at each end. One boy, "Paul," took a toy telephone from the other boy, "Bill," gave it to Bill's mother, talked with her for a few minutes, and then left the couch to play. After a few minutes, Paul returned, took the telephone from Bill's mother, gave it to his own mother, and told her to talk to Bill's mother. It seemed that Paul wanted to redress the earlier imbalance when his mother had been left out of the conversation.

Behaviors indicative of shame can be observed by the end of the second year but usually appear during the third year. The ability to feel shame requires not only inference of another's thoughts—someone is entertaining a critical evaluation of self—but also some awareness of self. One sign of self-awareness is the ability to recognize one's reflection in a mirror; another is manipulating the behavior of others; a third is verbal reference to the self in terms like "I," "my," "mine" or saying one's name.

The next stage, occurring late in the second or the beginning of the third year, is marked by acquisition of the semantic concepts "good" and "bad" and their application to objects, events, people, and self. The semantic concept "good" is usually applied to four related but nonetheless distinct states—the receipt of praise or affection, the avoidance of punishment, anxiety, shame, or guilt, semantic consistency between an action and a standard, and a feeling of sensory delight. By contrast, criticism, punishment, semantic inconsistency, and pain or discomfort belong to the category "bad." A mother in one of our studies found her three-year-old boy pinching himself with considerable force. To her request for a reason for the self-inflicted pain, the boy replied, "I don't like myself." This boy was aggressive with peers in the neighborhood and was aware that both the children and their parents disapproved of him. Many parents have noted that their four-year-olds deliberately misbehave in order to be punished, and then ask, "Do you love me?" One four-year-old girl told her mother she had done something naughty because she had a dream in which her infant brother had died after being stung by a bee. Now children suppress certain acts because of the wish to avoid assigning the concept "bad" to self.

A small number of children settle on a category for self that has "bad" as a central feature. Chronic sexual abuse can persuade a child that she or he is irredeemably bad; a very small proportion become unusually aggressive. An eleven-year-old British girl who had been sexually abused at an early age by her mother's male clients murdered two preschool boys.[12] The girl's categorization of herself as "bad" made it easier for her to murder without anger or desire for material gain. Fortunately, the vast majority of children are uncertain of their virtue and dread the onset of shame or guilt.

The next phase, usually seen by age four to six, is characterized by feelings of guilt following an action that violates a standard. Guilt requires the simultaneous activation of four psychological networks. The first two, which usually appear by the second birthday, are the awareness that self can control its behaviors and the ability to infer the feelings of others. The second pair of abilities appears later. The child must be able to relate an action performed in the past to a victim's current state. The regular integration of past with present is usually not seen until the fourth birthday. The automatic habit of relating the present moment to the past motivates the child to wonder about causal connections between events. Finally the child has to be able to "re-run" mentally the sequence that began with an action—disobedience, striking another, or destruction of property—and ended with the distress of another and to recognize that this sequence would not have occurred if he or she had shown restraint. Therefore, the child is responsible for the distress of another and has temporarily lost some virtue. The distinct feeling of guilt is the result of a loss of worthiness in the account book kept by self. It should be appreciated that if the feeling of lost virtue were due to the actions of another instead of self, shame or anger would flood consciousness.

Once the capacity for self-blame emerges, guilt is added to fear of harm, anxiety over future calamity, and sadness over loss. Guilt is more closely tied to suicide than the other emotions, and the provocations for suicide in contemporary America are not very different from those in ancient Greece— an illicit sexual experience, rejection by a lover, feeling responsible for the death of a child, and task failure. Cultures vary in the balance between the guilt that accompanies self-blame and the shame that accompanies concern over how others regard self following a behavior that violated a standard. All societies have concepts for both states. The Chinese and Japanese place a greater emphasis on the latter state than Americans. American children are socialized to believe in a private conscience in which self, not others, is the only proper jury. Thus Americans have to rely on laws rather than the opinions of neighbors to keep their society civil. It would be arrogant to declare that one strategy is more mature or more natural than the other.

Soon after they enter school children acquire an understanding of the concepts of fairness and justice. Some examples include beliefs that the severity of punishment should match the seriousness of the crime, that the amount of praise should match the talent or benevolence of an action, and that the difficulty of a task assignment should match the competence of the person completing it. I had failed in earlier writing to acknowledge that older children, like adults, construct representations of ideals and try to command them. Adolescent girls want to be the best exemplar of their gender category, just as surfers seek to tame the perfect wave. Every pregnant woman holds an image of the feelings and actions appropriate for the best mother; every adolescent who plays soccer has an idea of the perfect performance. Some Jewish prisoners in Nazi concentration camps ordered to build a brick wall for their oppressors could not help but build the best wall their skill and the materials allowed. As chairman of the psychology department, I felt an obligation to take B. F. Skinner to lunch because he had been retired for several years and was beginning to show signs of aging. After exchange of the usual niceties, I asked him why he had chosen psychology. His reply surprised me, for Skinner said that as an undergraduate he had no interest in psychology. His ideal was to change the world and he thought this was best accomplished by writing — Sartre came to the same conclusion. After he read John Watson's book on behaviorism, however, Skinner changed his mind and decided that psychology was the better strategy to achieve that prized goal.

The concept of equality is an ideal that is inconsistent with the serious variation in talent, courage, strength, kindness, and attractiveness that exists among one's friends. Nonetheless, many American and European intellectuals in the second and third decades of the twentieth century were attracted to the socialist philosophy of the young Soviet Union because they believed that a capitalist system that maintained inequality in wealth and power had brought on the depression of the 1930s and that a system that minimized inequality would lead to a more perfect society. They, like Marx but unlike Darwin, held an ideal conception of human communities. George Orwell's journalistic description of the lives of unemployed mine workers in northern England in 1936 in *The Road to Wigan Pier* illuminates the attractiveness of socialism to writers, scientists, and college professors during that harsh decade.

Social Categories

Children gradually realize that they belong to several social categories and feel guilty when they behave in ways that are inconsistent with the features of these categories. Each category has a set of obligatory actions and intentions. All children acquire membership in the social categories for family, gender, and developmental stage, and for others, religion and ethnicity are added to the list. When older, many will add categories for their social class, nationality, vocation, and roles as spouse and parent. The power of a category to monitor self's behavior is enhanced when its features are distinctive. Thus, loyalty to the obligations of one's gender is felt more urgently than loyalty to one's nationality. Because each family is unique, loyalty to this category is usually felt most intensely.

If the child believes that he or she belongs to a social category and, in addition, experiences a vicarious emotion—joy, pride, shame—when a member of the category has an experience with emotional implications, psychologists say that the child is identified with the category. The sadness I feel over Europeans' criticism of the United States because of the war in Iraq is a sign of my identification with my nation. Obviously, a child need not be identified with every category that he or she believes is appropriate. But an emotionally tinged identification necessarily limits the personal autonomy Americans celebrate as an ideal. A Navajo adolescent girl unable to leave her reservation because of an identification with her tribe, despite an intense desire to be an opera star in San Francisco, has a compromised autonomy. Rational analysis is impotent against the emotional force of an identification.

The important point, however, is that individuals try to maintain consistency between the features of the categories to which they belong and their evaluation of the actions that define each category. The detection of an inconsistency can be accompanied by an uncomfortable feeling of shame or guilt. A disloyal thought toward a friend can provoke guilt because of the inconsistency between the thought and the features that define "a good friend." Many college-educated women who are enjoying professional careers experience more inconsistency than their grandmothers over the category "mother." Adults with parents who belonged to different religious categories are also vulnerable to the tension of inconsistency. J. D. Salinger, author of *The Catcher in the Rye*, had a Jewish father and a Catholic mother, and his daughter has described the uncertainty her father felt as an adolescent in the 1930s when American anti-Semitism was virulent.

Nominal Categories

There are two kinds of social categories. Nominal categories, which have relatively fixed features, appear first. Gender and stage of development (baby, child, adolescent) are obvious examples of early categories; ethnicity and religion appear later. The ethical obligations attached to these categories are not tied to a specific person and apply to everyone in the category. Boys know they should not wear lipstick, even though they have never done so and have never been punished for such behavior. A mother had been pressing her two-and-a-half-year-old daughter to give up her pacifier by reminding her that she was no longer an infant. After months of nagging, the girl finally told her mother that she would do so on her third birthday, and to the mother's surprise, the daughter threw her pacifier away the day she turned three. The nominal category "child" had replaced the category "baby." A cartoon in the *New Yorker* of December 2004 illustrated a mother saying to her child, who was sitting on the floor pouting, "You're five now, Lance, you got to let go of four."

The recognition that one is a member of a particular family has special salience because family members are likely to receive special resources, especially affection, recognition of their value and selfhood, and the security that comes from believing that help will be given should catastrophe occur at some time in the future. The emotional power of these prizes is one reason for the strong emotional reaction against gay marriages among many Americans. The traditional definition of "family" is a kin group derived from the marriage and procreation of a woman and man. Any attempt to change that definition, even in the spirit of tolerance, can threaten the meaning and certainty of those resources and evoke serious dissonance. When the buying power, and therefore the meaning, of a German mark changed during the disastrous inflationary spiral in Germany in the early 1930s, many in that society became sufficiently anxious to vote Adolf Hitler into a position of power. The meanings of some categories are taken very seriously, and tinkering with them, even for benevolent reasons, exacts a social cost. Imagine the unrest that would follow a legislative or judicial decision that forbade Americans from using the terms "Catholic," "Protestant," "Jew," and "Muslim" and permitted only the general category "religious." I am not bothered by the concept of "gay marriage," but if the Massachusetts legislature passed a bill declaring that a person's astrological sign contained true information about personality that should be included in all psychological courses, I would become seriously disturbed by this change in the meaning of "truth." I suspect that everyone has at least one word in their vocabulary whose meaning is so sacrosanct that any alteration in its referents would provoke confusion.

Relational Categories

The second class of social category is defined by a particular social relationship with another and includes friend, son, daughter, sibling, parent, spouse, lover, grandparent, and citizen. The moral obligations attached to relational categories, which usually call for loyalty, affection, honesty, and nurture, are tied to a specific person. Hence, the required behaviors vary with the immediate social context. A person with two close friends, one dominating and the other anxious, will feel obligated to be deferential to the first and nurturant to the second. One of Eugène Delacroix's journal entries in 1823 reads, "I have 2 or 3 friends but I am forced to be a different man with each of them, or rather to show to each the side of my nature which he understands."[13] Although the distinct olfactory qualities of infants facilitate the bonding of mother to infant in both chimpanzees and humans, only humans add an imperative to be loyal to the relational category "mother." Some professional prostitutes who are mothers of infants report a palpable increase in guilt on evenings when they must work and cannot remain home with their child. A section in Leviticus in the Old Testament presents the moral dilemma of two men in a desert with enough water for only one to survive. Should the one with the water drink it and, as a consequence, reach safety while permitting the other to die? Or should he share the water in a nurturant gesture, guaranteeing that both will die? Rabbinical notes on the text report that a prominent rabbi advised that the man with the water should drink it and escape to safety. But if the pair had consisted of an elderly grandparent with the water and an adolescent grandchild, the rabbi might have arrived at a different solution. Once the social context is specified, the moral conflict becomes easier to resolve.

Individuals who meet the criteria that their category requires have moral authority and can use it to persuade others in times of conflict. Each university department usually has one or two faculty with such authority because they seem to put the vitality of the department or the university ahead of their own interests. Robert White had this enviable position when I arrived at Harvard; Roger Brown enjoyed a similar authority until his death.

Egalitarian societies award greater significance to the ethical demands of relational categories because nominal categories imply unearned status and privilege. The possession of distinct physical features makes it easy for persons to assign themselves to a nominal category. Social properties can be potent, however; the elite as well as the downtrodden believe themselves to be members of significant nominal categories. When a nominal category, such as ethnicity or religion, loses psychological power, the obligation to treat others equally is felt more urgently. This change, which occurred in England in the eighteenth century, was transferred to the new American nation, although Indians and African slaves were initially denied this dignity. Some individuals feel proud simply because they are members of a nominal category. The British during Queen Victoria's reign provide an example. My former colleague David McClelland told me that he felt a surge of pride after reading the David and Goliath story as a child because he had the same name as the biblical hero.

The extraction of pride from a relational category requires the person to implement the obligatory actions. Egalitarian societies want their members to feel more virtuous because of how they behave with others, and not because they belong to a particular group. A priest, physician, and teacher can feel good at the end of the day if they have been benevolent toward others; they are not entitled to feel good because of their vocation.

The moral power of nominal or relational categories derives from two different emotions. One is a feeling of cognitive dissonance created by inconsistency between the obligations and the person's behavior. The child's first words are for objects and events with fixed features, like "milk," "dog," "food," and "fall." All objects called "dogs" should bark, have fur, and be playful. If not, they are less than ideal dogs. Thus, when children learn the names for nominal categories like "boy," "girl," "Catholic," and "Hispanic," they believe that those words, too, name a set of fixed characteristics that define the categories and feel that they ought to be loyal to the features that define the categories to which they belong. Children experience as much dissonance if they stray from these obligations as they would if an animal without fur that never barked was called a dog.

A second basis for loyalty to the rules of one's category is the enhanced virtue that can accompany membership in the category. Residents of Boston in the 1830s were proud that most Americans regarded their city as the hub of the young nation. Fewer current Boston residents feel virtuous simply because they live in this urban setting, rather than in Chicago or San Francisco, despite the recent championships of the New England Patriots and the Boston Red Sox. The obligations and values associated with each nominal and relational category vary in their power to exact an unquestioned loyalty. When a person's major categories agree on an ethical demand, tension is minimal. When they do not, the person confronts the psychic pain of choice. Most of the time, but not always, the personal ethics that emerged from lifetime membership in the categories for family, gender, and ethnicity assume precedence over those associated with friend, vocation, class, religion, or community. But whistleblowers are always possible.

America's desire to honor an egalitarian ethic requires a denial of special privilege to nominal categories that, two centuries earlier, were sources of virtue. Nineteenth-century white, Christian males whose parents and grandparents were born in the United States and attended college could reassure self simply by reminding themselves of their membership in this five-featured category. The rejection of this basis for self-satisfaction, which accelerated in America in the late 1960s, denies this prize to any nominal category. My former colleague George Homans, who experienced frequent moments of distress because he was doing poorly in school, had no friends, and was incompetent at the skills boys value, reassured himself of his goodness by silently rehearsing the fact that his family pedigree could be traced to the second president of the United States.

Membership in some nominal categories can threaten self's virtue. Czeslaw Milosz felt ashamed of his Lithuanian origins because so few Lithuanians had achieved world eminence. The category "ethnic minority" can provoke uncertainty, shame, or anger, even though these emotions are less intense today than a century ago. On February 13, 2005, the citizens of Dresden, Germany, commemorated the sixtieth anniversary of the Allied fire bombing of their metropolis, hoping that the world would reclassify them as victims rather than perpetrators of World War II. Many Americans are required to obtain their daily supply of virtue through personal accomplishments rather than by reminding themselves of their nominal categories or remaining loyal to their relational ones.

There are two different types of achievements. Regaining muscle strength after recuperation from a broken leg and making the last payment on a thirty-year mortgage are victories with fixed features that allow pride when attained. But the desire to be rich or have higher status lacks this quality, for there are always others with more wealth or higher status. Hence, many who seek these goals are never satisfied and experience chronic uncertainty instead of pride. They discount the present moment, for all that matters is tomorrow, next month, or next year. And when those times arrive, they, too, are trashed by the next set of future dates.

The desire for wealth, which has this quality, has ascended to the top of the list of accomplishments in American society for at least two reasons. First, it fits the egalitarian American ethic because it has the appearance of being attainable by all, whereas becoming an accomplished cellist, physicist, novelist, or architect seems to be out of reach for many in the society. Becoming rich, therefore, has become a significant source of virtue in America. Listen to Friedrich Hayek, an economist who won the Nobel Prize in 1974, "Money is one of the greatest instruments of freedom ever invented by man. It is money which . . . opens an astounding range of choices to the poor man."[14] A recent Harvard graduate, speaking for his age and class cohort, stated it more bluntly, but with sadness rather than joy: "We have dropped the old ideals but we still must believe in something, and so we believe in success. And God knows, nothing succeeds like success."[15] No goal as glittering as true equality of dignity can be had without a price. The single-minded pursuit of wealth, and the status it brings, balanced by no other motive, is the price we must pay for social harmony. The materialism that penetrates every aspect of American life, which many find distasteful, is the tax exacted in return for the muting of civil unrest. I suspect that most readers who remember the burning of American cities following the assassination of Martin Luther King, Jr., are willing to pay this fee gladly. Few Americans would prefer a return to the harsh prejudices against African Americans, Jews, and Asians that existed less than a century ago.

A second reason for money's ascent in the moral order derives from the human desire, stronger in the West than the East, to distinguish self from those perceived to be less worthy. Early-eighteenth-century American colonists who could read and write were able to use their literacy as a sign of superiority because these talents were still uncommon, especially in communities west of Philadelphia and south of New York. A century later, a college degree and, in the decades before World War II, foreign travel or a position as lawyer, doctor, or professor served this function. These, along with other early marks of distinction, have become easier to attain and therefore more common and have lost some of their power to honor those who are willing to work for them. Yet because the accumulation of one or two million dollars is difficult, and uncommon, it can function as a symbolic sacrament. This change in the symbols of accomplishment exacts a social cost. Loyalty to community, friends, employers, or clients is being swept aside by the insatiable hunger for material gain, which at the moment is one of the few goals whose anticipated attainment excites and persuades self of its worth.

The preference for rational, rather than emotional, bases for decisions, which is so strong in the West, is easier when money is the salient prize. Economists love to compute cost-benefit ratios in which the amount gained or lost in dollars (or euros) is the primary criterion for judging the rationality of a decision. This practice requires estimating the cost of preserving a forest, supporting an orchestra, subsidizing education, or prolonging a life. Sole reliance on a monetary metric leads some economists to conclude that government should not pay for the vaccination of all children against measles because the cost of the mass program is more than the cost of caring for the children who catch measles. The children's suffering is ignored in the equation. If every parent about to close a business deal that would earn them two hundred thousand dollars suddenly left the room because his or her child was giving a recital at school or had been taken to the hospital with a broken leg, some economists loyal to this principle would accuse the parents of irrational behavior. Cost-benefit analyses could appeal only to those who were profoundly uncertain of the absolute validity of any ethical value other than personal material gain. But what is sadder is that no one laughs at a cost-benefit economist who ignores a parent's feeling of serenity or virtue because of the fear of relying on sentiment rather than a rational rule when one must choose among alternatives. If every citizen applied a cost-benefit analysis to every important decision, life, already dysphoric, would be emotionally uninhabitable. Those saddened by this state of affairs can take heart, for this ethic will change at some future time. Service to the community, loyalty to institutions, or concern with the Earth's health may once again compete with wealth as a criterion for choice and a sign of virtue. During the decades before the Civil War, Americans regarded paying laborers who worked for commercial enterprises as amoral, and in 2005 more high school seniors applied for admission to religious colleges than did so in 1950. A society's values do change.

At the moment, however, loyalty to self takes precedence over the obligations imposed by relational categories. The novel *The Unconsoled* by Kazuo Ishiguro dissects the feelings of obligation social categories generate.[16] Ishiguro caricatures this state in an encounter between a celebrated pianist and an older porter carrying his luggage to the hotel room where he will stay for a few days. After only minutes of conversation in the elevator the porter, who knows that the celebrity will give a public lecture on music a few days hence, asks if the pianist might, at some point in the lecture, say some kind words about all the porters of the city. (The reader does not know but learns later that the porter is the pianist's father-in-law.) The pianist reflects, agrees to do so, and over the next two days thinks about how he might honor the assignment he accepted. The extraordinary imbalance between the fragility of the social bond to the porter and his feeling of responsibility to keep his promise will motivate readers to examine the obligations their life circumstances have forced them to assume, whether as son, daughter, sibling, parent, spouse, employer, employee, lover, friend, or teacher. I confess to a feeling of freedom—a lightness of being—that followed my retirement and release from the continuing obligation to find financial support for my graduate students.

The fraying of social obligations has become a serious source of weakness in our society. When the social cloth is torn completely, each person is transformed from a dolphin in a group to a predatory, solitary shark. In a *New Yorker* cartoon illustrating a middle-aged couple in a living room, the wife declares to her husband, "I've decided to sell you on eBay." This remark is funny because Americans understand that the wife's feelings are only a little discrepant from the community's conception of many marriages. The cartoon would not have evoked a smile in 1805. A sixteen-year-old who was recently asked, "What do you want from life?" replied, "I want to matter to someone." I suggest that this answer would have been rarer in the nineteenth century, when most adolescents were so certain of their social relationships that they treated them as they did the air they breathed. This reply could occur only in youth who recognized the frailty of human bonds.

Cultures vary in the power of the individual's social categories to direct daily decisions. The Western celebration of personal freedom to enhance self, unconstrained by any ethic other than not harming another without provocation, has slowly eroded the force social categories used to exert, as ocean waves, over time, reduce a five-hundred-pound boulder to a pebble. The form that the resolution of the current conflict between the West and the rest of the world will assume hinges on how this difference in perspective is managed.

A growing number of citizens in the affluent West feel free of strong obligatory relationships to people, ideas, or institutions. The malaise of loneliness that accompanies this freedom prevents the feeling of vitality that can occur only when one believes that some goals are worth working for and others must be shunned. When no experience is absolutely good or bad the energy that should accompany each awakening is depleted. Pär Lagerkvist did not anticipate that there might come a time when some would be satisfied with nothing.

The Politics of the 1960s

An egalitarian ethic that emphasized justice for, and nurturance toward, the disenfranchised was essential to the morality of a majority of Harvard undergraduates during the late 1960s, when students on many university campuses led large protests against the Vietnam War and against prejudice toward African Americans and women. The Harvard faculty recognized the students' frustration over their apparent passivity toward these issues and their desire to proceed with "business as usual." One moment during a meeting of the arts and science faculty confirmed professors' suspicions. The newspapers had announced that President Richard Nixon had ordered the bombing of Cambodia, which expanded the already unpopular war in Vietnam. Liberal faculty members were outraged and wanted the university to break from its usual posture of political neutrality and make a public statement. Most meetings of the faculty draw about a hundred members from a roster of more than 650. But this afternoon most of the arts and science faculty were in attendance, and the venue had been moved from its usual place in University Hall to the large auditorium in Memorial Hall, built to honor Harvard graduates who served in the Civil War. An agenda is sent to the faculty several days before and is available on the day of the meeting, usually Tuesdays at 4 p.m.

The agenda indicated that the first item of business was the reading of an obituary of a faculty member who had recently died. As soon as the president—Nathan Pusey—called the meeting to order, a professor rose and requested that the printed agenda be aborted so that the faculty could discuss the war. Many in the audience indicated their strong approval of this request. President Pusey thought for a few seconds and then declared, in a calm, steady voice, "We will proceed with the agenda as printed," which we did.

The student demonstrations against the joined themes of war and racism derived their energy from both selfish and idealistic motives. The draft was law and many male students did not want to be sent to Vietnam. An end to the war meant elimination of this threat. But I held the belief, shared by many, that the students were genuinely empathic to the plight of the Vietnamese civilians, whom they saw suffering each night on television, and distressed by the racism of American society. They believed that their university had a responsibility to contribute to the elimination of these stains on their identification with their country. An undergraduate woman in one of my courses confessed that she and many of her friends were bothered by the inconsistency between the apparent irrelevance of the courses they were taking and larger social tensions. This phenomenon is rarer today, even though many tensions remain. The protesting students also sensed that some faculty members who agreed with their views were deriving vicarious pleasure from the protests their teachers were reluctant to join.

What was unusual about the mood at Harvard was the assumption that the violent disruptions on other campuses could not occur in Cambridge. After all, Harvard students enjoyed a superb faculty that treated each student as if he or she were a prince or princess destined for great futures and high positions. It did not serve their interests to disturb this happy state of affairs. Why would honored guests at the best hotel in the world burn down the dining room and trash the tennis courts? Hence, many faculty members, especially those over age fifty, did not understand why students would break the unwritten contract between themselves and the university, seize the central administration building, and refuse to leave when ordered. What would be gained by destroying the trust, civility, and respect they enjoyed? When Pusey, in desperation, ordered the Cambridge police to eject the students forcefully, the undergraduate anger turned to rage.

A particularly sad moment occurred months later, when the faculty committee appointed to decide the punishment for the small group who had occupied and refused to leave the building that housed several deans held a meeting in a packed Memorial Chapel. Although the punishments were mild, the students screamed obscenities at the faculty member who read out the judgment, even though he was deeply empathic with their cause and was in part responsible for their relatively light sentences. That hour provoked in me, and I assume in many others, the same shock that the Nobel Prize-winning novelist Elias Canetti felt in July 1927, when he saw Viennese police quelling a riot kill ninety members of a crowd that had gathered because a judge had acquitted the men who had killed a group of workers.[17] Many older faculty members never recovered from what they viewed as disloyalty and a lack of gratitude, and it has taken more than a generation for the bad taste of those months to dissipate.

The faculty's anxiety that spring is captured by a short speech at a faculty meeting held in a large auditorium where plays are performed. The major decision that afternoon was whether to vote for the establishment of a department of African-American studies. Students with grim, angry faces paced outside the building, and the faculty feared that serious unrest would follow a refusal to approve the new department. They were not concerned over their personal integrity but for the integrity of the community they loved and, more important, over the threat to their faith in the reliance on rationality, rather than sentiment, when making institutional decisions. The case for the new department did not rest on the claim that there was a rich corpus of organized knowledge that most students should possess. The persuasiveness of the request grew out of an empathy for the small number of African-American students and a subtly felt need for penance over the faculty's earlier indifference to student demands. As the vote approached, and it looked as if the new department would be approved, a respected gray-haired professor of economics, Alexander Gerschenkron, who was worried about the mood of expediency, asked to be acknowledged. The audience became quiet as he began telling a fairy tale about a king who had his heralds announce that the man who performed the most extraordinary act would be awarded his daughter, the princess, as a bride. Three finalists were selected, and a large crowd gathered in the main hall of the palace to witness the contest. The first contestant brought a beautiful harpsichord to the front of the hall, and the king declared that the instrument was an extraordinary object. The second suitor brought a painting of the palace and the surrounding woods, which the king acknowledged to be extraordinary. The final contestant was carrying a porcelain clock toward the king, who, as soon as he saw it, declared, "That is the most extraordinary object," and was about to award the princess's hand to this artist, when a man sitting in the front row holding a sledgehammer rose and smashed the clock to pieces. The king gasped and declared, "*That* is the most extraordinary thing I have ever seen." Gerschenkron sat down and there was a long silence as the faculty brooded on the moral message intended. Minutes later, the new department was approved.

Many of our wisest faculty, reflecting on these and similar events across the nation, declared that the university and American society would never be the same. We were witnessing the beginning of a barbarous era that would permanently change the quality of college life. It is only thirty-five years since that anarchic spring term, and classes are orderly, students are civil, and professors are still flying to distant places to give scholarly presentations for reasonable fees. The storm passed, the damage has been repaired, and the student anger has disappeared. Harvard, like most colleges, now admits many more minority students; the Department of African-American Studies flourishes under Henry Gates, and any pockets of prejudice that existed in 1969 are essentially gone. Most undergraduates would experience a sharp feeling of self-reproach if a prejudicial idea bubbled up spontaneously from their unconscious. A student's dress in 1969 differentiated those who grew up with wealth from those who were on scholarship. This discrimination is impossible today because almost all students wear the same costume of jeans and sweaters. The ethic of the "gentlemen's C" held by undergraduates from wealthy families has vanished as academic achievement became the symbolic sign of virtue for all, simply because these students were born after 1970 rather than before. The change in values is a result of historical events, rather than childhood conversations with parents, as Alex Inkeles told me five years earlier over coffee.

I celebrate the new morality. But there are no free lunches. If a twenty-one-year-old cannot use her skin color, religion, parents' occupations, or education as automatic marks of virtue and must rely primarily on her personal accomplishments, we will have to accommodate to the excessive self-interest and lack of institutional and group loyalty that are more characteristic of the current student cohort than of the one that graduated the year I arrived in Cambridge. Humans demand that events, ideas, and persons be sorted into bins labeled "bad," "good," "better," and "best" so that they know what to do each morning. Personal autonomy is only a gift for those with a moral compass.

A second change wrought by the new morality was the addition of an ethic of "fairness" to the traditional criterion of merit when decisions regarding the recipients of prizes, honors, and admission to honorific societies were being made. Committees feel an obligation to ensure a just representation of gender, ethnicity, and geography. Although some might be frustrated by this change in the symbolic meaning of the honor, it has the advantage of reducing perceptions of prejudice. Because the primary function of these "prizes" is to permit the recipients a few moments of pride, it is easy to defend the new practice by pointing to the social dividend it reaps. After all, the practice of relying primarily on test scores and grades in picking freshman classes at Ivy League colleges is less than sixty years old. When the community enjoys a reasonably coherent harmony, the spotlight can be directed at the perfected individual; when the coherence fails, it is not unreasonable to try to reduce the social dissonance in order to move closer to the ideal of a more perfect society.

Virtue in Pleasure

An inevitable consequence of the abandonment of nominal and relational categories as a basis for deciding what to do, and judging whether one is living life properly, was an increased reliance on self's pleasures, rather than the states of others, as the criterion for choosing one action over another. Americans are reminded regularly of Jefferson's declaration that personal happiness is a right, and by implication a moral obligation. This imperative weakens the ethics linked to the relational categories. Although individuals feel freer when their social categories lose some power, they remain vulnerable to uncertainty if they do not know what goals they should pursue. Humans who do not have to spend most of each day finding sufficient food and protecting self and family from danger need a reason for selecting one action over another. The establishment of the first agricultural civilizations, about ten thousand years ago, allowed many choices that had been denied the first humans. The opportunity to choose what was best was accompanied by the selection of personal properties—wealth, talent, beauty, freedom, status, power, or spirituality—as moral goods. About seven hundred years after the consolidation of Christianity Europeans replaced piety with rationality, and less than two centuries later added sensory delight. Many Americans would smile upon learning that Frances Hutcheson, an eighteenth-century Scottish philosopher, was certain that humans were happiest when they were kind to others. Most Americans and Europeans forgot, or never knew, that John Locke regarded the denial of personal pleasure as a hallmark of virtue.

An important advantage of awarding self-denial a bright halo is that everyone is capable of willful restraint; therefore, each person can provide self with frequent, albeit small, doses of satisfaction whenever they wish. When a feeling of virtue requires gaining external prizes that willpower alone cannot guarantee, those who cannot do so must live with the emotions that accompany failure. Put plainly, it is difficult for the poor, powerless, or lonely in contemporary America and Europe to feel virtuous because they successfully resisted seduction by desires for wealth and the status awarded for unusual accomplishment. The anger of young Muslim citizens in England provoked by their marginality, which is mounting, poses a serious threat to the status quo. The range of material comfort and privilege in our society, compared with Europe or Japan, has grown over the past 50 years, making it more difficult now than earlier for a poor American child to become upwardly mobile and move from the bottom to the top 25 percent in the distribution of income. This social fact may be one reason why more Americans than Europeans are committed to a religious faith. Those who are unable to feel smug because of their new automobiles, winter vacations, and smartly dressed children, or who reject these values as superficial, can find some measure of grace in their faith.

Humans seek two distinct psychological states. One originates in sensation; the other in a cognitive judgment. The attainment of either permits a brief bout of joy, followed by hours, days, weeks, or months during which one tries to re-experience the lovely moment. Although a small proportion spend many hours of each day trying to capture the pleasures that originate in sensation, a much larger number spend the same amount of time gathering evidence that permits the judgment that self has matched its features to an ideal. Darwin recognized the critical difference between these two states. On May 5, 1839, he wrote in one of his notebooks that humans feel they ought to follow certain lines of conduct and must learn that "it is his interest to follow it . . . by interest I do not mean any calculated pleasure but the satisfaction of the mind."[18] He had acknowledged months earlier that happiness consists of doing good and being perfect. The dissatisfaction with contemporary life in many industrialized societies, a partial product of the bleaching of worthwhileness from most activities, was captured in a cartoon in a March 2005 issue of the *New Yorker* illustrating three scenes. In the first a man working at his computer is imagining playing golf. In the second the same man is playing golf but imagining a naked woman. In the third he is making love to a woman but imagining his computer. It is hard to be happy for more than a few moments if one is unsure about the moral validity of one's actions. The contemporary demand to honor all ethical positions, which I celebrate, purchases the increased tolerance necessary for social harmony in diverse societies. But the price is not cheap. I fear that humans cannot have it all. If I award ethical legitimacy to pro-life advocates I necessarily lose some of my emotional commitment to a pro-choice posture.

Although a feeling state is the aim of both sensory delight and consonance with an ideal, the language that describes each feeling is far leaner than the vocabulary for the objects, people, and events that make the feelings possible. As a result, most adults, when asked what they want from life, reply that they want money, power, friends, respect, love, recognition, acceptance, or a particular prize, when the essential desire is the feelings these events create. Surfers enjoy the excitement of the activity and need large waves to attain this feeling. The target of their desire is not a large wave but the state created by the act of surfing. A very small number of unfortunate adults who suffer from a disease that prevents them from feeling any sensory pleasure are perfectly able to execute the behaviors that used to bring them joy, and the objects that produced these feelings in the past are present in their environments. However, they have no desire for them because their actions provoke no feeling.

A writer once noted that the lover takes more pleasure from a relationship than the beloved because of the excitement that accompanies the plans, thoughts, and acts of loving. A line from a popular song of my youth was "If I'm not near the one I love, I love the one I'm near." I acknowledge, however, that erotic love does have a unique status among the human pleasures because, unlike satiety and excitement, which can be gratified by many foods and activities, only a small number of persons can generate the delicious feeling. The "beloved" does have a status that steak and Hawaiian waves do not.

Sex as a Source of Virtue

Everyone requires information, usually delivered on an irregular schedule, informing them of their value. Rehearsal of self's nominal categories, loyalty to the obligations of relational ones, and acquiring signs of wealth, status, and accomplishment are effective messages. At least among Americans, however, nominal categories have lost much of their earlier power to reassure. The increasing distrust of strangers, due in part to geographic mobility, frustrates loyalty to relational categories while exacerbating loneliness. And the deterioration of the public schools has cast a shadow over the idealistic hope that any talented person who perseveres can expect wealth and status. Because of these losses, being a partner in a sexually satisfying relationship (with someone of the same or opposite sex), which is always gratifying, has become more essential to the judgment of self's value than it was a few centuries earlier. At the least it reassures those individuals who feel lonely or anonymous that at least one other person knows and cares about them, if even for a few hours.

The capacity to be aroused by the physical beauty of another, to enjoy the unique sensations of sex, and to feel enhanced by the vicarious possession of the admired qualities of a beloved are inherent features of our humanity. The conception of the relations between men and women in ante-bellum America idealized an inseparable blending of sexuality, companionship, tenderness, loyalty, and mutual respect. This combination, which defined love, was regarded as the richest gift nature had given humans. The sexual component in this ensemble has ascended to a preeminent position in this list, as well as in the larger set of life's delights, because other sources of happiness have descended. The third-ranked chimpanzee in a troop becomes the alpha male if the two more dominant animals suffer mortal wounds, even though his inherent characteristics remain unchanged.

A sexual relationship has two properties, in addition to sensory delight, that distinguish it from a gourmet meal, a deep sleep, and a warm room on a cold night. First, the specific times, places, and love objects are not completely predictable; hence, the excitement that hovers over uncertainty adds to the pleasure. Uncertainties over serious illness, the premature death of a loved one, a violent attack, gossip, a pregnancy before marriage, insufficient food, or the anger of a dead ancestor, which had been dominant concerns during much of human history, have become muted for many in modern industrialized societies. Most Americans have never been robbed, mugged, or raped, have ample food in the refrigerator, are indifferent to the opinions of the strangers in their community, and do not worry excessively over unwanted pregnancies because of condoms, diaphragms, and the pill. As these concerns lost their ability to disturb consciousness, those that had been a whisper earlier gained a stronger voice.

A second distinctive feature of sexuality is that the acts involved in attracting a love object, preparing for love, and executing its postures have become domains of mastery for many Americans. The covers of magazines stacked near checkout counters of supermarkets announce new and better ways to please both self and partner. The advertisements for Viagra resemble those for Eveready batteries announcing their reliability and endurance for whatever purpose the user intends. Few Americans care about the skill they display in eating pasta, taking a shower, or preparing for sleep, but they do care about their ability to attract, arouse, and satisfy an erotic partner. A successful sexual experience thus adds the joy of mastery to the sensual moments. One psychologist has discovered that reduced blood pressure is an additional benefit of regular sex.[19] Unlike the more limited opportunity for serious improvement in playing the piano or writing poetry, many more are capable of perfecting their skill in making love. Almost everyone can extract some degree of pride from improvement in this domain.

Other historical events have made heterosexual relationships more gratifying because unions flourish when each partner possesses desirable qualities that the other lacks but wishes to command, be it beauty, gentleness, honesty, loyalty, wisdom, celebrity, intelligence, sensitivity, power, pedigree, or property. In Bernhard Schlink's novel *The Reader*, a fifteen-year-old boy falls in love with an illiterate older woman because she treats him as an adult in their sexual encounters.[20] The participation in a mature sexual relationship permits the boy to feel enhanced. Medieval knights felt more vital after a romantic encounter with a woman of nobility than after bedding an equally attractive peasant woman. The increased dignity women have attained in Western societies over the past few centuries has rendered a love relationship more gratifying than it was in the fifteenth century, when women were seen as diminished spirits or accomplices to the Devil. Seventeenth-century manuals of advice for suitors instructed them to select women from the same social class who were mature, chaste, and brought a substantial dowry. There was no mention of their beauty or sexual appetite.

This enhancement of women exacts a cost, however. The high divorce rate in the United States and Europe has many causes. One is the heavier burden placed on each marriage. A century earlier, husbands and wives had stable sources of companionship outside the home (for example, a weekly card game or visit to a local club), and mutual involvement in the lives of members of the extended families living in the same town or county supplied pleasure. As these resources disappeared, marriage had to supply not only sexual gratification but also the pleasures derived from companionate relationships.

The replacement of the complementary psychological properties of husband and wife, characteristic of the eighteenth and nineteenth centuries, with a more similar profile of autonomy, self-assertion, and ambition is a second contributory cause of divorce. Many contemporary wives do not need to gain power or status vicariously through their husbands, and men, whose grandfathers gained gentleness and innocence through marriage, are less able to enjoy this prize vicariously. As a result, sexual pleasure has become a more critical foundation of a stable marriage. When the excitement generated by the uncertainty of sex and the unfamiliarity of the beloved are removed, couples are left with the joys of children and companionship. Although these are not unimportant sources of happiness, the culture's insistence on the necessity of multiple orgasms that propel the soul skyward tempts partners to decide that their sex lives could be better and they search for someone closer to their image of the ideal.

These historical events have created an obsession with the ability to love and to be loved sexually. It is hard to find a novel in which sexuality is not a prominent theme. The plot lines of many celebrated American films center on anger, envy, jealousy, and loneliness, but there are always several thirty-second erotic scenes to remind audiences that making love provides the most effective release from the anguish or ennui of daily life. A former Iranian colonel, now an émigré living in California, whispers "We are blessed" only once in the two-hour film *House of Sand and Fog:* after a satisfying sexual union with his wife. Opponents of gay marriage worry that changing the meaning of marriage will erode the sanctity they impute to acts of marital love. A nineteen-year-old college junior at the end of a pleasant first date is likely to say to her new acquaintance, "I'm on the pill," not "You're an interesting guy."[21] A fifteenth-century book of guidance for aristocratic women, written by a woman of the same class, advised young women to be chaste and older ones to avoid promiscuity, protect their reputation, respect their husbands, curb all pride, and care for their children. There was no mention of the importance of having a sexually gratifying love relation. Indeed, religious medieval Europeans regarded virginity and chastity as the more desirable state, and the eighteenth-century Shakers of New England, admittedly a minority, regarded the renunciation of sex as the highest form of purity.

Commentators on human nature from ancient China, Egypt, and Greece or Victorian England would have disagreed with today's self-appointed experts on mental health who declare, without wincing, that the ability to love another person sexually is (and presumably has always been) quintessential for a healthy personality. This statement may be true for many contemporary adults, but it was not true in the Athens of Plato, which, viewing women as inferior, did not regard a heterosexual union as the high point of the day. The tenets of Taoism, a popular Eastern philosophy, advocate the avoidance of an emotionally deep relationship with another—need no one and be needed by no one are the ideals to pursue. It is morally arrogant to declare that the ancient Greeks and Taoists were emotionally suppressed or intellectually limited. It was only a century and a half ago that Søren Kierkegaard suggested that loyalty to one's obligations, not being in love, was the absolute requirement for psychological health. I recall feeling annoyed one afternoon in a cathedral in northern Spain when I saw American tourists with cameras snapping photographs of the altar while a dozen local parishioners were on their knees in a state of worship. I imagined a future time when tourists with cameras would wander through our national parks taking pictures of lovers locked in ecstatic embraces. Modern citizens of Madrid or London who, five centuries earlier, were excited by the stoning of a witch were now aroused by watching a young woman on a stage slowly take off her clothes to reveal a blood-red heart pasted over her pubes.

The majestic position of erotic love is likely to be maintained until the uncertainties that hold it aloft lose salience and another uncertainty, perhaps a safe food supply, a warm hearth in winter, mutual loyalty and affection among members of an extended family, or the honesty, kindness, and civility of neighbors, displaces sex as the alpha obsession. If and when that happens, the ability to love a sexual partner and to receive love in return will retain their traditional and very secure place in the list of human joys but will lose their current, historically unique status as an absolute requirement for psychological health.

The Contribution of Science

The broad dissemination of biological research announcing that humans share important psychological and biological features with chimpanzees has weakened the ethical obligations of the relational categories that call for altruism, cooperation, and loyalty. The biologists, writing in a Darwinian perspective, emphasize the continuities rather than the differences among species. The facts of evolution, citizens are told, imply that humans are biologically prepared to be self-interested and motivated to maximize their status, pleasure, and reproductive potential. These scholars simply ignore the glaring fact that the first human groups were cooperative and that contemporary societies that have enjoyed long periods of peace, including the Balinese and the Batek of Malaysia, discourage intense competitiveness and encourage cooperation. If maximizing our reproductive potential is the most urgent human need, it is puzzling that during the opening decades of the seventeenth century more than one in five adults in England remained unmarried because of economic conditions that motivated many to avoid the shame of being unable to support a family. Among humans, preserving one's virtue trumps the motive for maximizing one's inclusive fitness every time.

Evolutionary biologists remain frustrated by their inability to construct a compelling explanation of why so many adults cooperate with strangers and are loyal and kind toward many who are not kin. Some try to explain this fact by arguing that people cooperate to maintain a favorable reputation with others. Although some cooperation is driven by this goal, I suspect that most is not. This explanation contains the same flawed assumption held by orthodox behaviorists fifty years ago. These biologists refuse to recognize that humans help others because their biology demands that they try to meet personal standards for nurturing others, even if they receive no external reward for the behavior. Several years ago I conducted an intervention project designed to help poor first-grade children with no reading skill. Retired adults visited individual children at their schools for an hour a day, five days a week, over the school year, helping the children learn to read. Most volunteers were motivated by a desire to meet a standard of usefulness to their community. In most cases, their neighbors knew nothing of their effort and their local "reputation" was not enhanced by the volunteer work.

The evolutionists also have difficulty explaining why many societies have invented a transcendental, spiritual force—a God or gods residing in the sky or in nature. Evolutionary biologist Richard Dawkins is irritated by this habit, which he believes defies the canon of inclusive fitness. Dawkins is reluctant to acknowledge that human biology demands that each individual strive to regard self as good and that most individuals need continual reassurance. Belief in a metaphysical force, and the practice of rituals that presumably please that force, can, for some, mute the uncomfortable tensions that compromise the ability to meet the responsibilities their societies demand. Faith in some absolute good—whether God, motherhood, the sanctity of life, love, art, writing, nature, or adding to the corpus of scientific facts—is necessary for engaging the day with enthusiasm. Einstein's marvelous insights about space-time contribute no more to the inclusive fitness of our species than a Muslim pilgrim walking from Amman to Mecca.

Although scientific evidence has become an arbiter of many issues that have moral implications—Is an embryo alive? Is violence on television bad for children? Does affirmative action have a benevolent effect on the education of college students?—it is an error to assume that any ethic is an obvious derivative of any form of animal behavior. The human moral sense is a unique evolutionary phenomenon with a foundation in the human genome. It is not an obvious derivative of any known competence in apes or monkeys.

The public is told regularly that biological facts deny the power of individual will and the significance of humans in a universe devoid of any distinction between good and evil. These declarations trouble many because they mechanize human nature and rob the concepts of procreation, marital fidelity, and consciousness of some of the mystery on which their emotional power has rested. If a donor egg from Mary Smith can be fertilized in a petri dish with sperm from Richard Jones and then implanted in the uterus of surrogate mother Ruth Williams so that Richard Jones's wife can be a mother, the meanings of "parent" and "reproduction" are changed sufficiently to make many feel that the mystery of conception is disappearing and, with it, the feeling of agape that infuses the idea of humanness with a sacred quality. A mourning over this loss is one reason why George W. Bush won the election of 2004 and why some state legislatures are requiring teachers to devote as much time to discussions of intelligent design as to evolutionary theory.

Americans today are divided over two different views of humanity. One group insists that the family, headed by a man and woman, is the primary unit in society, the family's freedom from state coercion is a primary imperative, and heterosexual love is a sacred experience. The meaning network for this group links human specialness, heterosexuality, Christianity, family, and patriarchy in a coherent and meaningful structure. The second group sees the individual as the primary unit, personal achievement as salvation, sex as a natural, not a sacred, experience, and rationality based on science as the basis for decisions. The meaning network for this group combines the individual, rationality, achievement, sexual pleasure, egalitarianism, and science. The advocates of the first perspective feel threatened by the second and are rebelling.

The evolutionary argument became attractive over the past few decades because citizens expect science to explain their intentions and to rationalize the behaviors their communities require. The behaviorism I was taught zealously in 1950 was born several decades earlier to quiet those who argued that the children of the recent European immigrants were genetically tainted. Politically liberal Americans wanted experience to be the sculptor of development. Freudian ideas were popular among many Americans at about the same time because the availability of inexpensive contraceptives made sexuality outside marriage free of risk, and, therefore, erotic images were permitted fuller access to consciousness. But because these images were still not completely free of shame or guilt, many felt a tension that Freud described as a conflict between id and superego. Psychoanalytic sessions were supposed to free self of this discomfort. These ideas, which seemed intuitively correct, rationalized the sexual longings that were beating at the entrance to conscious life.

A little less than a century later, the extraordinary increase in geographic mobility, bureaucratic forms of employment, ethical diversity, and competition for a small number of vocations with high status and income forced many Americans, who were already favorably disposed to self-actualization, to turn up the gain to a level that was becoming uncomfortable. Postdoctoral fellows working in a biological laboratory with twenty other young scientists are reluctant to share their discoveries with peers for fear that someone will beat them to the next, more significant finding. Youth who chose science because they anticipated the pleasures of sharing ideas with others now find themselves in a battle zone. The employee who has been loyal for twenty years and learns that the president of the company has used his or her pension funds for a selfish purpose is entitled to justified anger. Graduate students in many universities support themselves by teaching small groups of undergraduates enrolled in large lecture courses. One student who needed extra money placed signs on campus the first week of term that promised fifty dollars to students who would drop out of a course they had already selected and instead enroll in the course he was scheduled to teach. When I told him this act was ethically dubious, his reply, offered with no shame, was that we live in a market economy, and therefore he did not violate any moral standard.

Historical changes have forced many Americans to cater to self first. For those who find this imperative uncomfortable or are prevented by their history or class position from taking full advantage of the opportunity to enhance self's status, it is soothing to be told by biologists that because all animals are selfish, their attitude is no reason for shame or guilt over indifference to the feelings of others. It saddens me to hear honest, competent, responsible American adolescents say, with conviction, that a long period of world peace is impossible because humans are inherently selfish. They have assimilated the messages in textbooks and on television shows and assume that the basis for their pessimism is a set of proven scientific facts, not an ethical stance. No character in Shakespeare's plays suffered because of social isolation; these heroes and heroines were troubled by the conflicts their obligations had created. John Updike's anti-hero in the Rabbit novels is desperate because he has no obligations. The individualism that Ralph Waldo Emerson believed would allow the human spirit to soar, like all ideas taken to excess, has become corrosive of confidence, trust, and serenity. Montaigne was right; moderation above all.

Every seat in a large auditorium at the Massachusetts Institute of Technology was filled—and many were denied a seat—for a meeting in the fall of 2004 in which the Dalai Lama, along with some Buddhist monks and psychologists, discussed the power of meditation to reveal the secrets of the human mind. The main theme of the presentations was that anyone, with practice, could learn to meditate and, in so doing, gain a more profound understanding of mind. In my summary of the meeting on the final day, I suggested that, had this meeting been held in 1950, only a third of the auditorium would have been filled, and I asked, rhetorically, why so many had traveled so far to attend this conference. I answered by noting that many Americans were bothered by scientists telling them that they had no free will, that their actions and emotions were determined by their genetic constitution and childhood conditioning, and that their primary urge, whether they knew it or not, was, not to love, cooperate, and show kindness, but to maximize their health and status so that they, and their closest genetic relatives, could sire the greatest number of children. They found this description of humanity unattractive and desired a kinder alternative that returned some control to their ability to choose while legitimizing both their altruistic intentions and wish to believe in an ideal. The Buddhist ideology supplied this healing conception. They came to Cambridge to nod their assent to this more pleasing description of their humanity. I added, however, that my comments should not be interpreted as a defense of the biological determinists or a celebration of the Buddhists. Humans do have the freedom to decide whether they will or will not visit a sick neighbor, and their decision is not knowable from measurements of their brains. But that fact, which renders the Buddhist philosophy attractive, does not necessarily render it valid.

An important function of a moral standard is to permit individuals greater freedom to practice a behavior that social conditions demand or to prohibit actions that are causing unrest. Impoverished young women in seventeenth-century Milan, forced into prostitution, rationalized their behavior as ethically acceptable. Luther, bothered by the fragility of the marital bond caused by the widespread use of mistresses by sixteenth-century German husbands, commanded young men to celebrate marital bliss and choose women who would be reliable housewives, good mothers, and sexually gratifying love objects. When life circumstances force an action that is inconsistent with local morality, the mind usually finds a way to explain its necessity and bleach the behavior of some of its taint.

Commitment to an ethical standard permits each person to decide, without excessive delay, what actions to implement when they have a choice because humans resist the conclusion that it makes no difference which response is selected. We insist that our lives have some purpose other than begetting the next generation. But most of us are silent if asked to provide a foundation for our decisions. The inability to justify one's moral intuitions with more than the weak reply, "It feels right," generates unease in societies that celebrate rationality. For this reason, any person or group that announces that it has a logically compelling answer to the question, "Why do I believe this is right?" will be celebrated. The church was an effective source of justification for Europeans for more than fifteen hundred years until science raised its hand and volunteered to be judge, leading many citizens to assume that the facts of nature would provide a rationale for ethical decisions.

The problem is that humans are selfish and generous, aloof and empathic, hateful and loving, dishonest and honest, disloyal and loyal, cruel and kind, arrogant and humble. Most feel a little guilt over excessive display of the first member of each of those seven pairs. That feeling is uncomfortable, and we are eager to have it ameliorated. Church attendance or psychotherapy is effective for some if the message and the character of the priest or therapist enjoy respect. Some people do feel better when they learn that their less social urges are natural consequences of the fact that they are close relatives of gorillas. The currently high status of the biological sciences has made it possible for students of evolution to serve as therapists to segments of their community. For those who are unable to accept this picture of humanity, biologists are villains—hence the current challenge to the validity of evolutionary ideas.

Many books published over the past quarter-century claim that because self-interest is present in all animal species, humans need not feel ashamed of consistently catering to self first. A motive to enhance one's perfectibility leads many couples to control their fertility so that one or both can enjoy the pleasure of personal accomplishment gained through education, vocational advancement, travel, artistic pursuits, and a host of other activities.

Yet anyone with a modest knowledge of the natural world—and minimal inferential skill—could find examples in nature that support almost any ethical message desired. If you wish to sanctify marriage, point to pair-bonding gibbons. If, however, you think that infidelity is more natural, nominate chimpanzees. Elephants should be emulated if one believes that women should be in positions of dominance, but elephant seals are the model if you believe that men should dominate harems of beautiful women. Nature has enough diversity to fit almost any ethical taste.

Science is one of the most powerful — some might say the most effective — ways to illuminate nature. The propositions constructed from the mysterious marriage of the concrete and the imagined can bring clarity, comprehension, and, on occasion, a feeling that combines delight, awe, and wonder into an emotion for which we have no name. Science deserves to be celebrated. But we ask for more. Not satisfied with the gift of understanding, we demand that the fruits of research also tell us what we ought to do when we must choose among alternatives. In this Hobbesian world we, not the king, must provide order.

Knowledge and morality are not independent, for facts can point to an incorrect basis for a moral conviction. For example, if the threat of the death penalty has no effect on the frequency of homicides, then perhaps our society should eliminate this harsh sentence. In addition, social conditions can require actions that have to be rationalized with a moral position. Some arguments for and against slavery during the century before the Civil War hinged on whether negroes and whites belonged to the same species. If yes, slaves had to be awarded freedom; if not, slaveowners were justified in denying them liberty. Facts were to be the basis for deciding an ethical issue. Why didn't eighteenth-century Americans choose a different defense, either adherence to some absolute principle (like equality) or the word of authority? Why did they, and why do we today, regard scientific evidence as the preferred way to defend or to oppose a moral proposition? The Supreme Court, for example, decided in 2005 that adolescents who committed murder must be tried as juveniles rather than as adults. This meant that a death sentence for these criminals was less likely. The rationale for this conclusion cited scientific evidence on brain maturation rather than acknowledge the true basis for this position — namely, an ethical urge to permit the young another chance. I suspect that some author, at this moment, is writing a play in which a Nobel laureate in biology, in the role of judge in a courtroom, is questioning a creationist accused of irrationality. The roles were reversed four hundred years ago when Robert Cardinal Bellarmine was accusing Galileo of heresy.

One reason for our current faith in objective evidence as the guide to social rules is that science has gained community respect through useful inventions that permitted humanitarian advances, technical feats that magnified our sense of potency, and the prediction of a few future moments. Science and a rational approach to decisions have acquired golden haloes denied to other institutions. Citizens thus expect scientific knowledge to be the best guide to the resolution of moral dilemmas because facts are objective and, presumably, most likely to be just.

The Limits of Science

Three ethical issues that were debated in 1980, the year my colleagues and I finished our research on the effects of daycare, centered on the legal rights of homosexuals, a woman's right to an abortion, and the legitimacy of attempts to reduce racial segregation in neighborhoods and educational institutions. These issues remain controversial. The arguments for and against each are supposed to be responsive to facts. For example, it is assumed that defense of a pro-life position would be strengthened if scientists could determine when life began. And yet the question "When does life begin?" cannot have an answer with the certainty of "When will the next solar eclipse occur?" Advocates of liberal legislation on homosexuality applauded when research showed that homosexuals were not unfit soldiers, and many assumed that the resolution, voted by the members of the American Psychiatric Association, that homosexuality was not a mental disease had scientific content. Legal opinions on bussing to reduce segregation in schools and promote affirmative action in colleges are supposed to be influenced by evidence bearing on the academic achievement of black youth bussed to integrated elementary school settings or matriculating at our better colleges.

But the factual information is secondary to the ethical question. The debate on abortion centers on whether a woman is free to decide about her body. The moral dilemma pits the mother's right to autonomy of personal choice against the fetus's right to life. This question cannot be decided by an appeal to evidence. Because our society holds individual freedom sacred, the Supreme Court's last ruling on abortion sided with the woman. Future courts might defend the fetus. In either case, the facts are not very relevant. Legislation on homosexuality turns on whether adults are free to behave as they choose, as long as they harm no one, and court rulings, until now, have used this premise to arrive at decisions. The moral conflict raised by bussing to achieve racial integration in schools places the sacredness of each family's liberty against society's need to move toward integrated communities.

Little in nature can affirm or refute any one of the opposed positions in this trio of ethical dilemmas. Science confessed at the beginning of the twentieth century that nature has no values, and therefore empirical evidence has minimal implications for moral questions. Citizens must look elsewhere for this guidance. As the nineteenth century ended, many scientists, philosophers, and writers were elaborating Kant's distinction between knowledge and values and assenting to Kierkegaard's plea that we recognize the chasm between what is known and what is good. Ethics is to be found not in reason but in each person's faith.

But because the power of science remained intimidating, there was a need for a philosophical statement that justified the separation of fact and value. Allan Janik and Steven Toulmin have suggested that Ludwig Wittgenstein published his dense but famous work *Tractatus Logico-Philosophicus* in 1922 for that very reason.[22] Wittgenstein intended a defense of the transcendental nature of ethics and its independence from objective knowledge when he suggested that ethics and aesthetics were one and the same.

Unfortunately, Americans were not receptive to this abstruse declaration, for they wanted a respected, external support for their moral decisions. Because neither the church nor philosophy filled that void for a large proportion of the society, scientists stepped forward and promised to resolve ethical issues by gathering objective information on issues of community concern. It is not clear that psychology, sociology, anthropology, or biology can keep that promise.

Some scientists claim that investigations of less modern cultures will reveal what is basic about human nature and tell us how to adjust our ethics to be consonant with nature's plan. Other cultures cannot serve that function. Middle-class Americans allow their children to express some anger because they believe it is in accord with human nature. Jean Briggs challenged the universality of that principle in her pioneering study of the Utku Eskimo of Hudson Bay.[23] In this culture, every display of anger after the second birthday is followed by an adult ignoring the child. Despite this "silent treatment," few children display tantrums, and the colitis and migraine headaches presumed to result from the suppression of anger do not occur among these people. Hence, the answer to the question "Is it basic to human nature to express anger or to suppress it?" is "Neither." The consequences of suppressing anger depend on the social context. In the United States, where children leave home to play with friends and the social norm is to defend self if attacked, it is adaptive to permit children some display of anger in the service of self-defense. But anger is not adaptive for children restricted to an igloo for nine months of every year. Anyone who lived with smoldering anger in a small space for so long would probably develop somatic symptoms. Neither can elegant research on chimpanzees, which has illuminated the psychology of these animals, make the problem of deciding right from wrong easier to resolve. The least aggressive chimps are the most subordinate in their group. The exact opposite occurs in humans. The most violent adolescents in America are among the poorest and least powerful in their society because the causes of killing in apes and humans are different. Thus ethical decisions regarding the prevention and punishment of crime should not be based primarily on the scientific facts investigators gather on animals.

The plea for relevant research by Congress and citizens is based on the assumption that objective facts should guide decisions about daycare, abortion, affirmative action, the death penalty for criminals, and education. Scientific research tells us that high levels of talent in geometry are more common among boys than girls, adolescent boys are more violent than adolescent girls, male chimpanzees are sexually promiscuous, and bipolar illness has a genetic component. But a majority of Americans would defeat referenda calling for the separation of boys and girls in geometry classes, more severe punishment of aggressive behavior in boys, the acceptance of adultery as ethically neutral, and the sterilization of adults who have bipolar illness. Scientific evidence can reveal why some select one action over another, why some events are classified as "good," and why humans can detect an invalid argument. But science cannot supply the constructive basis for any moral standard. Moral propositions imply that one action is better than another, but it is rarely the case that a particular action is good for all potential beneficiaries. A person at risk, that person's family, and the society in which he or she lives are three beneficiaries, and I can think of few actions that would be of equal benefit to all three. Daniel Callahan took the bold step of questioning the popular premise that generous public support of medical research that might prolong an individual life is an inherent good that invites no challenge.[24] Callahan wonders whether our society might benefit more if some of this money were used to reduce poverty and improve our educational institutions. The results of research cannot be the sole guide for judging what is psychologically beneficial for children, their families, or their communities. Each must make a value decision informed by prior assumptions that originate in sentiment.

Although scientific facts help us understand the world and are interesting topics for conversation, citizens who choose to ignore them when deciding what is morally preferable are neither uninformed nor irrational. Suppose, for the sake of argument, that future scientists discover that the presence of higher levels of male sex hormone in male compared with female fetuses is one reason, among many, why more men than women are attracted to careers in mathematics and physics. That hypothetical fact does not imply that women cannot do creative work in these fields. Hence, one could argue, on ethical grounds, that our society is better served by allowing women equal access to high positions in these disciplines. This ethical decision would dilute feelings of discouragement in freshmen women selecting a concentration. Critics will reply that this practice might deprive the society of significant discoveries because the most talented students were not allowed to realize their abilities. Yes, that is possible. I chose this example to point out that both positions have an ethical component, and it is not obvious that we should always choose the alternative that is in accord with scientific evidence.

A society whose laws were always in strict accord with scientific facts would be far more disheartening than any contemporary community. About 50 percent of Florida teenagers have their first sexual experience in the four warm months from May to August.[25] This sturdy fact has no ethical implication whatsoever, and no state legislature is considering a law that restricts lovemaking to either the summer or winter months. Each community holds ethical positions regarding equality, socialization, and education of the young.

Citizens are neither irrational nor unintelligent when their response to scientists presenting new facts with relevance to social issues is: "Thank you for working so hard to provide us with this interesting knowledge. We shall brood on it but at the moment do not wish to act on its implications for our social practices."

Yet if not from science, where can the foundations for a community's ethics originate? Where can a person or a community find a basis for its moral imperatives? The answer lies with the sentiment of the majority in the community, acknowledging that sentiments change with time. Many moral issues are placed on local ballots each election, indicating the community's receptivity to using local sentiment as a guide to resolving ethical dilemmas. When the Supreme Court recognized how difficult it was to define pornography objectively, the justices declared that local attitudes should determine which books and movies violated community sensibilities. The court legitimized each individual's private emotional reaction as a participant in the maintenance of values. The executives at the Public Broadcasting System also allow each member station to decide which programs are acceptable for viewing in their area. As long as members of our society hold different values, each of us will have to acknowledge the legitimacy of the other without losing faith in our own ethics. This diversity in ethical positions resembles the differences between tigers and sharks. Each is potent in its own territory but impotent in the territory of the other.

It is difficult to rely on sentiment for all moral issues in our society because of the extraordinary range of opinion and a resistance to having legally binding propositions rest on emotional rather than rational grounds. This is one reason why science has been placed in the position of moral arbiter. Although science can help by providing evidence that disconfirms the factual foundation of an ethical premise, it cannot supply the basis for any moral proposition. Facts prune the tree of morality, but they cannot be its seedbed.

It is a tribute to our respect for rationality that Darwin's thesis on the evolution of animal forms led many to question their faith in creationism. But had Europeans not been prepared for Darwin's argument, his evidence and thesis would have been ignored. Thus, data, presuppositions, and logic mix in a mysterious way to influence the values of persons and communities. "Sentiment is not enough, logic is not enough, and experience is not enough, if we wish to know and to know what to do. Each should be given its due by the intelligent man as he tests his stock of beliefs and actions."[26]

Which Criteria Should Guide a Life?

Economists and evolutionary biologists have an advantage over social scientists because they have achieved a temporary consensus regarding the criterion to use when evaluating one phenomenon as better or more useful than another. Economists rely on the easily measured variable of cost. Evolutionary biologists rely on the concept of inclusive fitness to evaluate the differential significance of an animal's features.

Inclusive fitness is measured by the number and vitality of an individual's offspring, and the reproductive success of all genetic relatives, compared with the fecundity of other animals living in the same ecology. This idea presumably explains the changing distribution of animal species, from life's origin 3.5 billion years ago to the present. The survival of a species does not imply a correlation with any other desirable psychological property. The fact that large numbers of animals survive over thousands of generations carries no ethical implications. Gazelles prefer fewer tigers; tigers prefer fewer humans; humans prefer fewer flies. Biologists simply wish to understand why the numbers are the way they are.

Unfortunately, some authors write about fitness with a cognitive bias that focuses on the features of particular genetic profiles rather than a perspective that acknowledges that fitness is a relational concept that must take into account the animal's setting. Genetic profiles that are fit in one ecology are less fit in another. A male sea lion, for example, is more fit if he lives with very few males and lots of females but less fit if there are many males and few females. The historical context affects the relative fitness of human groups. The children born to marriages of black and white partners in the pre–Civil Rights South were at high risk for ostracism or, in some cases, lynching. The same class of children born today, in a more tolerant environment, has far greater fitness.

Unlike economists and biologists, social scientists cannot agree on a criterion that awards priority to any one of the large number of human qualities that wax and wane over a lifetime, century, or millennium. Casual reflection on this question reveals that no candidate has the ethical neutrality of cost in dollars or number of healthy offspring. Every property nominated—social status, wealth, years of education, number of friends, number of orgasms, co-operation, self-interest, children nurtured, charitable works, promises kept, books written, discoveries made, places visited, or days free of anger—hides a value bias and frustrates a desire for a rational answer to what is best. Each candidate is a culturally limited, ethical premise.

One possible candidate that can be defended as a criterion for choice is a consciousness minimally perturbed by the dysphoric feeling that accompanies the recognition that self has violated a personal standard or failed to attain a goal regarded as praiseworthy. Each person strives for a feeling that is attained, always momentarily, by behaving, thinking, or feeling in ways that are in accord with one's understanding of what Plato described as "doing the good." Cultures differ in how this state is achieved and in the depth of their faith in the validity of the target chosen. Buddhists value detachment from external goals and obligatory relationships because the passions surrounding desire perturb serenity. Kant located this state in acceptance of the categorical imperative. For G. E. Moore, the state was attained through intimate relations with others and encounters with beautiful things. When historical events create doubt, or confusion, over an absolute distinction between good and evil, youth who find it difficult to accept a relativistic view of morality try to repair the loss of certainty. It is not a coincidence that many more American seventeen-year-olds in 2004 than in 1954 chose to matriculate at colleges with a clear religious philosophy. When life in American communities had more order, greater predictability in the trustworthiness of others, and far less violence, some wise commentators (Erich Fromm is an example) suggested that those who sought a religious commitment were trying to escape the burden imposed by freedom of choice.[27] Less than a century later, under conditions of enhanced disorder, distrust, and aggression, few self-appointed purveyors of wisdom are satirizing those searching for an ethic that infuses each day with a meaning that transcends eating, sleeping, and protection from harm. Each of the major world religions was born at a time when history had created a mood of increased uncertainty in large segments of the society. A cartoon in a February 2005 issue of the New Yorker depicts a mother standing at the entrance to a living room where a large party is in progress and saying to her three-year-old at the foot of the stairs, "Mommy and Daddy and their friends are pretending they don't have horrible lives now." No American in 1950 would have smiled because he or she would not have understood the referent for the mother's message. No refugee in western Sudan would have smiled because he or she understood it too well.

The genomes of the current generation of humans are essentially similar to those our original ancestors had 150,000 years ago. But those first humans, who emerged in a warm climate with a social organization consisting of foraging bands of thirty to fifty individuals, many of them genetically related, were cooperative with, and loyal to, their group. Successful adaptation demanded the suppression of excessive competition and self-aggrandizement. Although the first humans were capable of placing self's interests above those of others, unchecked displays of that trait would have provoked rejection, exile, or in some cases murder.

The psychological differences between the first humans and ourselves are sufficiently dramatic to motivate a curiosity over whether the current romance with unconstrained self-interest is a biologically prepared propensity with a natural priority or a posture demanded by the conditions history created and rationalized as a standard in perfect accord with nature's plan. Most young monkeys in natural settings play with other monkeys. But infant monkeys taken from their mother and placed with an inanimate wire object that is a source of food become juveniles who sit crouched in a corner of a cage far from their peers. The capacity to crouch alone in a corner is inherent in the genes of the monkey, but actualization of that odd behavior requires very unnatural conditions. Thus, we might ask, "Does the current obsession with self's pleasure, status, wealth, and power in many industrialized societies have to overcome a biologically stronger urge to be a loyal, caring, and cooperative member of a stable group that can be trusted to reciprocate in kind, or are both traits, lion as well as lamb, equally friendly to our genome and the historical setting determines which one will be dominant?" I cannot be sure but have the intuition that the former is closer to the truth.

SIX

Acknowledging Temperament

Community pressure for government-funded daycare centers grew in the 1970s as more working mothers found it hard to find suitable surrogate care for their children. Some members of Congress, appreciating the reasonableness of this need, responded to President Nixon's request to prepare legislation that would establish child-care centers under government supervision. The bill was never passed, and today's Congress would not consider such a law because of the greater suspicion of government control of an institution that is so closely tied to family values.

Although most parents had not noticed serious problems in their three- and four-year-olds who attended nursery schools, they, and most psychologists, were far less sanguine about the innocence of surrogate care for infants. One reason for the worry was the recent dissemination of John Bowlby's ideas on attachment, although years earlier psychologists had written that adult talents and personality had their origins in infancy. It is easy to nod in assent to the declaration that the infant's first task is to establish an emotional attachment to a caretaker. Mothers who read this statement would have an additional, presumably more rational, reason for caring for their child.

The anxiety that hovers over the proper relationship between mother and infant has always been part of the American ethos. Witness this sermon by a nineteenth-century New England Congregational minister:

It will readily occur to you that irreparable damage may be and must often be done by the self indulgence of those parents who place their children mostly in the charge of nurses and attendants for just those years of their life in which the greatest and most absolute effects are to be wrought in their character. . . . They give over to these faithless and often cruelly false hirelings of the nursery, to be always with them, under their power, associated with their persons, handled by their roughness, and imprinted day and night by the coarse, bad sentiments of their voices and faces, these helpless, hapless, beings whom they call their children, and think they are really making much of, in the instituting of a nursery for them in their keeping. . . . Now is the time when her little one most needs to see her face and hear her voice and feel her gentle hand. Now is the time when her child's eternity pleads most entreatingly for the benefit of her motherly charge and presence. What mother would not be dismayed by the thought of having her family grow up into the sentiments of her nurse and come forward into life as being in the succession to her character! And yet how often is this most exactly what she has provided for.[1]

The significance of an infant's attachment to the mother, wedded to the older intuition that biological mothers necessarily provide better care than a hired caretaker, supported the conviction that infants must have the caresses only a biological parent provides. Rene Spitz enjoyed brief fame among child psychologists and psychiatrists in the 1950s when, after observing apathetic infants in a foundling home, he declared that their pathetic state was caused by inadequate mothering rather than an absence of variety or a physical illness. Citing this observation, Spitz warned mothers to stay close to their infants and not abandon them to surrogate caretakers. Although muted in intensity, the safety of daycare for today's infants remains a source of uncertainty. The National Institute of Child Health and Human Development has spent millions of dollars in the past two decades assessing the consequences of out-of-home care for infants placed in varied forms of surrogate rearing. The clearest result is that the social class of the family has a far greater influence on cognitive and emotional development than the person caring for the infant or the place where the care is given.

The Unexpected Face of Temperament

Richard Kearsley, an older graduate student in our department who had left his pediatric practice to obtain a doctorate in developmental psychology in the 1970s, was friendly with physicians in the Massachusetts Department of Health, who thought it useful to conduct a study of the effects of daycare on infants. Kearsley suggested that he, Philip Zelazo, a postdoctoral fellow in my laboratory, and I request funds from the National Institutes of Health for a project evaluating infant daycare.

My prior research had little or no practical implications, and my conscience was occasionally pricked by the seeming selfishness of spending public money on issues that were of interest to my colleagues but did not immediately illuminate a question that the public cared about. The feeling generated by the belief that one is working for the public good is discriminably different from the emotion that accompanies the discovery of an unexpected regularity in nature. Pride of discovery is distinct from the "high" accompanying recognition that one has helped another. It is not unimportant that the zeitgeist of the 1960s, punctuated with protests against the Vietnam War and for civil rights, had sensitized the consciences of social scientists who wished to participate in the benevolent reforms being advocated.

Kearsley, Zelazo, and I could have compared infants attending existing daycare centers in Boston with those living only at home, but this design was flawed because the centers would have been of different quality. We decided that a better strategy was to run our own daycare center, staffed with people we trained, and observe the children over time. Because working-class mothers were under an economic burden and their children performed less well in school than those born into middle-class homes, we decided that as long as we were doing the research, we would add a second gold star to our mast and establish a center in a working-class neighborhood. The Roxbury section of Boston had a large number of African-American families. If we established the center close to this neighborhood, we could hire African-American women, many of whom needed employment. We would not only find an answer to our question but, at no extra cost, would be helping economically burdened African-American women.

The research proposal was funded, and we rented a large space in the south end of Boston, hired staff, prepared a curriculum, and designed the assessment procedures. The plan called for enrolling infants between three and a half and five months and following them until they were about two and a half years old. We matched each infant who attended our daycare center with one raised at home with respect to birth order and mother's age. All infants were born at term, without serious physical compromise, and were African-American.

Several months after the project began we confronted a serious political problem that forced us to change the sample. Though it seemed calamitous at the time, this obstacle had an unexpected happy ending, for it led to a discovery that motivated the fruitful research on temperament. Racial tension in Boston was high in the 1970s, and a small political group, the Boston Black United Front, did not want a white Harvard professor and his two white colleagues imposing themselves on the Roxbury community. They asked to meet with us to explain our goals and procedures and, after we did, told us that any result we might find would fuel racist ideas. If the African-American infants in our daycare center were not advanced over the infants raised at home, prejudiced Americans would conclude that not even Harvard professors could help black infants. And if the infants in our daycare center were advanced over those raised at home, racists would declare that African-American mothers were inadequate and needed the help of white professors. They insisted that we terminate the project.

We had three options. We could stop the project and return the funds to NIH, we could establish the center somewhere else, or we could stay where we were and enroll infants who were not African-American. The savior in this tight situation was a minister at a church in Boston's Chinatown. This benevolent cleric suggested that if we enrolled some Chinese-American infants in the project, he would protect us from political pressures—a promise he kept. Our final sample consisted of Chinese-American and Caucasian infants who attended our daycare center matched with Chinese-American and Caucasian infants who were being raised at home. We admitted some African-American infants to our daycare center, in a spirit of tolerance, but promised the Boston Black United Front that we would not assess them. We kept our promise.

One incident should provoke a smile. When the weather was warm, a staff member often put two or three infants in a carriage and strolled to Boston Common, about twenty minutes away. One afternoon the three infants in a stroller consisted of a Caucasian, a Chinese, and an African American. As the staff member passed Shreve, Crump and Lowe, an expensive jewelry store, an older woman was leaving the shop and saw the staff member and her three charges. "How wonderful," she declared, "You have three infants," and she bent down to see them more clearly. According to the staff member, her face paled as she gasped, "But, my dear, they are different colors!"

The rationale behind the assessments resembled the one used in prior work. We avoided a priori concepts like "attachment" or "emotional regulation" and chose derivatives of our earlier research on children in the first and second years. Infants differ in attentiveness and affective reactions to discrepant events. We filmed each infant's behavior to a variety of discrepant episodes, observed them playing with toys and other children, evaluated their language development, and administered a standard scale of intelligence. Each child was assessed eight times from three and a half to twenty-nine months of age. We summarized the seminal results of this effort in 1978 in our book *Infancy: Its Place in Development.*[2]

The first two chapters were written during the preceding few years as part of my attempt to arrive at a synthetic statement about development. I was deeply frustrated by my inability to pierce the impenetrable wall that separated limp ideas from a deeper understanding and, in the spring of 1975, experienced a bout of depression that lasted about four months. Had I gone to a psychiatrist, I would have been diagnosed as clinically depressed and put on a regimen of drugs and therapy. I began to keep a diary in 1970, and the entries for this period reveal my terrible pain. The depression lifted spontaneously in the fall, but having peered into the abyss, I was changed permanently. Most adults who have had a serious depression vow to avoid any repetition of a similar episode. I took a private oath to make each day as beautiful as possible. Family, friends, forests, reading, tennis, and exploring rich corpora of data have been effective defenses against the recurrence of that deep, dark melancholia.

The evidence revealed no important differences between the infants in daycare and those raised at home on our measures of cognitive and emotional development. We also affirmed, this time with nonsocial stimuli, that attention to unfamiliar events increases after eight months of age. In one episode, each infant saw a sequence in which the examiner's hand moved an orange rod in a circular arc until it contacted a row of three lights that lit on contact. After ten repetitions of this sequence, the infants saw a discrepancy. The examiner touched the rod, but it did not move and the lights lit four seconds later. We regarded this procedure as a way to assess the infant's reaction to discrepancy. Some contemporary developmental psychologists might have used the same procedure to decide whether infants understand the concept "action at a distance."

The infants looked longer at the discrepant event than at the last few repetitions of the original sequence. But the more important point is that the developmental change in attention showed a U-shaped function for both the daycare and home-reared children, with a trough in attention at about seven and a half months. Duration of attention was long at three and five months, minimal at seven months, rose thereafter, and was longer at twenty-nine than at five months. This fact supported our earlier conclusion that a new cognitive competence emerges during the last half of the second year. The daycare and home-reared children showed almost identical patterns of attention over time, strengthening our faith in the power of maturation.

The third finding, which required the Chinese-American infants, was that the two ethnic groups, whether raised at home or attending our center, differed in emotionality and in heart rate. The Chinese-American infants, compared with the Caucasians, smiled and babbled less often, cried more when their mother left them during a brief separation, and had less variable heart rates to the discrepant stimuli. In addition, their mothers described them as more timid and vigilant compared with the Caucasian children. Ethnicity turned out to be a more important determinant of our behavioral and biological measures than surrogate care. These results, which made a deep impression on me, were the major reason why I pursued the study of temperament the following year.

Inhibited and Uninhibited Temperaments

The minimally variable heart rates of the subdued Chinese-American infants, which reminded me of the stable heart rates of the adults in the Fels

study who had been avoidant children, refocused my thoughts on temperament. Howard Moss and I had suggested in *Birth to Maturity* that a "constitutional" factor—we meant temperament—probably contributed to the
avoidant behavior some children displayed during the first three years. I did
not pursue this idea in 1962, however, because I did not know how to begin.

Alexander Thomas and Stella Chess reintroduced the concept of temperament in 1957 after a half-century of exile.[3] Almost every textbook described
their nine temperamental dimensions based on interviews with parents—
words again—rather than on watching children. I was critical of concepts
that bubbled up from intuition rather than plucked from the red-hot kiln of
direct observation. Psychology possessed too many ideas dreamed up in quiet
rooms with the shades down because they seemed pleasing to the creator or
to the community being courted.

I cannot think of one theoretically important psychological concept originating in intuition, without the support of reliable observations, that survived
more than twenty-five years. John Watson, the American behaviorist who
popularized the significance of conditioning in the 1930s, was wildly mistaken when he announced that he could produce any behavior if he were
able to control a child's life for the first five years. Sandor Ferenczi, a disciple
of Freud who had never seen a patient with Tourette's syndrome, made an
equally serious error when he wrote that the frequent facial tics of people with
Tourette's were the result of a repressed urge to masturbate. Freud guessed incorrectly when he wrote that paranoid adults had not passed through the oral
stage of development successfully. John Bowlby went too far when he predicted that anxious adults had been raised by inaccessible, insensitive caretakers during their first year of life.

Psychologists like abstract words—"emotion," "memory," and "learning"
—that bury the natural phenomena under a blanket of semantic networks.
Too many investigators begin their research with concepts like "intelligence"
or "reactivity" and look for evidence to prove their existence. It is not obvious
that intelligence and reactivity are unitary phenomena in nature; the ability
to remember a series of eight numbers and crying to a stranger are natural
events.

Biologists, by contrast, more often begin their work with a trusted phenomenon. Rosalind Franklin was trying to determine the crystal structure

of DNA molecules because scientists suspected that it was the constituent of genes. Franklin probably had a favorite answer tucked away in the back of her mind, but she knew that this gift could be opened only if observations permitted. If Johannes Kepler had not had access to a rich set of observations gathered by Tycho Brahe and his associates, his insight that the Earth had an elliptical, rather than a circular, orbit around the Sun would have been delayed.

I had not probed temperamental biases earlier because I first needed to believe in reliable evidence that pointed to some phenomena to measure. The behaviors and heart rates of the Chinese-American infants provided two such variables. It was also important that I had seen two different types of children in prior decades—the avoidant compared with the bold toddler when each encountered unfamiliar people, places, or objects. I trusted these observations, and both were described in the Thomas and Chess list of temperaments, although their dimension, called "slow to warm up," implied that the differences in avoidance were displayed primarily with people. My observations suggested that some children were subdued and timid to many unfamiliar events, not just to people they did not know.

Cynthia Garcia-Coll was searching for a thesis topic in 1979, and I suggested that she study these two temperamental types by exposing twenty-one-month-old children to unfamiliar but not dangerous events, such as rooms, people, robots, and temporary separation from the mother, and determine which children were consistently avoidant and which consistently bold. The selection of twenty-one months seemed reasonable because the children in the daycare project first displayed obvious timidity to unfamiliarity when they were between eighteen and twenty-one months old.

I needed funds to support this work and called Thomas James, president of the Spencer Foundation in Chicago, told him of my need, and he agreed to send me the money. A similar act of generosity after a fifteen-minute telephone call is far less likely today. I then left for a sabbatical year at the Center for Advanced Study in the Behavioral Sciences on the campus of Stanford University to write a chapter for the next edition of the *Handbook of Child Psychology* and complete the manuscript of *The Second Year*. But I kept in close contact with Cynthia and felt confident that the work would proceed well, despite my absence, because several students and, especially, my future son-in-law, Steven Reznick, were at the laboratory.

On my return in the summer of 1980, I learned that Cynthia had discovered that a small group of children were consistently avoidant (inhibited) and an equally small group were consistently bold (uninhibited) across the unfamiliar events. Further, more children in the extremely inhibited group had a higher and less variable heart rate. This was the third time we had found a relation between a tendency to show restraint to unfamiliarity and a minimally variable heart rate. Cynthia and I graphed the results and put them on the wall of my office with a question that read, "Do you believe this?" I later learned that breeds of dog that are timid have higher heart rates than do less timid breeds.[4]

The fates added an additional generosity by sending Nancy Snidman to my laboratory. Nancy had learned the technique of spectral analysis of heart rate—a more powerful way to evaluate sympathetic tone in the cardiovascular system—and wanted to apply this technique to young children for her thesis. She was officially a graduate student at the University of California in Los Angeles but had moved to Boston for personal reasons. I welcomed her to the laboratory, and she has become a close collaborator and friend for more than twenty-five years.

Nancy observed thirty-one-month-old children in two unfamiliar situations. She selected the older age because a spectral analysis required children to remain still and twenty-one-month-olds are restless. Nancy used a different set of unfamiliar events because a robot or an unfamiliar room is insufficiently novel to a two-and-a-half-year-old whereas an unfamiliar child is a better incentive. Nancy had pairs of unfamiliar children of the same age and sex play together. At the end of the play session, a woman with a plastic cover over her head and torso entered the room and invited each child to play. About 15 percent of the children were timid and avoidant with the unfamiliar peer and unfamiliar woman; another 15 percent were bold and sociable. The data Cynthia and Nancy gathered marked the beginning of the project on inhibited and uninhibited children.

It is not a coincidence that within every animal species studied there are always some animals who avoid unfamiliarity and some who will approach.

T. C. Schneirla, who worked at the American Museum of Natural History in New York City and pursued this idea for a large part of his career, suggested that the intensity of a stimulus determined whether approach or avoidance was the behavior of choice.[5] I believed that it was the unfamiliarity of the stimulus, not its physical intensity. The intensity of a light or sound, relative to the background, can be measured absolutely, but discrepancy cannot, because the unfamiliarity of an event is always relative to the past experiences of the agent.

The next question was to determine whether these two behavioral categories were preserved and, if so, to what degree and to look for biological properties that would support the belief that these differences were temperamental in origin. An important clue to the selection of biological measures came from the work of Robert Adamec of Memorial University in St. Johns, Newfoundland. Adamec, who was studying house cats, had discovered that timidity to novelty emerged in kittens at the end of the first month, when, following brain maturation, the amygdala begins to exert more control over behavior to unfamiliar events. More important, timid cats showed a more reactive amygdala than bold animals.[6] Nancy Snidman and I visited Adamec and talked with him about our mutual interests. We left with greater confidence in the hypothesis that the excitability of the amygdala, due, we believed, to the inheritance of different neurochemistries, was a distinguishing property of inhibited and uninhibited children.[7] We began to search for biological measures, other than direct recording from the child's amygdala, that might be indirect indexes of amygdalar excitability. We chose heart rate, heart-rate variability, muscle tension, and pupillary dilation because the amygdala affects these qualities.

The inhibited children had higher and less variable heart rates, larger pupils, and greater muscle tension. But the correlations among these biological measures were low—a finding repeated in many laboratories. Some inhibited children had high heart rates but low muscle tension; others showed the opposite profile. Every measurement permits only a partial view of the events scientists are eager to understand. A large curtain with many tiny holes placed in front of a vista of great beauty provides an analogy. The view from each hole, like the data supplied by a single measure, offers a restricted glimpse of the scene. Although scientists get closer to the natural event over time, they will never have an unrestricted view. An Indian philosopher likened the pursuit of truth to a person in a large, many-walled labyrinth walking toward the center, where truth resides. The destruction of a wall, represented by a new fact, permits our hero to move forward, but he never reaches the center. Kant and Bohr were right, although for different reasons, when they claimed that we have to be satisfied with the small gifts nature sends. Despite these obstacles, some scientists continue to rely on just one biological measure—skin conductance, heart rate, cortisol, or a potentiated eyeblink reflex—to measure levels of anxiety, arousal, or fear. This practice fails because no single biological or behavioral variable is a sensitive index of a psychological state for all persons. There are no silver bullets.

I had been invited by the editor of *Science* to submit a paper on our research because social scientists had been complaining that the magazine published too few technical reports in psychology, sociology, and anthropology. A friend who knew the editor had suggested that our work on temperament might be of interest to the scientific community. Our first major summary of these two temperaments, titled "Biological Bases of Childhood Shyness," appeared in *Science* in 1988. We suggested that biological measures should be added to behavioral variables in order to distinguish groups with similar psychological profiles. The final paragraph applauded Jung's prescience when he wrote to Freud that temperamental factors could contribute to the development of social anxiety, then called hysteria. Freud rejected Jung's suggestion.

About one of every four children originally classified as inhibited (at twenty-one or thirty-one months) remained shy and subdued at age seven and a half; one of every two children classified as uninhibited was sociable during the school-age years. Only three children changed their behavioral status from inhibited to uninhibited or vice-versa. This fact, affirmed in our subsequent investigations, and by other psychologists, means that the primary effect of a temperamental bias is to constrain the development of other profiles. Although it was common for some inhibited two-year-olds to lose their shyness and for some uninhibited two-year-olds to become subdued in unfamiliar situations, very few inhibited children became extremely exuberant and very few uninhibited children became intensely shy and consistently avoidant.

An essay written by a thirteen-year-old boy who had been a fearful two-year-old described how he conquered his timid personality through will, even though he confessed that he lacked the relaxed spontaneity of the typical uninhibited boy. An early temperamental bias prevents the development of a contrasting profile. The probability that an inhibited child will not become an ebullient, sociable, fearless child with low cortical excitability is very high. Yet the probability that this child will become extremely shy and show high cortical excitability is much lower. And the prediction that an uninhibited child will not become an extremely shy adolescent with high biological arousal is more certain than the prediction that this child be exuberant with low biological arousal. The child's temperament is more effective in constraining the development of the opposite profile than in determining a particular profile. This principle that a temperamental bias eliminates more possibilities than it determines also applies to the effects of environments. If all one knows about a group of children is that they were born to economically secure, well-educated, loving parents, one can be confident that they are unlikely to become criminals, psychotics, drug addicts, or homeless beggars, but one cannot predict what they will become. Similarly, among children born in poverty to single parents who did not graduate from high school, it is possible to predict the adult occupations they are unlikely to choose—curator of a museum, Wall Street stockbroker, or cellist—but not those they will select. Imagine a stone rolling down a steep mountain over a five-minute interval. An observer of this scene can eliminate a great many final locations after each few seconds of descent, but not until the final second will the onlooker be able to predict exactly where the stone will come to rest.

Categories or Continua

Some colleagues were unhappy with our decision to concentrate only on the children who were extremely inhibited or uninhibited and to ignore the children in the middle. They believed that nature intended a continuum from extreme timidity at one end to extreme spontaneity at the other. This time I did defend an a priori idea because our interest was in the biological bases for the two profiles. I interpreted the biological literature as implying that distinctly different phenotypes often originate in qualitatively distinct genomes.

Very tall, very short, and average-height children are the products of different sets of genes. Although Thomas and Chess described easy, difficult, and slow-to-warm-up children as if they belonged to categories, they treated the variation within each of the nine temperamental dimensions as continuous. For example, the dimension called "approach-withdrawal" implied a continuum from sociability to shyness. By failing to say otherwise, Thomas and Chess rejected the possibility that infants who almost always approached unfamiliar people might be qualitatively, not just quantitatively, different from those who usually avoid strangers. The different connotations of a continuous trait and a qualitative type are captured by the comparison between "Mary has uncommon beliefs" and "Mary is paranoid." Although some psychologists think of masculinity as a single continuous property of males, it turns out that two distinct biological mechanisms are in operation during fetal development, at least in mice. One mechanism enhances male sexual behaviors while a second eliminates female sexual responses and defeminizes the male. Thus there are distinct types of males. One has a combination of enhanced male sexuality and muted female sexuality whereas another has the enhanced features of both sexes. From a biological point of view, there is no continuum of maleness.

The temperature and volume of a saucepan of water are continuously measured values, but ice, liquid, and steam are qualitatively different phenomena that emerge from particular values of these properties. Because the most popular statistical procedures assume continuous magnitudes, many psychologists believe that most psychological phenomena will be understood, eventually, as the result of the addition of continuous variables. Yet the physicist Pierre Duhem noted that nature consisted of qualitative phenomena that cannot be formed by adding quantities, and asked facetiously, "How many snowballs are needed to heat an oven?"[8]

The modern concept of species, fundamental in evolutionary theory, is a qualitative category defined by distinct clusters of correlated features in reproductively isolated groups. The many dimensions that characterize a particular species—weight, length, metabolic rate, and life span are not of equal importance. Two species that share ten of eleven features are not always more similar in phylogenetic history than those that share only seven of eleven qualities. Mice and dogs have two eyes, two ears, and four limbs, rely on internal fertilization, and nurse their young, but only dogs bond to humans. That single feature is a vital component of the cluster that characterizes dogs, and it cannot be removed without changing the category in a serious way.

This issue is germane to current practice among psychiatrists who assign category names to patients based on their most salient psychological symptom, even though most have a cluster of characteristics. Common psychiatric categories are depression, bipolar disorder, schizophrenia, general anxiety disorder, panic disorder, social phobia, specific phobias of animals, blood, or situations, psychopathy, and obsessive-compulsive disorder (OCD). For example, many patients who report a depressed mood have somatic problems, among them headaches, allergies, abnormal immune function, dizziness, and diarrhea.[9] One of every two patients with bipolar disorder reports a medical condition; one of every two men with social phobia suffers from premature ejaculation.[10] Thus there is some degree of arbitrariness in diagnosing a patient as depressed rather than as suffering from chronic headache. In some cases the physical problem could cause a depression; in others it could follow a depression.

An analogy with fatigue is appropriate, for "feeling tired" is a feature of many different diseases. The restrictive focus on the emotions of depression or anxiety can blind the clinician to the complete cluster of complaints and prevent a more accurate diagnosis. Psychiatrists deal with this fact by using the term "comorbid." They say that Mary's compulsive symptoms are comorbid with her depression. It is probably more fruitful to recognize the combination of compulsions and depression as one diagnostic category and compulsions without depression as a different psychiatric category. Consider an analogy to the symptoms of influenza. Physicians do not tell patients that their fever is comorbid with their sore throat because a sore throat and fever are both characteristic of the flu, whereas a fever without a sore throat is likely to be the sign of a different illness. It seems wise, therefore, to invent new diagnostic categories that are faithful to the complete cluster of symptoms and to stop using the term "comorbid," which simply means that a symptom is correlated with the one of primary interest. It is rare for a single feature to define a species. Different animals groups live in the ocean. Whales have internal fertilization, but sea bass do not. Sharks attack humans, but sea scallops do not. Thus "living in the ocean" is not an informative guide to the proper species category.

However, the advantage of assuming continuous dimensions or discrete categories depends, in the end, on the scientist's purpose. Those wishing to explain a particular event—for example, why an adolescent with a good academic record failed a test—are likely to choose a continuous dimension, such as fatigue. Yet psychologists wishing to explain a large number of different behaviors preserved over a long period are more likely to favor a category. We should distinguish between a single behavior limited to, and created by, a temporary condition (impatience while sitting in a car on a crowded highway) and a cluster of behaviors that is part of a stable personality. The sentence "Mary was happy at her birthday party" implies a temporary state that lies on a continuum with her normal feelings. The sentence "Mary is a happy person" implies a more permanent cluster of features and a category that distinguishes Mary from those who are usually sad.

I was convinced that the temperamental types we were studying differed qualitatively in their susceptibility to emotional states because they inherited qualitatively different neurobiological profiles. Hence, I was attracted to categories. Studies of twins supports this belief, for different genetic factors are associated with panic attacks, on one hand, and phobias, on the other.[11] Had I assumed that inhibited and uninhibited children differed quantitatively on a biological variable, for example, the concentration of a neurotransmitter or the density of its receptors, I might have treated the two types as falling on a continuum. A preference for continua or categories rests, in the end, on the explanation the investigator favors.

Infant Reactivity

The modest preservation of inhibited and uninhibited behavioral profiles and their relation to some biological measures motivated a search for earlier signs of these two temperaments. Audiences had reminded me that experiences at home during the first two years could have created an inhibited or uninhibited profile. A second reason for studying infants was that the early form of these temperamental biases might provide a clearer guide to the brain circuits that were the foundations of the toddler profiles. Finally, research by Lewis Lipsitt and his colleagues at Brown University suggested that we might find signs of inhibited or uninhibited behavior early in life.[12] In this study two-day-old infants sucked on a nipple connected to an apparatus that measured the rate and amplitude of their sucking. Most infants suck in bursts; they suck five or six times, pause for a few seconds, suck again, pause, and so on. After the newborns had received water for sucking over a two-minute period, the liquid suddenly changed to water sweetened with sugar when the sucking reached a particular value. Two minutes later, an even sweeter sugar solution was delivered. Most infants showed briefer pauses between sucking bursts (resulting in a faster rate of sucking) following the change from water to sugar, reflecting a heightened level of arousal. Some infants showed a dramatic increase in sucking rate; others a relatively small rise. Because the sensation contained in the sugar water activates the central nucleus of the amygdala, which in turn affects the motor component of sucking, the variation in sucking rate could reflect differences in the excitability of this structure. When these children were observed in unfamiliar situations two years later, the children who, as newborns, displayed large increases in sucking rate to the sugar water were more inhibited than those who showed minimal arousal to the sweet taste.

Nancy Snidman and I began with one hundred healthy Caucasian infants born at term to middle-class families. Evidence gathered by neuroscientists had suggested that limb activity and crying to unfamiliar events might provide an index of amygdalar activity. Had I had been unaware of this evidence and reflected only on responses that might be early signs of inhibited behavior in two-year-olds, I might have frustrated infants or presented them with a conditioned stimulus for an aversive event. My thoughts would have been attracted to words like "fear" rather than concepts like "quality of arousal to novelty."

We presented four-month-olds with unfamiliar but ecologically natural events that included mobiles constructed from colorful toys, tapes of human speech without the visual support of a person, and very dilute solutions of alcohol applied with a cotton swab to the nostrils. I took the hundred video-tapes to a quiet room and began watching each with a relatively open frame of mind. I focused my attention on motor activity and crying but suspected that the quality and timing of both reactions contained information. I was not certain which qualities would be most useful and therefore did not invent a code and ask graduate students to go to their offices, study the tapes, and put numbers on the behaviors. I did not know what behaviors they should code.

The first eighteen infants showed reasonable variation: some pumped their legs and arms to the mobiles; some lay still. Some fretted to the onset of the human voice; others babbled. The variation in motor activity and crying could be described as a continuum of reactivity. Then I put the tape of the nineteenth infant—a girl—into the video recorder and within ten minutes saw a qualitatively distinct profile. This infant began to arch her back to the moving mobiles, and a few seconds later, her face assumed a pained expression, followed by crying. This infant was not just a little more aroused than others, she was displaying a qualitatively different form of arousal. On another day I saw an infant who lay completely still without a cry during the entire battery. The temperamental categories we later called high- and low-reactive were invented that week. Several years later a Chinese pediatrician, who had spent a year in my laboratory, tested a large number of Beijing four-month-olds and sent me the videotapes. The Chinese infants were very different from our Boston children, verifying the evidence from the daycare study. Most were motorically still, quiet, and rarely cried. Over 80 percent were low-reactive. It was hard to resist the conclusion that Chinese and Caucasian infants began life with different temperaments.

I have had several other epiphanies that resembled the moment the concepts of high- and low-reactive were imagined. The contrast between the apathetic, retarded San Marcos infants and the vital seven-year-olds in the village represented one instance. The evening I plotted the age that separation fear first occurred in infants from Boston (at home or attending our daycare center), Israeli kibbutzim, Mayan villages, and homes in Antigua, Guatemala, and Botswana was a second occasion. The infants in all these settings showed no cry of fear before six months, and the likelihood of crying following maternal departure was greatest between eight and fifteen months. A cry of fear to separation seemed to be a growth function monitored by brain maturation. The third exhilarating moment occurred the first time I saw a twenty-month-old cry after the examiner, who had modeled some actions, said that it was the child's turn to play. The child's cry led to the insight that a moral sense and self-awareness emerged in the second year.

The arches, pained facial expression, and intense crying of the nineteenth infant was a fourth occasion. I do not believe that I would have invented the concept of high-reactivity by sitting at my desk brooding on the most fruitful temperamental concepts or by asking mothers to describe their infants on questionnaires because mothers are poor informants of their own infants. Once again, a faith in constructs inferred from observations proved fruitful.

When the high- and low-reactive infants, who returned to the laboratory in the second year, differed in their tendency to cry and retreat from or approach unfamiliar events, I was more certain that high- and low-reactivity were early signs of the later inhibited and uninhibited profiles. With the help of Doreen Arcus, we gathered similar data on more than four hundred four-month-old infants. This part of the story, which I told in *Galen's Prophecy: Temperament in Human Nature* (1994), also suggested that many young children classified as "insecurely attached" to their parent because they could not be soothed by the mother when she returned following a brief absence were likely to be high-reactive infants with perfectly sensitive, loving mothers. Later research has supported this claim.[13]

We saw these children again at four and a half, seven and a half, eleven, and fifteen years of age. When they were eleven and fifteen years old we gathered a variety of biological measures that were indirect indexes of amygdalar excitability. The high-reactives generally had higher values than the low-reactives on every measure, but as we found earlier, there were low correlations among the measures—once again, no silver bullets. For example, most children and adults have greater neural activity in the left hemisphere, as measured by the electroencephalogram, especially the frontal lobe on the left side. The smaller proportion of people who have greater activity on the right side are often, but not always, more tense or anxious. As we expected, more high- than low-reactives had greater activity on the right side. However, some high-reactives who were very tense and anxious over friendships and test performances showed greater activity on the left rather than the right side, and some low-reactives who were sociable had greater activity on the right side. A few highly exuberant, confident, fearless low-reactive females showed extreme right-hemisphere activation. Thus, this measure, considered alone, cannot be used as a highly reliable index of degree of uncertainty or anxiety.

The same conclusion also applies to the other measures. As I noted earlier, few biological or behavioral measures have the same meaning for everyone. This suggestion is supported by the relation between greater activation of the left frontal area and each adolescent's self-description as "being happy most of the time." The modest relation between the report of a sanguine mood and greater left-hemisphere activation is restricted to a small number of individuals who have a low-reactive temperament. Most adults who say they are usually very happy do not show greater left-hemisphere activity than others, and most who show clear left-hemisphere activation do not report being happy most of the time. Twelve of the fourteen adolescents we interviewed (about 15 percent of the group) who said they were usually happy and, in addition, had left-hemisphere activation, had been low-reactive infants. This fact implies that the psychological meaning of both measures varies with the person's temperament. This result should not be surprising. The subjective judgment that one is or is not happy has many determinants. Some individuals rely on a cognitive analysis of their current life conditions, compared with the past, to make the judgment. Others rely more on their current feeling tone. I suspect that more low-reactives use their usual feeling tone, whereas more high-reactives rely on an assessment of whether they are meeting their personal standards for accomplishment. These are very different reasons for "feeling happy." *The Long Shadow of Temperament*, written with Nancy Snidman and published in 2004, summarizes the information gathered on these children when they were eleven years old.[14]

The influence of biology on temperament was affirmed in a study of twins at the University of Colorado's Institute of Behavioral Genetics. This project, which was both extensive and expensive, was made possible by the generosity of the John D. and Catherine T. MacArthur Foundation in Chicago. I noted earlier that the foundation had decided that research in the social sciences would benefit from more collaboration, and less competitiveness, among scientists and funded several consortia composed of scientists with a common interest working in different institutions. The groups met regularly to plan collaborative work. The group devoted to early development, with

Robert Emde of the University of Colorado as its director, included Robert Plomin, Elizabeth Bates, Marshall Haith, and Marian Radke-Yarrow. Plomin, who was then at Penn State, took the lead in organizing a collaborative venture that would explore the heritability of cognitive functions, empathy, and inhibited and uninhibited behavior in large numbers of same-sex identical or fraternal twin pairs. The children, who were seen at fourteen, twenty, and twenty-four months of age in a laboratory at the University of Colorado under the direction of Joanne Robinson, were exposed to unfamiliar people and objects. The results of this work, summarized by Robert Emde and John Hewitt in the edited volume *Infancy to Early Childhood: Genetic and Environmental Influences on Developmental Change* (2001), revealed that inhibited and uninhibited profiles were moderately heritable.[15] That is, identical twins were more similar than fraternal twins in their tendency to be inhibited or uninhibited.

But it is important to appreciate that the heritability of any characteristic is higher when most members of the community are exposed to the conditions that evoke the characteristic. Because most American children frequently encounter strangers and novel objects and places, biological factors are likely to influence early differences in timidity. But if only a few children see strangers or new places, as might occur in rural Tibet, differences in inhibited behavior are more likely to be the result of experience. Robert McCall had used the prevalence of tuberculosis to make this point. When the bacillus was common centuries ago and many were exposed to this infectious agent, those who became tubercular were likely to be genetically susceptible. But because most contemporary Americans are not exposed to the bacterium, those who get the disease are likely to live under unsanitary conditions. Strong sanctions against violent behavior in Puritan New England resulted in rare occurrences of extreme aggression by youth. The few who were violent probably possessed a special biology. These sanctions are far less strict today; hence, most cases of adolescent aggression are the result of childhood experiences and current life conditions. Once again, our interpretation of a behavior depends on the social context in which it occurs.

A small proportion of infants are born with a biology that renders them especially susceptible to a strong biological reaction to events discrepant from their experience. The four-month-old infants saw a speaker baffle with a schematic face pasted on its front and moments later heard human voices speaking short sentences. This event is discrepant because there was no person in front of the infant who could be the source of the speech. About 15 percent displayed a fearful face and moments later cried. More high- than low-reactives cried to this event, and half of this fearful group were inhibited at eleven years. One of these children, interviewed at age sixteen, reported strong feelings of tension and unsureness when she had to interact with people she did not know. A vulnerability to becoming uncertain to discrepancy is preserved in some children from early infancy to adolescence. About one-third of the high-reactives, but very few low-reactives, showed a large cortical reaction to discrepant pictures (a person with a tomato for a head) at both eleven and fifteen years of age. These adolescents had been unusually fearful and emotionally subdued over a dozen years earlier when they were twenty-one months old. If a genie were to appear and grant me an answer to only one question, I would ask this generous spirit, "What is the inherited neurochemistry that contributes to this quality?" The selection of that question is a measure of the dramatic changes in my premises over the past five decades.

Years after Francis Crick and James Watson had published their famous paper describing the structure of DNA, more than fifty years ago, Crick published a series of lectures. One paragraph summarized his belief that future research would reveal that brain neurochemistry had a major influence on human behavior and its variation.[16] I wrote in the margin of that page, "No!" Stubborn facts have forced me, kicking and screaming, to relinquish the pleasing premise of biology's irrelevance that attracted me to psychology so many years ago.

To my surprise, inhibited and uninhibited children differ in select physical features that are under genetic control. For example, more inhibited than uninhibited children—not all—have a small body size and light blue eyes—all the children are Caucasian. Scientists have bred a population of tame silver fox that, like our uninhibited children, show little fear to unfamiliar people or objects. After twenty generations of selective breeding of pairs of tame foxes the offspring had lower blood levels of the stress hormone cortisol, white spots on their fur, and softer cartilage in the tail and ears.[17] Comparisons of domesticated strains of guinea pigs and sheep with their wild forms reveal that the domesticated animals are tamer and possess a biology characterized by less activity in the circuits that produce cortisol and excite the sympathetic nervous system.[18] These differences help to explain why dogs are gentler than the wolves that are their ancestors. These facts mean that the genes that contribute to tame, fearless behavior to unfamiliarity might also affect aspects of anatomy and physiology.

Finally, time of conception might contribute to these temperamental profiles for children conceived in August and September in the Northern Hemisphere (or in February or March in the Southern Hemisphere) are a little more likely to be inhibited than those conceived at other times of the year.[19] The human brain produces more melatonin when daylight hours are decreasing. Thus, American mothers who conceive in August and September, when the hours of daylight are decreasing, produce large amounts of melatonin. This molecule crosses the placental barrier and affects the unborn infants. Melatonin can slow the rate of cell division and suppress processes that monitor the production of antibodies. Hence, excessive melatonin could lead to excessive antibody production, which in turn could affect brain development. It is interesting that children conceived in spring or fall, when the mother is secreting much less or much more melatonin than usual, are more likely to have small deviations from symmetry in parts of the body, like the face, ears, or fingers.[20] The early astrologers may have had a correct intuition, even though they had the wrong mechanism. When this knowledge becomes well known, couples planning to conceive may decide to avoid early spring and fall. I can imagine a future *New Yorker* cartoon illustrating a wife, index finger waving, saying, "No, honey, it's September."

This rich corpus of evidence honed earlier intuitions to create my current view, which is still speculative. About 15 to 20 percent of healthy, Caucasian infants born to stable families inherit a neurochemistry that renders the amygdala unusually excitable when the brain sites that detect an unexpected or unfamiliar event project that information to it. Unexpected events are familiar but unanticipated, such as an itch on the skin, the sound of raindrops on the window, or the sudden onset of a bright light. Unfamiliar events are discrepant from knowledge gained in the past, such as meeting a stranger or visiting an unfamiliar home. Because high-reactive infants are biased to become inhibited children, their hyper-responsiveness to unexpected events at four months might be due to the same biology that produces an avoidant, vigilant reaction to unfamiliar, discrepant events in the second year. The low-reactive infants inherit a different chemistry, accompanied by a less reactive amygdala, and are biased to become uninhibited toddlers. It is reassuring that others have come to similar conclusions, especially Nathan Fox of the University of Maryland and Cynthia Stifter of Pennsylvania State University.[21] Stifter and her colleague Samuel Putnam found that one-year-olds who delayed before reaching for flashing red lights and objects making sounds, which are discrepant, were inhibited at age two whereas those who reached for these toys quickly were more often uninhibited a year later.

Environments receive the children with these temperamental biases and, through processes we do not yet understand, produce distinct personality profiles that are the joint result of their temperaments and subsequent experience. About two-thirds of the high- and low-reactive infants develop a behavioral persona not seriously different from that displayed by a majority of adolescents in their community. Only one-third of high-reactives preserved a shy, timid, subdued profile through adolescence, and only one-third of the low-reactives preserved an exuberant, sociable, bold persona. Thus, consistently timid or bold behavior to unfamiliarity is not an inevitable adolescent outcome of these temperamental biases but the product of a specific temperament developing under particular circumstances. Class of rearing represents a significant context of development. A high-reactive infant who maintained an inhibited style is likely to seek a job in which frequent interaction with strangers is minimal. Secretary in a large insurance company or bank clerk are likely choices for those who did not pursue graduate training for a specialized profession. Poet or bench scientist are more likely paths for those who attended college and grew up in economically comfortable homes. Both the poet Sylvia Plath and the biologist Rita Levi-Montalcini were inhibited as young girls.

Shy children growing up in China in 1990 were regarded as having a desirable trait and were popular with peers. By 2002, following the national emphasis on a market economy and a self-assertive style, shy children had become less popular and were seen as having a handicapped personality.[22] The writers John Cheever, who died in the second half of the twentieth century, and Alice James, William James's sister, who died a hundred years earlier, probably inherited the same temperamental vulnerability to a de-pressed mood.[23] But Cheever's ideas about human nature were formed when Freudian theory was ascendant and because he assumed that his depression was caused by his childhood experiences, he tried to overcome his distress with drugs and psychotherapy. Alice James's understanding of her mental anguish was influenced by the biological explanations of the nineteenth cen-tury. Hence she concluded, after trying baths and galvanic stimulation with little success, that as long as she could not change her heredity, she wished to die. The historical era in which these two writers lived had a profound influence on their coping strategies and emotional lives.

An infant's temperament can be likened to an ancestral form in evolution, for each temperament can result in a variety of different personalities. The specific personality profile that emerges is determined by the historical era, culture, and family in which development occurs. I noted earlier that the so-cial class of the family, analogous to living on an island for an animal species, provides a unique combination of values, opportunities, and role models that, over time, shapes an envelope of personality types from the initial tempera-mental bias. And as with a new species, new temperaments appear when human groups that had been isolated from one another for millennia mix and mate. The ease of travel in the world has made it possible for a Hindu who grew up in Delhi to marry a Mexican immigrant who grew up in Cali-fornia. The children born to these marriages can have novel temperaments. The mechanisms that turn a temperamental type into a personality in dif-ferent settings include the rewards and punishments experienced at home and the child's identification with his or her gender, ethnicity, social class, religion, and nationality.

High-reactives may be at a greater disadvantage in contemporary America than they were in colonial New England. Americans are barraged with mes-sages urging them to seek the new and experience the exotic and exciting. The basis for deviance in this century is not a physical feature, like skin color or a cleft palate (which can be corrected surgically), but a reluctance to adopt a life-style that is more stressful for high-reactives than for others. Unfortu-nately, a temperamental bias present at birth cannot be observed as a distinct feature in an adult because experience has sculpted it into a specific form. A physical metaphor is helpful. A drop of black ink placed in a rotating cylinder of glycerine disappears into the clear liquid within a few minutes, and from that time forward cannot be seen as separate from the glycerine in which it is embedded.

The concepts "high-reactive" and "low-reactive" infants and "inhibited" and "uninhibited" children refer to behaviors in unfamiliar contexts rather than feelings or brain states. Because psychologists cannot measure brain states accurately I was reluctant to name the feeling states of the inhibited and uninhibited children, even though I appreciated that their public behaviors represented only the surface. I had been burned earlier by leaping too quickly to conjectures that turned out to be mistaken; remember my conviction that the sorting of figures by the Fels adults measured conflict.

Feeling Tone

Interviews with these children when they were fifteen or sixteen years old indicated that many high-reactives who confessed that they often feel uneasy with strangers or in crowds did not appear unusually shy or tense when talking with an interviewer they did not know. Some were emotionally spontaneous. Nonetheless, these adolescents reported a penetrating tension when they anticipated entering a crowd, meeting a stranger, traveling to a new place, rejection by a friend, or the temptation to violate a moral standard. One confessed to worrying excessively whenever she had a headache or a cold because she imagined a more serious illness. A few high-reactive adolescents who appeared full of energy, spontaneity, and vivacity told the interviewer that they disliked being touched, had trouble sleeping before examinations, or experienced profound periods of sadness. A common confession was that they did not like the feeling that accompanied their inability to predict the future, phrased usually as "I don't like not knowing what's going to happen." As a result, they have a strong need to be in control of their life circumstances.

Each person's environment determines which everyday experiences are unpredictable and therefore capable of generating chronic uncertainty. Food is a paramount concern in refugee camps, gossip in small villages, suicide bombers in Baghdad. Most middle-class American adolescents are uncertain over two events: school performance and social relationships. Of the two, the behavior of others toward self is less predictable than a teacher's grades because disciplined study can reduce the uncertainty over test performance. But there is little one can do to mute the uncertainty of a future meeting with a stranger. Because high-reactives are especially vulnerable to events they cannot predict, they worry a great deal about their social encounters.

High-reactives are also at a higher risk for depression. Three of the four clinically depressed adolescent girls in our group had been high-reactive infants, suggesting that the biology responsible for high-reactivity at four months can place some children at an elevated risk for a seriously depressed mood in adolescence.[24] The nineteenth four-month-old, whose behavior was the origin of the notion of high-reactivity, was one of these depressed adolescents. This girl feels anxious and isolated in crowds, worries continually about the opinions of peers, hates ambiguity, prefers solitary hobbies, and is planning to be a writer.

Several of the adolescents displayed frequent facial frowns during the four-month evaluation. This response is uncommon at that age. Although none was particularly shy as an adolescent, many reported high levels of tension or anxiety. Their biology affected their feelings more than their observable social behaviors. This result affirmed the intuition Howard Moss and I had formed forty years earlier, but today I believe I have gained a deeper understanding. T. S. Eliot wrote in "Four Quartets":

We shall not cease from exploration
And the end of all our exploring
Will be to arrive where we started
And know the place for the first time.[25]

Carl Jung, who wrote a book on the differences between introverts and extraverts, noted that each adult displays one psychological face with others, which he called a persona, and another that represents private feelings, which he named the anima.[26] Jung recognized that it is hard for a friend or an observer to know the person's anima from their persona. Some adults who appear sociable and animated live with high levels of worry and doubt, while others who appear quiet and subdued are internally serene. The maxim "You can't judge a book by its cover" has some truth.

Many years ago I visited Mardi Horowitz, a psychiatrist in San Francisco who had gathered a unique corpus of information. A small number of patients in psychoanalytic treatment had agreed to be filmed and to accept sensors for a large number of biological measures during their therapeutic sessions. The measures included heart rate, blood pressure, skin conductance, and muscle tension. The original hope was that the content of the patient's statements would be lawfully related to changes in the biological variables. I watched, simultaneously, the film of the therapeutic interaction and the moment-to-moment changes in the biology that were displayed on a bank of monitors. Surprisingly, the two sources of data had little correspondence. I remember watching one patient confessing a deep feeling of guilt over a sexual act and noting no change in any of the biological measures as he made this statement. I am no longer surprised by this dissociation because our observations on the high- and low-reactive adolescents yielded the same conclusion. Words with emotional content can, in some individuals on some occasions, float free of the expected changes in brain and body. Psychologists acknowledge this truth when they hear political speeches but forget it in the laboratory. That is why self-descriptive statements in interviews or on questionnaires have ambiguous meanings, for identical answers can be accompanied by very different biological profiles. Herbert Weiner of the University of California in Los Angeles came to the same conclusion in 1992 in his book *Perturbing the Organism: The Biology of Stressful Experience.*[27] But this is a message no one wants to hear because ideas that rationalize habitual scientific practices, even though flawed, are stubbornly held until they can be replaced with better ones.

A major change that accompanies development is the construction of a wall between the psychological face shown to others and one's inner life. Few friends of the artist Eugène Delacroix realized how anxious he felt when he was with men who possessed a strong personality. He wrote in his journal, "I am afraid of such people and is there anything more calamitous than being afraid?"[28] Roger Brown, whose insights into language development brought acclaim, surprised every one of his friends who read his memoir, *Against My Better Judgment.*[29] Roger described behaviors and emotions that were dramatically inconsistent with the face he had shown to others for many years. The dissociation between social behavior and quality or level of internal arousal is managed by the prefrontal cortex, which, by placing a heavy hand on the amygdala, prevents it from disrupting well-worn habits. Patients with damage to the prefrontal cortex have no difficulty reporting that a picture of a snake is unpleasant and arousing but do not show the biology that should accompany this verbal judgment.[30] It takes at least fifteen to eighteen years for the prefrontal cortex to gain complete control of activities in other parts of the brain. By their first birthday infants can retrieve what happened in the immediate past; by age three they can inhibit acts that have been punished; by age four they reliably integrate the past with the present; by age seven they can persevere toward a future goal despite fatigue or fear; and by adolescence they can control the disruptive penetration of feelings into their routine behaviors.

Temperament and Morality

Humans vary in the relative weight they assign to their ethical beliefs, compared to their anticipated pleasures, when a decision must be made. Consider a college senior planning to attend a Saturday night party who learns on Friday that a relative who lives a hundred miles away has been taken to the hospital with a broken leg. A significant determinant of the decision of what to do is the estimate of how much guilt will be felt if one does not honor an obligation to the relative. Because high-reactives are prone to more intense guilt when they violate a standard they are likely to forego the party. Some adults are so dogmatically loyal to their ethical beliefs that they appear to friends as inflexible. The loyalty to private premises is a protection against the guilt that is anticipated should self fail to honor a salient ethical standard. When the fifteen-year-olds were asked to remember the last time they felt guilty, most named a time when they actually hurt someone or performed poorly on a test or an athletic contest. Less than 20 percent recalled an incident when they violated a personal standard on disloyalty to another or had a hostile thought toward another. The high-reactives were more likely to name these last two causes for a moment of guilt, and those who did showed higher cortical arousal and greater activation in the right rather than left frontal area. Those who are less susceptible to extreme levels of guilt can afford to be ideologically flexible—some are perceived as hypocrites—and freer to rely on expected pleasures when a choice must be made.

Stephen Daedalus, James Joyce's hero in the novel A *Portrait of the Artist as a Young Man,* is an example of this personality type. When Stephen tells a friend that he is not going to attend Easter Mass because he has lost his Catholic faith, his friend reminds Stephen that the refusal will upset his mother. Stephen insists that he cannot be disloyal to his principles. The friend urges him to attend Mass to please his mother and to live with the moment of guilt provoked by his failure to be true to his convictions. Stephen refuses because he fears the self-reproach that will follow false homage to an idea he does not believe.

Ludwig Wittgenstein, a painfully shy child and melancholic adult, wrote in his notebook that he was too lazy to achieve anything of significance and could not imagine any future other than a ghastly one without joy or friends. The poet Czeslaw Milosz noted in his diary that he felt ashamed of his lack of virtue, and Leo Tolstoy described himself as a worthless creature unable to do anything good. It is likely that these intellectuals, like the fictional Stephen Daedalus, possessed a temperament that rendered them vulnerable to intense guilt when they failed to honor their private notions of what was moral, even though their actions hurt no one.

I noted in chapter 5 that once the brain changes of puberty have occurred, adolescents regularly check their virtue by asking silently whether their collection of features is sufficiently worthy. The answer consciousness returns, which varies across the year, depends on the qualities selected and the friends and relatives used for the comparison between self and other. The gnawing feeling of doubt that follows the decision that self is lacking in worth can be the result of two different histories. The more common feeling is rooted in experiences that produced the belief that parents do not value self, peers find self an unacceptable companion, teachers regard self as incompetent or lazy, or self's social categories imply psychological impotence.

The second, less frequent mechanism involves temperament. Youth with a biology that frequently generates a feeling of tension search for a reason for the unexpected pulse of uncomfortable mood. Those raised in Western societies, which emphasize each person's responsibility, accomplishment, and character, are tempted to conclude that their tension stems from a failure to meet one of their personal standards on achievement, courage, civility, honesty, loyalty, or kindness, even though their parents were loving, peers friendly, teachers approving, and their social categories desirable. As a result they are vulnerable to a moment of guilt. Over time this sequence becomes automatic. Each time they detect a rise in bodily tension they automatically reproach self for an ethical lapse and become vulnerable to the momentary guilt. In order to avoid this corrosive sequence these individuals try to eliminate the evidence for ethical failure and in so doing become risk-averse.

The low-reactives, who are less likely to experience spontaneous episodes of tension demanding an interpretation, orient to the world and try to avoid task failure and criticism from others. Thoughts of possible failure or criticism function as conditioned stimuli for actions aimed at gaining success and the praise of others. Thus a seminal difference between the two temperamental types is that the high-reactives focus on their internal states and the thoughts they provoke while the low-reactives direct their attention to events in the social world. Jung made a similar argument more than seventy-five years ago.

When self-doubt originates primarily in experience, without a temperamental contribution, individuals are motivated to prove their worth and, if life circumstances are not severely depriving, do so through extraordinary achievements, near-perfect loyalties, or exceptional altruism. These are the workaholics and Mother Teresas in our society. If life is harsh, and they perceive no opportunity for obtaining these goals, they turn angry. The group whose self-doubt originated in temperament is at a disadvantage because their biology continues to generate provocations for guilt; hence, worldly success is less effective at muting the self-reproach completely. As a result they are vulnerable to bouts of depression or bursts of anger. A small number become chronically dysphoric. John Calvin, Sylvia Plath, T. S. Eliot, and Ludwig Wittgenstein are examples of individuals who, despite talent, achievement, and acclaim, could not persuade self of an unblemished worthiness.

Advantages and Disadvantages

Although some readers might regard a high-reactive temperament as less desirable than a low-reactive one, nineteenth-century Americans would have wanted their daughters to be born with this bias because a timid personality was an appropriate trait to complement the tough, competitive, unsentimental male profile. And then historical changes in the nation's economy, which

brought women into offices and daily contact with men, made a shy, fearful persona an unattractive feature. Freudian ideas cooperated, for they asserted that anxiety was the primary cause of neurotic symptoms and a malevolent quality to be avoided at all cost. In less than a hundred years Americans had become persuaded that anxiety was a toxic psychological state to be eliminated.

A high-reactive temperament has some advantages in contemporary American society. For example, these adolescents avoid excessive risk and conduct their lives with considerable caution because they have learned that if they do not do so they will feel uncomfortable. As a result, they are less likely to be injured in accidents, whether in automobiles or on skis, and as adults watch their diets, have regular checkups with a physician, and probably live a longer life. They are also a little more likely to be committed to a religious ideology; twice as many high- as low-reactive adolescents were deeply religious. The profound satisfaction they derived from their faith appeared to mute their level of worry or depression, for they showed lower levels of anxiety and cortical arousal than the minimally religious high-reactives. Religiosity does protect some adults from anxiety disorder, and among those with a serious depression, a religious affiliation is accompanied by fewer suicide attempts.[31]

Although high-reactives are at greater risk for developing extreme levels of anxiety when they anticipate meeting strangers—called social phobia—a majority will not become social phobics. Further, many adults with social phobia were not high-reactive infants but acquired these symptoms for varied reasons, perhaps shame over their social class, physical appearance, or inadequate vocabulary. About ten of every hundred Americans had social phobia during part of their adolescent or adult years. I suspect that two or three of these ten were high-reactive infants and inhibited children but not more than one of these ten had been low-reactive infants and uninhibited children. Although more high- than low-reactives are at risk for social phobia, most high-reactives (more than 70 percent) do not become social phobics. The development of this symptom requires more than temperament.

By contrast, a relaxed, optimistic mood is a seminal feature of the adolescents who were low-reactive infants. They not only said that they were relaxed but talked freely and smiled often while talking with the interviewer. Most low-reactive adolescents smiled within the first two minutes of meeting the unfamiliar interviewer; few high-reactives were that spontaneous. One especially bubbly fifteen-year-old low-reactive girl declared, "Everything is fun." When shown pictures of two people entangled with each other at speeds too fast to permit perception of the details the low-reactives said that the people were hugging whereas the high-reactives reported that they were fighting. Although low-reactives do not want to fail examinations, perform poorly in athletic contests, or lose a close friend and say that they worry about these outcomes, their anxiety does not rise to an intensity that prevents a good night's sleep. Further, unlike high-reactives who report worrying about the same events, the low-reactives are apt to describe themselves as easygoing. Adults who report feeling good at the end of most days are likely to possess higher serotonin levels.[32] There is the possibility that low-reactives secrete more serotonin than high-reactives. But their sanguine mood requires a benevolent environment; serotonin alone cannot award that gift.

One low-reactive boy made a deep impression on me during the evaluation at four years of age. In one procedure the examiner asked each child to perform some innocent actions (for example, tap the table) as well as some acts that violated family values (for example, pour cranberry juice on the table). The examiner's final request provided the most interesting information. She showed the child a color photo of herself, said that it was her favorite picture, and then handed the photo to the child, saying, "Tear up my favorite picture." Most children became quiet and, after a few moments, tore a small piece from a corner of the picture. This boy gave the photo back to the examiner and in a confident voice announced, "No, it's your favorite, I won't tear it up." I was surprised by the lack of anxiety he displayed to an unfamiliar authority figure he was flagrantly disobeying. He was, at age fifteen, a classic uninhibited adolescent. He laughed often, spoke freely, had a healthy conscience, and struck me as one of the best-adjusted teenagers I had ever seen. He had all the features of movie heroes who marry fearlessness to a strong inner voice calling for responsibility.

A small number of adolescent boys who had been low-reactive infants comprised a unique category. They were supremely self-confident, immune to serious anxiety, pragmatic, and realistic, and had set high goals for their lives. They were also likely to possess a biology indicative of low cortical arousal to challenge. When an interviewer asked the adolescents what adult vocations they were considering, only two replied that they wanted to be president of the United States. Both had been low-reactive boys with the profile described above. One was the boy who refused to tear up the examiner's photograph. I suspect that if I could have seen Theodore Roosevelt, Lyndon Johnson, Ronald Reagan, and Bill Clinton at four months, all four would have been low-reactive infants. I am less certain about the temperaments of Woodrow Wilson, Harry Truman, and Jimmy Carter. Because testosterone (male sex hormone) suppresses signs of fear to danger in animals, it remains possible that the exaggerated boldness we observed in these low-reactive boys is a little more likely in males than in females.[33]

The small number of adolescents with unique behavioral and biological profiles supports my earlier defense of the utility of positing categories of children rather than placing all on one or more continua. The behavior of one girl is especially illustrative. She belonged to a small group of four-month-olds—about 15 percent of the sample—who displayed very vigorous motor activity but no fretting or crying. We called these infants aroused. This toddler showed an extraordinary level of vitality and energy during the assessment at twenty-one months. She laughed, screamed with delight at most episodes, and talked frequently. No child (from a total of 468) approached her in sheer exuberance. Her style of interaction with the interviewer at age sixteen was equally distinctive. She was exceptionally garrulous, criticized the grammar of the interviewer, and shared her philosophical views on life and nature as if she and the interviewer, who was fifteen years older, were colleagues at a scholarly meeting. She confessed to being stubborn and opinionated and, in a remarkably mature comment for a sixteen-year-old, said, "I don't need others to define myself. . . . I hope I never lose my sense of resonance with the world." This girl, who was clearly different from every other girl at every assessment, from four months to sixteen years, belongs to a special category for which no current psychological concept applies. Exuberant is the best I can do.

These two temperaments affect quality of performance on laboratory tasks that are boring and have minimal consequences for the person, except the satisfaction of knowing they did well. Because many high-reactives do not like the feeling that accompanies a less-than-perfect performance, they remain attentive and motivated and usually obtain higher scores than low-reactives on such tests. For example, researchers Rachel Pollock and Deborah Sorenson first let our adolescents listen to the sound of an abnormal heartbeat to familiarize them with this stimulus. They then asked the teenagers to detect the occasional appearance of an abnormal heartbeat embedded in a noisy sound background that resembled static. The high-reactives did better than the low-reactives on this difficult though boring task because a compromised performance would have provoked more shame or guilt in them than in low-reactives. Indeed, the high-reactives who did best had described themselves earlier as "taking themselves seriously."

Many laboratory procedures designed to evaluate a person's emotions or values in fact fail to do so because the motivation to avoid mistakes takes precedence over the deeper psychic phenomena the psychologist wishes to measure. Remember my error in assuming that the sorting of the paper figures by the Fels adults reflected conflict when it actually measured the person's preference for attending to the tiny details on the figures. The first two questions a mind asks in every test situation in a laboratory are: How unfamiliar is this task, and how important is it for me to do well? Because the answers to these queries affect every laboratory protocol, psychologists have been frustrated in their attempts to construct procedures that are sensitive indexes of beliefs, emotions, and values. They want to gain entrance to a house whose thick doors resist penetration.

Most youths who experience occasional doubt over their social acceptability, talents, attractiveness, status, or virtue do so because of their socialization rather than their temperament. A temperamental bias affects the chronicity and intensity of the feelings that accompany these doubts because the neurochemistry that is the biological foundation of a temperament influences the excitability of particular brain circuits. These circuits, which can become excited spontaneously or in response to an event, activate symbolic networks representing the sources of uncertainty established during childhood and adolescence. These networks are "well-worn" paths primed for evocation by a brain state. Consider a hypothetical high-reactive child with an excitable amygdala living in a family that demands an excellent report card every year, a clean bedroom every morning, polite behavior with strangers, and decorum at the dinner table. This child experiences continual uncertainty over parental criticism for failure to adhere to family rules and regularly activates a semantic network for self in which the adjective "bad" is a central node. However, a low-reactive child living with the same family who had a minimally excitable amygdala would be protected from frequent activation of this undesirable network for self.

A particular level of amygdalar excitability does not by itself create a particular emotion but generates an envelope of possible states. I agree with those who define a human emotion as an interpretation of a change in bodily feeling. A change in brain state, without any interpretation, either because it was not detected or because it was ignored, should be given a different name. There is no agreement on what to call these unrecognized brain states. But we should distinguish between a man who detected a rise in heart rate and muscle tightness as he entered a room of strangers and thought, "I am anxious," and a woman who failed to detect the same reactions, even though her behavior might have been affected by the altered bodily state. Freud called the latter state "unconscious anxiety," implying that it should be regarded as similar to conscious anxiety. I am not certain this decision was wise because the individual who is aware of a higher heart rate might decide that he was "excited" over the people he was about to join. The judgment that one is excited leads to behaviors different from those accompanying the decision that one is afraid.

Equally important, cultures vary in the most likely interpretations of a change in feeling tone. Some who feel their heart beating unusually fast on awakening might decide that a deceased ancestor was displeased because they had violated a moral standard on civility the previous day and would experience a moment of guilt. Others, with the same bodily change, might conclude that they were apprehensive over the day's heavy responsibilities. Still others might decide that their beating heart is the delayed consequence of a frightening encounter with a snake several years earlier and become anxious because they believe they are losing their vital spirit. This phenomenon, common in Latin America, is called "susto." Finally, those who conclude that they have been cursed by a woman in the village believed to be a witch would experience a blend of fear and anger.

Thus all of these profiles of brain activity, which are components of a temperament, resemble the verbs "take," "hit," and "give," which can be followed by a number of different objects. One brain state could generate fear, guilt, loneliness, or sadness depending on the person and the local context. Another state might provoke interpretations of ambition, excitement, or a resonance with the world. The important point is that scientists should give one set of names to the brain states and their accompanying bodily changes and another set to the interpretations the person imposes on the detected feelings. Because rats and mice, and perhaps apes as well, do not interpret their bodily changes, scientists should not equate the emotions of animals and humans. Although some scientists attribute "fear" to both rats and humans, the psychological states in the two species are far from identical. Some scientists say that mice that freeze in a place where they had been shocked a day earlier or do not enter a brightly lit alley are "anxious." But readers should understand that the brain state of the mice is quite different from that of adults who refuse to fly because of anxiety over a possible crash.

Finally, we should distinguish between a chronic feeling tone, whether tension or serenity, which can be temperamental in origin, and the briefer emotions of anger, shame, sadness, fear, joy, or sexual pleasure that last from a few seconds to a few hours. The latter are difficult to re-experience. It is hard to retrieve the sensations that accompanied making love, an elegant meal, anger toward a stranger, or a last-minute victory on the tennis court that occurred days earlier, but it is easy to retrieve the settings, actions, and actors. One reason is that the brain circuits that create an acute feeling differ from those responsible for the registration of places, people, and things. This difference might be adaptive. The ability to recall the places where food and predators were encountered in the past has an obvious advantage. But re-experiencing a feeling of satiety when one has not eaten for three days, or reliving anger when one is not frustrated, seems less adaptive. Perhaps the difficulty of retrieving feelings of fear, anger, sadness, or shame is a benevolent property that makes maintenance of a good mood more likely.

Hippocrates and Galen appreciated, two thousand years ago, that the temperaments they called sanguine, melancholic, choleric, and phlegmatic referred to susceptibilities to particular moods and not to behaviors. A vulnerability to a brief episode of anger, fear, anxiety, or sadness, or a chronic mood of tension, irritability, or apathy, is more likely to be preserved over time than a particular class of public behavior because the emotions are more closely tied to a brain state. But unfortunately, acute emotions and moods are not measured as easily as behaviors that can be recorded on film. The verbal descriptions and facial expressions that psychologists use to infer emotions are not highly correlated with the brain states that are their presumed foundations. That is why, for some women, there is no relation between their report of the intensity of sexual arousal they are feeling while watching an erotic film and simultaneous measurement of degree of vaginal engorgement.[34] This frustration has led some scientists to ignore the person's psychological state and to treat profiles of brain or bodily activity as signs of an emotional state — for example, interpreting amygdalar activity to a photograph of a fearful facial expression as reflecting a related emotional state in the viewer. I now address the serious problems raised by this assumption.

SEVEN

Celebrating Mind

Natural events can be described and eventually explained in two ways. The first views each phenomenon as the result of a cascade of events. Some cascades, like the reflex withdrawal of a hand after touching a hot stove, are over in less than a second. The cascade that begins with the formation of a tropical depression off the West African coast and ends with a hurricane striking Palm Beach, Florida, requires days. The cascade that began with Lyndon Johnson's birth in rural Texas and ended with his assumption of the presidency in 1963 required decades. The important fact is that when novel properties are added to a new phase, it is often necessary to describe them with a distinctive vocabulary. The properties of velocity, pressure, opacity, temperature, and direction, appropriate for hurricanes, are not useful descriptions of the air and water molecules that are its elements, either currently or when it was a tropical depression. Transparency is a quality of glass but not a property of the silica atoms from which the glass emerged. This view, usually summarized by the statement "The whole is more than the sum of its parts," regards every observed event as an emergent form that depends on, but is not identical with, its elementary foundations. When applied to psychological phenomena, this perspective implies that the meanings of words that refer to perception, feeling, belief, intention, and habit will differ from those describing the biological events that permit those functions to be actualized. Put simply, stars, stones, squirrels, and sadness are useful names for coherent outcomes but useless for their constituents.

An alternative view, called reductionism, maintains that it is both possible and theoretically desirable to translate an emergent phenomenon into the vocabulary that describes its foundation. A more permissive form of reductionism argues only that the emergent event be explained by the more fundamental forms. Although physicists have managed to describe a small number of chemical phenomena with the vocabulary of physics, most chemical events have until now resisted such a translation. Roald Hoffman notes that the process of oxidation, in which an electron is removed from an atom or molecule, often resulting in a deleterious effect on body cells, cannot be translated into the vocabulary of physics without losing the essential meaning of this idea.[1] I confess to feeling surprised one February evening in 1980, while sitting in a Stanford University auditorium, when the late Willard van Orman Quine, one of America's most admired philosophers, told a large audience that all psychological events could, in principle, be described as physical events and that one day there would be no need for any psychological terms.

Scientists who subscribe to a reductionist philosophy assume that when the power of machines that measure the brain is enhanced, many phenomena now described in psychological terms will be replaced with a language referring to neurons, molecules, receptors, and activated neural circuits. My schema of my wife's face and my feeling of affection for her will be explained with a vocabulary referring only to brain structures and states. The images and emotions will be epiphenomena that can be ignored if the primary goal is explanation. This hope resembles the physicists' aspiration to find one set of equations that will explain both the gravitational properties of large bodies, like planets and stars, and the quantum characteristics of atomic particles. String theorists hope they have invented a set of mathematical equations that will permit an explanation of the large from the small, but the jury remains out on this bold claim.

The reductionists' dream of explaining the "large" behavioral phenomena from the activity of groups of "tiny" neurons blossomed a century ago when machines that could amplify small voltages made the first measurements of brain activity possible. The English physicist Edgar Adrian wrote an influential book on the physical basis of perception in 1947, the year after I began college, promising this victory.[2] Years later, many hundreds of scientists, including the Nobel laureates David Hubel, Francis Crick, and Eric Kandel, suggested that this hope was not only rational but, in principle, attainable. This assumption led to the unfortunate habit of attributing psychological states to profiles of brain activity and implying that the brain state, which is necessary for the psychological one, is a proxy for it (note that physicists do not make this error, for they do not attribute gravity to atomic particles). The strict reductionist strategy is flawed because the names for the elements and functions that comprise neuronal activity cannot be used to describe perceptions, thoughts, feelings, or actions. Should the difference between the gravitational force governing planetary orbits and the quantum events within atoms be analogous to the difference between neuronal activity and a psychological phenomenon, the current vocabulary for neurons, transmitters, and circuits can never replace the psychological terms, and a completely new vocabulary that describes the relations between brain profiles and psychological events—a string theory for brain/mind—will be needed.

The Need for Distinct Terms

The heart of the controversy pits language purists, who are made uneasy by the messiness of multiple vocabularies, against pluralists, who accept the fact that no single set of terms can cover all we observe and wish to explain. Biologists do not use the vocabulary of DNA base pairs to describe the proteins in the muscles of the heart; chemists do not rely on the language of quantum events to describe the salt shaken on a salad. Niels Bohr told a frustrated Edward Teller that physicists must use the concepts of classical physics, not those of quantum theory, to describe the results of an experiment, even though the quantum events were the foundation of the measurements. When Teller challenged this dualist position, Bohr replied that if the younger scientist were correct they would not be having their conversation over a cup of tea but imagining both events. In a quantum world there are no flowers, faces, fears, conversations, or teacups.

Children growing up with parents who have not attended college usually have smaller vocabularies than those living with families that have some college training. The usual explanation is that the former parents are less likely to talk with and read to their children than the better-educated families. However, the psychologists who found this relation in six-year-olds concluded, to my surprise, that the sparser vocabulary of the children from less well educated parents reflected compromised functioning of the brain area involved in language.[3] This is an odd way to explain this result. I cannot play the violin because I have not had lessons, but this lacuna in my training does not mean that the areas of my brain that are normally active when someone plays the violin are structurally deficient. This study illustrates the problem that arises when a psychological term (language ability) is replaced with a biological one (neural structure). If a window shatters because a boy threw a ball at it, we can attribute this event to the ball striking the glass, the boy's intention and subsequent action, or the profile of brain activity that accompanied the motor response. The problem with the last explanation is that the coherent psychological component vanishes into a long description of neuronal firings the more closely we examine the changes in brain activity over the interval from planning to execution. As a viewer slowly approaches Claude Monet's painting of the Seine at dawn there comes a moment when the scene dissolves into tiny patches of color.

Different Metrics

Distinct vocabularies for mind and brain are necessary because the meaning of a word has two related components. One is the complete collection of thoughts it evokes; the second is the thing, or things, in the world it is intended to name. The latter is called the referent. The word "justice" evokes many thoughts, some of which have no referent in the world. But if one person thought of the Supreme Court's ruling on desegregation of the schools whereas another thought of the Nuremberg trials at the end of World War II, the meaning of "justice" would not have identical meanings for the two. Neuroscientists and psychologists often use the same words for a psychological process (for example, "fear," "consciousness," "arousal"), but the meanings differ because the referents for the neuroscientist are brain circuits, whereas they are reports of feelings and observed behaviors for the psychologist. Stated differently, the meaning networks for words that name psychological events are distinct from those that name brain activity.

Acts, for example, have an intended goal, thoughts have a semantic coherence, and feelings have a quality. Neuronal activity has none of these properties, and it is not possible to replace the psychological terms with biological ones without losing some meaning.

Consider, as an illustration, a scientist who wanted to know the immediate change in quality and intensity of a conscious feeling of "fear" in a person with a snake phobia who is presented with pictures of rattlesnakes with open jaws—a question asked by many investigators many times. The use of an interview or questionnaire to obtain this information relies on semantic networks containing such terms as "tense," "afraid," "upset," or "anxious." Unfortunately, these words do not capture the nuanced details of the sensations evoked by the pictures. Remember that adults who cannot experience the beating of their heart or the sweat on their palms can accurately describe the emotional expressions on faces and the feelings of the characters in a story. Brain-damaged patients, who are as accurate as normal persons in describing the quality and intensity of the emotion provoked by pleasant and unpleasant pictures, have a very different biological reaction to these pictures. There is little or no relation between verbal reports of the intensity of anxiety or fear to pictures of angry or fearful facial expressions and the amount of activity in the amygdala.[4]

The phobic could be placed in a magnetic scanner to measure changes in degree of oxygenation of the blood in parts of the brain that mediate conscious feelings. There are several problems with the inferences drawn from this procedure. First, the measure is an index of the amount of input to a set of neurons and is not necessarily correlated with the amount of output from that site. Second, the change in oxygenation of the blood is usually not detected until several seconds after each snake picture is shown and, therefore, might not reflect the change in conscious feeling that occurred during the first second. It is tortuous to assume that a psychological process taking place a fraction of a second after a stimulus appeared was reflected in activity in a brain site occurring several seconds later. Third, if a brain area without a rich blood supply was active during a psychological event, this method might not reveal that activity. A set of neurons became active when a person heard a discrepant sound (measured by placing electrodes directly into the neurons) but the blood-flow evidence failed to reveal any distinct activity in those neurons.[5]

Finally, most events activate many brain sites. The unexpected sound of a whistle while a person is listening for a particular tone, for example, activates twenty-four different areas.[6] And most of these twenty-four areas are not necessary for the detection of the novel sound. This means that scientists cannot assume that a brain site is necessary for a psychological process just because it was active during that process. Measurement of the activity of my sweat glands when I play tennis would reveal that they are more active than when I am sitting still. But this activity is not needed for the planning or execution of the motor movements involved in hitting a tennis ball.

Each form of evidence presently recorded from brains is influenced by a unique set of conditions that prevents scientists from knowing with certainty the psychological processes that accompany the activity. It is not unreasonable to compare these inferences with those of a person flying at night at thirty thousand feet peering at the ground below. Our observer would be able to discriminate areas with human activity from others by the presence or absence of lights but could not know whether the lights came from offices, factories, bars, or homes or whether the dark regions were farmland, rivers, parks, or forests. The discoveries to be made in coming decades will dilute the seriousness of these problems, but it is less obvious that they will solve them completely.

A thought experiment reveals the difference between the report of a conscious feeling of fear and simultaneous measurements of the brain. Imagine a woman with a phobia of snakes who is told to lift her finger the moment the appearance of a snake on a screen made her afraid and to lower her finger when the feeling of fear disappeared. Although her finger movements indicated that her fear state lasted four and a half seconds, the brain measurements changed continually over this interval, and the brain state during the first half second was distinguishable from the state during the last half second. Thus, we can ask which of the nine brain states (let us assume that each brain state lasts about half a second) represents her fear. It should be obvious that this question has no certain answer. And if we brought the woman back seven days later and repeated the experiment, we would record nine new brain states not observed a week earlier. Words for psychological states, whether reported by an experiencing agent or invented by a scientist to explain the data, freeze-frame a cascade of dynamically changing events to imply, incorrectly, that there is an essential psychological state that exists at a particular time in a specific place in the brain, not unlike physicist Ernest Rutherford's image of an electron orbiting the nucleus of an atom.

More important, it is not possible to use measures of brain activity as indexes of unitary states of anxiety, fear, or stress because there are multiple forms of these emotional states. Nature did not create one state of fear. Students of primate behavior agree that removing a monkey from its familiar cage mates is stressful. Some stressed animals emit distinct calls called coos; others become immobile and quiet. These two reactions are accompanied by different patterns of brain activation. Hence there is no clear answer to the question "Which group is more stressed?" The distinct combinations of behavior and brain activity shown by these two types of monkeys reflect qualitatively different forms of stress.[7]

The "uncomfortable" state of a person who has been conditioned to blink to a tone is contained in circuits that involve several structures in the brain. To ask where the uncomfortable state is located is like asking where the "group" is in a collection of twelve people discussing the presidential election of 2008. The best a scientist can do is to suggest that a particular brain profile has a certain probability of accompanying a psychological state and to recognize that this probability changes a little every time a measurement is made. To rephrase Niels Bohr, all we have are observations. Looking for the place in the brain where a person's feeling of fear is located is as fruitless as Diogenes' search for an honest man.

Meaning

The structures and functions of brains can be described with the well-understood metrics for space and time. A neuron has a length that can be measured in millimeters and a duration of activation measured in milliseconds. Unfortunately, psychological structures, like the representation, now more than seventy years old, of the scene in the rowboat and my feeling of fear when I yelled to my father that I was going to jump into the lake, require a metric of meaningfulness, which varies with the number and coherence of the structures it evokes. Thus, the representation of the moments in the rowboat are more meaningful than my representation of the windowsill in my study but less meaningful than the representation of my granddaughter. Unfortunately, psychologists do not yet know how to measure meaningfulness. But that failure, hopefully temporary, does not imply that this problem will never be solved. Nor does it imply that measures of brain will one day provide an index of meaningfulness, for different brain patterns can accompany similar meanings. A woman at a dinner party who wanted the saltshaker resting a foot away could say to the person sitting next to her, "Pass the salt, please," point to the saltshaker, or mimic the shaking of salt with her hand. Each of these three communications would evoke different patterns of brain activity, in the speaker as well as in her dinner companion, but the meaning intended and apprehended would be the same. Identical meanings can emerge from different brain profiles.

A critical feature of meaningfulness is that it varies with the agent's state and the context. The number of representations evoked by the schema of a glass of water will be larger when I am thirsty than when I am not. Hence, meaningfulness, like the judgment of simultaneity of two light sources, is relative to the agent's status at a particular moment. The suggestion that the meaningfulness of a psychological representation transcends measures of brain activity bears some resemblance to Kurt Godel's proof that some true mathematical statements about numbers transcend formal logical systems. Godel's celebrated insight held that no formal logical system was able to generate all the possible true statements in mathematics. This principle has an analogue in the claim that no set of rules for combining the base pairs that constitute the molecule DNA can predict all the possible bodily organs. Nor is there any set of rules for combining words and the rules of grammar that can predict all possible sentences, no set of sentences that can account for all possible thoughts, and no set of rational statements that can predict all possible emotional commitments to some ideal. Similarly, there is no set of statements about neurons and their functions that can predict all possible psychological states. Thus, mathematics transcends logic; thought transcends language; faith transcends rationality; and beliefs, intentions, and emotions transcend brain activity.

The nub of the problem is that the special properties of each measure are a barrier between scientists and the beloved target they wish to know because each measurement distorts the natural phenomenon. Mirrors of different curvature provide a metaphor for the products of different measures. A photograph of Abraham Lincoln placed in front of each of twelve such mirrors will appear different to observers, and no reflection is completely faithful to the photograph. Plato captured this idea by describing people in a cave who saw only the shadows cast on the walls by objects in the outside world but not the objects themselves.

That is why Bohr claimed that scientists can only know what they can measure and can never know a phenomenon in its natural, pristine form. This declaration is essentially similar to Kant's claim, almost a century and a half earlier, that the mind cannot know the "true essence" of any experience, which he called "noumena." If we accept Bohr's principle, and I do, it follows that the meaning of each inference depends on what was observed and how it was quantified. However, and here is the rub, we do not know how to translate the metric of a biological measure into that of a psychological one; say, a certain increase in blood flow to the amygdala into a rating on a seven-point-scale of the intensity of "anxiety" a person feels at the moment.

A scholar translating a poem from one language to another confronts the same problem. The Japanese use the word *amae* to describe the psychological state of a person who has complete confidence that another will always protect and care for him or her in all situations. No single word in English captures this meaning; hence, an absolutely faithful translation is not possible. I recall one afternoon when I tried without success to explain to a Japanese visitor the meaning of the feeling of alienation a mother felt toward her infant.

The Indeterminacy of Prediction

The greater the number of phases in a cascade, the harder it is to predict a later form from an early one because some determinacy is lost at the transition between phases. Stated a bit more formally, the predictability of an event close to its origin is higher than the predictability of an event distant from its origin. A bird leaves a branch on which it is resting and begins to fly. The direction of flight during the next three seconds is more predictable than the direction two minutes later because events, not knowable initially,

intervene to affect the course of flight. The correlation between the vocabulary of three-year-olds and their vocabulary one year later is very high, but
the correlation between the vocabularies at ages three and fifteen is lower
because of intervening experiences.

The products of each person's history influence the brain's reaction to an
event. All humans possess a gene that regulates the amount of serotonin in
the synapses of varied brain sites, but people differ in the length of that gene.
Some have a short form, others a longer one. When individuals with the short
form of the gene on both chromosomes were given a drug that promotes the
release of serotonin, those with more education and a higher income had a
brisker reaction than those with less education and a smaller income. The
inference is obvious. A person's past history affects the brain's reaction to a
challenge.[8]

The critical influence of experience is also seen in a comparison of one
group of children—five to fifteen years old—who were removed from their
homes because they were maltreated with a second group of children of the
same age and social background who lived with nurturant families. (I mentioned this work earlier.) Self-reported feelings of depression were highest in
maltreated children who had both the short form of the gene and minimal
support from relatives or the adults who cared for them. The children from
loving families with the short form were no more depressed than those with
the long form of the gene.[9] Thus, both the child's past history and the current
environment had a serious influence on the likelihood of depression.

The responsivity of body and brain to an allergen (for example, pollen)
is even affected by the immediate past. Adults who spent the hour before
they were exposed to the allergen in a room with their spouse or lover had a
smaller reaction than those who had been alone. And regular exercise affects
the usual measures of brain and body used to infer cognitive and emotional
traits. No measure of brain could reveal that a participant in a study had
been with a spouse an hour earlier or exercised four times a week. A hand
(representing brain) holding a string attached to a kite (the mind) provides
an instructive metaphor for the relation of brain to mind. When the string
is short, the kite's direction is under the strong control of the hand. But as
the string becomes longer there comes a moment when, in a stiff breeze, the
hand loses control and the kite determines how the hand moves.

What Is Assigned: Ideas or Processes?

When Neil Rudenstine became president of Harvard in 1991 following Derek Bok's tenure, he recognized that the faculty had become increasingly fragmented. Humanists rarely lunched with chemists, physicists did not attend the colloquia of biologists, and most molecular biologists had no interest in papers written by psychologists. One of Rudenstine's first acts was to establish informal groups of faculty representing most of the schools of the university—arts and science, divinity, medicine, law, education, business, and public health. The goal of one group, called the Mind/Brain/Behavior Initiative, was to allow neuroscientists, social scientists, educators, humanists, and lawyers to become acquainted with one another's vocabularies, methods, and premises. Steven Hyman was one of the first directors of the network, and when he left Harvard to become the director of the National Institute of Mental Health, Anne Harrington, a historian of science, and I became co-directors of this consortium. Hyman returned several years later to become Harvard's provost.

A primary, but not the only, activity of the consortium consisted of monthly dinner meetings at which someone spoke for about an hour, followed by a lively discussion. This format permitted the varied faculty groups to appreciate the epistemologies of the others. I am not certain, however, whether many minds were changed. Most neuroscientists remained convinced that when the story was complete, the brain would account for the complexities that the humanists and social scientists were probing. I recall an eminent neuroscientist's reply when I asked, "If you could measure accurately every event going on in my brain at this moment, would you be able to predict that I was about to leap onto the table at which we are sitting and begin to dance?" "Yes," was his reply, and nothing I said could persuade him otherwise. He was certain that because every action, thought, and feeling has its origin in brain activity, it necessarily followed that all psychological events had to have a distinct instantiation in brain that, once measured, would imply only one inference. Any other belief was irrational.

But it is not certain whether a brain location is the home of a particular experience or the place where a particular process is engaged. Although a face almost always activates a cortical site in the posterior part of the brain, called the fusiform gyrus, a picture of a spider activates this site in adults who are afraid of this animal, and photos of cars activate this site in automobile aficionados.[10] It is not even possible to use activity in the fusiform area to determine whether a person is actually looking at a face or merely imagining it, for this area is activated when individuals are looking not only at a photograph of a face but a photo of the arms and trunk of a man with a homogeneously gray circle that replaces the face.[11] A scientist examining brain activity in the fusiform area could not distinguish between these two states. This cortical area, it appears, is not slavishly reserved for registering faces but is prepared to process any frequently encountered visual event with detailed features requiring close analysis to discriminate between two similar examples from the same class (for example, two faces or two cars). This explains why an autistic eleven-year-old who spent a great deal of time examining a set of cartoon characters, which had facial features, showed greater fusiform activity to the cartoon figures than to human faces.[12] Most cortical areas will be understood best by discovering the processes each was prepared to engage in rather than by trying to determine the contents it was intended to store.[13] My thumb and index finger are prepared to pick up any object with a particular range of size and weight, not just teacups and pencils.

A good reason for doubting that a particular segment of knowledge is always stored in the same place in all persons is that a carburetor will activate different sites as a function of exposure to this object: in auto mechanics who have replaced thousands of carburetors over their careers and in adults whose carburetors failed when they were driving in a blizzard. To ask where a specific piece of knowledge is represented is similar to asking where a state of hunger is located. A feeling of hunger is the product of activity in many places in the body and brain, and these places may vary across individuals. Adults lying in a brain scanner watching the same movie segment displayed different patterns of brain activity in the frontal lobe because the scenes provoked different thoughts.

Nonetheless, some scientists continue to believe that particular ideas are assigned fixed places in the brain. I was surprised by a report in which one person lying in a brain scanner was given the role of investor while another, a stranger lying in a separate scanner, had the role of trustee. The investor could invest any part of twenty dollars with the trustee, who then decided how much of the profit to share with his investor partner. The patterns of brain activity, across many pairs of investors and trustees, revealed that after a number of exchanges, the trustees who began to return more money to their partners showed increased neuronal activity in a brain structure called the caudate that is usually involved in motor activity. The scientists concluded that the neurons in this site evaluated "trustworthiness toward another."[14] The likely flaw in this bold inference is that the caudate is usually active when a person is evaluating incoming information in order to make a motor response indicating a decision. That is exactly what the trustees and partners were doing in the experiment. Because the trustees were more likely to feel ambivalent over being exceptionally generous than over being selfish, we would expect the caudate to be more active under the former mental state. The brain generates a unique waveform whenever a person is instructed to hit a key when he or she sees a particular target appear on a screen. The activity in the caudate is probably reflecting the trustee's state of indecision over which movement to make (be generous or be selfish) and does not represent "trustworthiness."

The neurons of the motor cortex are activated when a basketball player prepares to shoot a basket in the closing seconds of a game in which his or her team is behind by one point. But no one would claim that the "hope of winning the game" is represented in this site. There is an important difference in meaning between "required for" and "represents." A psychological state, the judgment of pleasure following a good meal, for example, requires particular brain structures, but it is not represented by them because the psychological state is an evaluation that can be mediated by different brain states. Therefore, the mental state need not occur every time these structures are activated and might occur when they are not activated.

The hope of finding a place in the brain that is the essence of a thought or feeling is as futile as trying to discover the most essential basis for the taste of a piece of milk chocolate. Remove the milk, the sugar, or the chocolate, and the usual sensory experience vanishes. The mind likes the notion of essences, but like the tooth fairy, nature failed to provide examples of this pleasing idea.

Those who hope to find the place in the brain that represents the material foundation for a psychological event forget that many physical phenomena are the product of a relation between structures and are not "in" any of them. The ocean tides and the heat of a stone at high noon under a bright sun are examples. Thoughts, feelings, and action plans are the products of relations among collections of neurons in different places and, like the contagion of a crowd, are not locatable in a particular spot in the brain.

The seminal point is that each brain profile permits more than one inference about a psychological state. To reduce the number of possible inferences, scientists must know something of the individual's previous history. But that history, whether years of education or talking with one's spouse an hour earlier, cannot be described with the words appropriate for brain activity. Conversely, the same psychological event can be the product of different brain states. If asked to name a picture of a maple tree, I would give the same correct answer whether I had just awakened, had exercised for two hours, had drunk a bottle of wine, or had been administered a mild anesthetic. Each of these conditions would have altered my brain in a nontrivial way. I would also have given the correct answer a year later if I had developed Parkinson's disease during the interval. If a psychological measurement can remain unchanged despite alterations in brain, it follows that measurements of brain alone cannot, in principle, be proxies for a psychological phenomenon.

A paper in the official journal of Britain's Royal Society argued that scientists one day will be able to state that a particular brain state precedes each freely willed decision or action.[15] They suggested that if my brain could be measured with the powerful machines of the future when I was trying to decide between soup or salad, there would be a moment when my brain was in a particular state that would predict my choice of salad. I suggest that this hope cannot, in principle, be realized because there cannot be a single brain state across all individuals that precedes the selection of salad over soup. More seriously, my brain state the moment before I decided on salad will be different at varying times of day, in different restaurants, and in a state of fatigue versus intoxication. If future neuroscientists were able to measure my brain across a hundred occasions when I selected "salad," they would record a hundred different brain states, but the choice of salad would have remained the same. Thus, the assumption of a deterministic relation between a brain state and a psychological decision is overly optimistic.

Fortunately, scientific work supports this judgment. The leech's nervous system is considerably simpler than our own and far easier to study. A trio of California neuroscientists stimulated varied groups of neurons to see if they could predict whether the subsequent motor pattern would be a swimming or a crawling movement if the leech were in its natural state. They could not make this simple prediction 100 percent of the time because the response following stimulation of the neurons depended on the prior state of the nervous system and unpredictable "noise" in the neuronal matrix.[16] There is an inherent unpredictability at the level of the neuron that resembles the uncertainty of a photon in quantum mechanics. If scientists with complete control of a simple nervous system cannot predict with perfect accuracy which one of two acts will occur, it is highly unlikely—I am tempted to write impossible— that any future scientist with the most elaborate equipment will be able to predict whether I will order soup or salad.

The predictability of a psychological reaction must always be a probability estimate. Remember Erwin Schrödinger's cat, enclosed in a box containing an apparatus that, upon detecting a photon, releases a toxin that will kill the cat. An observer cannot know with certainty, following the release of the photon, whether the cat is dead or alive. He or she must open the box to answer that question. Moreover, in the quantum world the act of observation alters the state that existed before the observation was made. Imagine a man wanting to know the postures, facial expressions, comments, and moods of a group of people talking in a room behind a thick door in the seconds before he entered the room. The moment he opens the door he has disturbed the properties he wished to know. Hence, it is impossible, in principle, to be certain of the psychological or biological state of a person before these states are measured because the act of measurement alters those states. I am afraid that the observers monitoring my brain will have to wait until I tell the waiter whether my preference is for soup or salad on any given evening. Free will resides in that narrow corridor of unpredictability that nature built to frustrate humans who entertained the illusion that one day they might know it all.

The Need for Biology

This critique of the reductionists' hope should not be construed as an argument for ignoring the contributions of biology to a deeper understanding of psychology. Every psychological phenomenon is ambiguous with respect to its historical origins, and adding biological information often illuminates the meaning of a behavior, thought, or emotion. The evidence from brain activity can provide a more profound appreciation of the behavior. For example, the blink of an eyelid that had been conditioned to close at the sight of a clenched fist is mediated by a circuit different from the one activated when a person blinks voluntarily or when startled by a loud sound. The research on temperament I described in chapter 6 suggests that the biology associated with shy behavior in adolescents who had been high-reactive infants is different from the biology that accompanies equally shy behavior in low-reactives. For example, among the eleven-year-olds described by their mothers as shy, quiet, and worried about the opinions of others, failure, and the future, more adolescents who had been high-reactive as infants showed signs of high cortical arousal, whereas most of the shy, anxious low-reactives did not. And among the fifteen-year-olds who were seriously anxious over social interaction, only the high-reactives had high cortical arousal; the few low-reactives who reported similar worries did not display this feature. The socially anxious adolescents who were high-reactive might profit from therapeutic regimens different from those given to socially anxious adolescents with a different biology.

The syndrome called autism, characterized by seriously impaired social behavior, consists of different types of children, and measures of brain might allow clinicians to detect the distinct types. For example, only some children diagnosed as autistic, not all, fail to scan the eyes in photographs of human faces, suggesting that they may have a dysfunction of the amygdala, because adults with lesions of the amygdala scan the mouth and nose but do not look at the eyes. This fact implies that there is a small group of autistics who have a very particular abnormality. The argument for gathering biological information is the same that explains why physicians order blood and urine tests for patients complaining of exactly the same symptoms, for example, headache, back pain, or fatigue. The body chemistry revealed in the laboratory tests permits the physician to arrive at a more accurate diagnosis and to prescribe more effective therapy.

The meaning of a single psychological feature is analogous to the meaning of a verb in a sentence. Many verbs can follow different nouns and be followed by different objects and in so doing assume distinct meanings, as in "The boulder struck the car," "The clock struck noon," and "The man struck the spectator." As in language, the more prevalent a psychological feature, the more ambiguous its meaning; the less common, the more restricted its meaning. An extensive vocabulary is more common among children raised in upper-middle-class homes than in children raised in families where no one has a high school diploma. Thus a large vocabulary in a child from a less-educated family is more likely to be due to a special biological talent, and biological measures might reveal that fact.

A second, equally important reason for gathering biological evidence is that it can lead to rejection of an incorrect explanation of a psychological phenomenon. The discovery that the brains of many autistic patients are abnormal has led to rejection of the popular explanation in 1950 that their mothers were cold and aloof. The popular interpretation of separation fear in eight-month-old infants thirty years ago was that the cry of distress when the mother left the child unexpectedly in an unfamiliar place meant that the child was anxious over the loss of its target of attachment. In plainer words, the infant missed its mother. But, as I noted in chapter 3, the more correct explanation is that brain maturation permits the eight-month-old to retrieve the representation of the mother's former presence and to compare it with the present moment while still being unable to understand the discrepancy between the two. The resulting uncertainty leads to the cry of separation.

Many more examples are possible. The important point is that the addition of biological to psychological evidence often illuminates the meaning of a feeling, thought, or action, even though the psychological phenomena will have to be described with a distinct vocabulary. When astronomers added the information on microwave radiation originating in the cosmos to the observations of stars and planets obtained with telescopes, they gained new insights into the formation and rate of expansion of the universe, even though the mathematics that describes the gravitational force between Earth and Sun is different from, and cannot be reduced to, the mathematics of the energies in the radiation.

The addition of a novel form of evidence is often followed by an expanded appreciation of a puzzling phenomenon. Telescopes, microscopes, accelerators, and magnetic scanners are obvious examples. Although psychologists interested in language, perception, and memory are using machinery that

permits measurement of brain activity, social scientists curious about personality and pathology have been more resistant to taking advantage of the engineering advances, and they continue to rely on the relatively restricted information that questionnaires and interviews provide. A limited set of evidence
usually leads to a restricted understanding of a phenomenon of interest.

The current field of personality illustrates this problem. People vary in
their social behavior with strangers and authority figures, caution in settings
of risk, ease of anger arousal to domination, vulnerability to guilt following a
violation, receptivity to new ideas, and a host of other qualities. We assume
that the stable traits on which people vary form clusters; that is, those who
are cautious when driving in snow and quiet with strangers are also likely to
take their family responsibilities seriously. The task is to discover the clusters.
Because some traits in a cluster have a partial foundation in biology, it should
be fruitful to gather biological evidence. At present, however, the popular list
of personality traits, including the notion of self-esteem, is based solely on
evidence from questionnaires. It is unlikely that this restricted source of information could reveal the most fruitful personality types. If scientists added half
a dozen biological measures to the questionnaire data they would discover
a larger and different set of personalities. Alfred North Whitehead wrote,
more than seventy-five years ago, that a new source of information resembles
travel to a foreign country because it generates a fresh perspective on existing
understanding.[17]

Sources of Justification

Because many events, real or imagined, have more than one explanation,
each person must decide which one is most trustworthy. When the events
are the stuff of daily life, most award maximal legitimacy to their personal
experiences. Adults who have enjoyed a gentle childhood are certain that
humans are basically kind; those who suffered harsh encounters are equally
convinced that human nature is inherently mean. When the events have no
referent in direct experience, many are willing to trust the declarations of
those who have, and they are receptive to accepting the explanations of authority, especially if they share similar values.

Most of the phenomena studied by university faculty, whether in the sciences or humanities, are not terribly relevant to the decisions citizens must make each day, even though these events, and their explanations, are inherently interesting and provide aesthetic pleasure. The age of the universe, size of the largest dinosaur, and origin of human language are three examples. Of greater relevance is the fact that scholars in various fields rely on different forms of evidence when justifying their assertions. Mathematicians trust justifications based on consistent proofs. Philosophers trust the logic and coherence of verbal arguments. Pascal's defense of the wisdom of believing in God—Pascal's wager—is one example. Historians trust the content of written texts, whether found on Mayan temples, in Cicero's writings, or in the records of a seventeenth-century English squire. Natural scientists reserve the judgment "correct" to observations, preferably those that can be repeated, free of the distortion imposed by human judgment. Social scientists have the same ambition, but unfortunately, many must rely on the semantic statements of informants or their subjective evaluations when they study humans. Many biologists regard such evidence as tainted, and an imperfect justification for a claim to truth.

Each group of scholars awards maximal legitimacy to the evidence it regards as defining its territory. As a result, a statement that refers to the same phenomenon or contains the same concept enjoys differential respect among historians, biologists, social scientists, and neuroscientists. A nice example is the claim that humans began to wear clothing about seventy-two thousand years ago. The evidence for this bold conclusion was not the discovery of the remnants of a loincloth but discovery of DNA differences between body and head lice. Body lice live in clothes, and their distinctive DNA pattern seems to have originated about seventy-two thousand years ago—hence the inference that humans put on clothes at this time.[18] Biologists probably have greater faith in this estimate than historians. A primary node of controversy in contemporary psychology centers on the type of evidence that justifies a conclusion. Should we trust the words a person uses, the behaviors he or she displays, or measures of the brain? The correlations among these three are usually quite low. One astrophysicist asked about the age of the universe answered that any estimate he might offer had little value, for it would change with time. What was of primary interest was the method used to arrive at any estimate.

Truth and Evidence

Because neuroscientists and psychologists rely on different evidence, they are differentially trusting of certain conclusions. Consider a woman in a quiet room who is told that she will hear a series of sounds, for example, "pa," and should strike a key the moment she hears the sound change in any way. A recorder is turned on, and she hears a "pa" sound twenty times, followed by a sound that is a very slight physical variant on the prior acoustic profile. Although the woman does not perceive any difference between this tone and the preceding twenty tones and therefore does not hit the key, her temporal lobe generates a distinct waveform at 250 milliseconds to the subtle change in sound.[19] If conscious perception of the deviant tone is the evidence, it is correct to conclude that the woman did not "perceive" any change in sound. If the brain's reaction is the evidence, it is correct to conclude that her brain "detected" the new stimulus. The evidence from the woman's consciousness and her neurons require different conclusions. Similarly, the concept "tendency to approach rewarding events" is usually measured with a questionnaire, but when biological variables are used to index a similar property, there is no relation between the two measures.[20] Thus the statement "Mary has a strong tendency to seek rewards" has one meaning if questionnaires are the source of evidence and a different meaning when biology supplies the information.

The adolescents in our temperamental study provided an especially nice example of the different meanings of psychological and biological measures of the same word. When the cortex is in a lower state of arousal, the electro-encephalogram (EEG) reveals more power in the range of frequencies called "alpha." But when the neurons become more active, there is greater power in the higher frequency range called "beta." Thus the ratio of beta over alpha values is assumed to correlate with the degree of cortical arousal. The fifteen-year-olds on whom we gathered EEG data, while they sat still with no task to perform, had several weeks earlier ranked twenty statements from most to least descriptive of their personality. The high-reactives who described themselves as serious, thinking excessively, minimally relaxed, and not easygoing had lower ratios (less cortical arousal) than the high-reactives who said that they were relaxed and easygoing. The conscious self-descriptions and the EEG evidence lead to different conclusions regarding an adolescent's "level of arousal."

Of course, we wish to know what is happening in the brain of a person who is planning a murder, a seduction, a performance, or the eating of a gourmet meal. The biological information could permit elimination of explanations that are not biologically reasonable, as facts can dilute the rational basis for believing a moral proposition. But that information cannot eliminate every possible account. Thus, as I noted in discussing morality, biological evidence can render a psychological explanation impossible, but it cannot be the seedbed for psychological descriptions and interpretations. The latter have an autonomous coherence and lawfulness. Roger Brown, a psychologist interested in language development, discovered that children learning English use the plural form—adding an "s" to a noun—before they use participles, like "going." That fact has a robust claim to truth, and it is unlikely that anyone will discover facts about the developing brain that would render that observation impossible.

Caveat Emptor

Citizens who trust the media to tell them truths about nature do not appreciate the importance of the empirical basis for a scientific claim. The public was told several years ago of Judith Rich Harris's declaration that parental behavior has little or no effect on children's development.[21] Harris's sources for this conclusion were reports in the existing psychological literature. Unfortunately, that body of research is woefully inadequate because psychologists have not studied in detail the relations between all the important actions and properties of parents and all the possible psychological outcomes in children. For example, there are no elegant studies of the effects of parents' practices or personal qualities or children's identification with each parent on the development of values and emotions. Harris's conclusion was as premature as Ptolemy's claim that the Sun orbited the Earth or Lord Kelvin's declaration that the Earth was too young to permit the gradual evolution Darwin posited. Although Harris's conclusion was based on insufficient evidence, citizens who trusted the media might have been confused by her counterintuitive statements. In this case, the public was right, and I suspect that no American mother stopped caring for or socializing her child after learning about Harris's declarations. Thomas Jefferson should be smiling for, as I noted earlier, he believed that if someone stated a moral dilemma to a farmer and a professor, the farmer would more often arrive at the correct solution.

A few years before Harris's book was published, many newspaper headlines reported that infants younger than one year could add small numbers.[22] The journalists did not tell readers that the evidence for this claim was a change of a few seconds in the duration of attention to a doll that was placed on a stage. Each infant first saw a single toy resting on a stage. An examiner then lowered a screen to occlude the stage, and a few seconds later the infant saw a hand place a second toy behind the screen. At this point the infant saw only the screen. The screen was then removed, and the infants saw either one toy or two toys resting on the stage. Most infants looked a little longer at the stage with one toy than at the stage with two toys. The psychologist concluded that the infants added their representation of the original toy to their representation of the second toy placed behind the screen and expected to see two toys. Because one toy was discrepant from their expectation, they looked longer at this event.

But the consensual meaning of "add" among teachers and mathematicians requires knowing a rule for combining cardinal numbers. That is, the meaning of "knows how to add" requires possession of the semantic concept of a cardinal number and the procedure involved in combining numbers. Because infants possess neither the concept of cardinal number nor the conceptual rule of addition, it is not obvious that infants can add. My colleague Susan Carey tells me that three-year-olds who can recite the sequence 1, 2, 3, 4, up to 10 have absolutely no idea what the words "three," "four," or "five" mean. All they know is that any one of these words refers to an array containing more than two objects. These words are like the child's recital of "do, re, mi, fa, sol, la, ti, do" with no appreciation that they name notes of a scale. The main point is that the word "add" has one meaning when it describes a pattern of looking in infants and a quite different meaning when ten-year-olds solve a page of addition problems. The word "bit" has different meanings in "The boy bit the apple," "The mouse bit the intruder," "The cowboy bit the dust," and "The president bit the bullet." The same conclusion applies to "add" in the statements "Ten-year-olds can add" and "Infants can add." I suspect that Einstein's understanding of time as he ate his lunch and thought of his late-afternoon appointment with Kurt Godel for their walk home from the Institute for Advanced Study was not the meaning he intended in his special theory of relativity. It is not the meaning my generation understood when it heard the romantic song that began, "Time waits for no one, it passes you by."

Many psychologists believe that each person's conception of their psychological and physical features, which is not completely conscious, is a critical determinant of behavior and mood. I suspect that most Americans assume that a self-concept and its close relative, self-esteem, are difficult to assess and that psychologists evaluating these qualities must be using an extensive set of sensitive procedures. They would be surprised to learn that many scientists who measure self-esteem use a ten-item questionnaire that can be filled out in less than ten minutes. One item, for example, asks individuals to rate how much they agree with the statement "On the whole I am satisfied with myself." It takes almost thirty minutes to evaluate the far simpler quality of acuity of hearing. It therefore strains credibility to argue that one of the most dynamic and intricate of human characteristics can be measured accurately in ten minutes. Hence, readers of newspaper headlines reporting that a scientist discovered that low self-esteem predicts poor school achievement or delinquency should understand that the conclusions have an extremely special and restricted meaning.

Many years ago I studied a group of ten-year-old boys who were described by both their teachers and their peers as unpopular and academically retarded. More than half of these boys denied these qualities when asked directly on a questionnaire. But more subtle procedures were able to detect the fact that these boys had a less desirable conception of themselves. Few individuals reveal their private understandings of themselves readily. Psychologists should be prepared to invest as much effort in measuring these beliefs as the person spent in establishing them. No biologist would announce that he or she has measured the health of a forest, the fitness of a species, or the age of a fossil in ten minutes. If the late Nobel laureate in physics Richard Feynman had learned of this ten-item questionnaire measure of self-esteem, he probably would have exclaimed, "Surely, you're joking."

Statements about the prevalence of mental illness around the world can also have different meanings. Psychiatrists and psychologists usually rely only on the verbal statements of thousands of adults who are asked to recall their emotions and moods since childhood. That information suggests that one of every three adults has suffered, or is suffering now, from anxiety or depression. This very high proportion implies a social fact we should worry about. Yet these technical papers fail to acknowledge that humans distort their past. It is common to worry over one's personal health and the health of relatives, job security, intimidation, robbery, social rejection, loss of a loved one, and task failure, and many who recall losing a job or a loved one ten years earlier guess that they must have been seriously depressed or anxious then, even if they were not. And many individuals forget a prolonged period of sadness, worry, or anger that occurred ten or twenty years earlier. I had forgotten the intense tension I experienced for about six years during the late 1970s. Had I been asked last year about my mood when I was fifty, I would have replied that I felt perfectly fine. I was reminded of this painful interval only after reading my diary entries for those years as I worked on this book. A friend told me he was absolutely certain that as a child he went to the roof of his apartment house and urinated over the edge. When he visited the place as an adult he was surprised to learn that his mischievous act was impossible because the roof had a brick wall several feet high on all sides.

Psychiatrists diagnose a patient as having an anxiety or mood disorder only if these emotions interfere seriously with daily functions. This practical criterion is not used for most diseases. A physician will classify a person as having leukemia or diabetes even if the features of the disease in an early phase have no effect on everyday responsibilities. One reason why anxiety and mood disorders are more frequent among the poor and less well educated is that their jobs usually require them to be at work eight hours each day. A lawyer, doctor, or architect who is feeling depressed can call in sick and not lose his or her job. If psychiatrists gathered biological information on every patient, in addition to the interview, they would have a more useful definition of mental illness and one independent of the ability to cope with life's demands.

The Fiction of Intelligence

The popular concept of intelligence provides a final example of the importance of the evidence used to justify a conclusion. Every society invents words to describe the variation in the talents that it needs or values. The claim that there is a single cognitive ability that is heritable, and as easily measured as height and weight, is usually attributed to Darwin's cousin Francis Galton, who in 1869 wrote *Hereditary Genius*.[23]

As with many psychological concepts, historical conditions made the concept of "range of intelligence" necessary. Most adults in rural, agricultural societies composed of many small villages can perform the tasks of planting, harvesting, cooking, cleaning, and caring for children that are needed for survival. The variation in the speed or agility with which these tasks are performed is not of great importance. Nineteenth-century industrialization, however, created a special set of conditions. Some tasks, especially reading, writing, and doing mathematics, required more skill than planting, cooking, and washing, and societies recognized that formal education was necessary to learn these talents. The attempts to teach these competences to children revealed variation in their abilities. That fact had to be named, and our society called it intelligence.

The tests of intelligence that Galton invented—excellent vision and hearing and the ability to react quickly to a stimulus—turned out to be poor predictors of success in school or in life. None of the talents Galton thought were signs of intelligence are evaluated on the modern intelligence test. Although that failure might have put an end to the concept, it could not die because our society needed a way to explain why some children learned to read and do arithmetic easily while others had difficulty. The French psychologist Alfred Binet recognized that tests of memory, learning, and reasoning resembled the talents needed for school success and therefore might be better predictors of which children found academic work difficult and which found it easy. He was right. The problems that he, with Theodore Simon, invented are the origins of the modern intelligence test. Binet and Simon, who did not compose either a biological or a psychological theory of intelligence, were satisfied with the practical fact that they had constructed a set of problems that could predict a child's educability. The brief summary sentence in the upper-right-hand corner of the first page of a newspaper does better than pure chance in predicting tomorrow's weather. Most of us do not care why that prediction is often accurate.

But the scientists who followed Binet and Simon did care about the meaning and origins of the scores on intelligence tests. Although some rejected the notion of a general intellectual ability and argued for the existence of many distinct cognitive skills, as Howard Gardner did in *Frames of Mind: The Theory of Multiple Intelligences* (1983), others were equally certain that a single general ability was a real, and not a spurious, natural phenomenon.[24] The latter view is unlikely to be correct. Adele Diamond, a former student of mine, discovered that the small number of children who inherit the disease called phenylketonuria possess a compromised function of the frontal lobes, but the cognitive skills dependent on other parts of the brain are spared.[25] These children have difficulty inhibiting an impulsive response or holding a great deal of information in working memory, but they have no difficulty discriminating among different shapes. That fact alone suggests that the psychological concept of "general intelligence" is inconsistent with the biology of the brain. Scientists can treat "intelligence" as a social construct with utility, because it accounts for some of the variation in academic performance. But they should reject the fruitfulness of this notion if they believe it is an inherited property of a brain. Almost one of every two white U.S. Army recruits who took the Binet intelligence test in 1919 had scores that indicated they were feebleminded.

The word "intelligence" occurs in sentences that ignore the age and background of the person; sometimes even the species is ignored. The following three statements can be found in many psychological textbooks:

1. Intelligence predicts academic grades in college.
2. Intelligence passes through developmental stages.
3. Intelligence increases with phylogeny.

The term "intelligence" has different meanings in those three sentences because each refers to distinct combinations of agents, contexts, and sources of evidence.

The fact that seven-year-old children in every community who learn to read, add, and compose stories easily obtain better grades in high school and college than first-graders who have difficulty mastering those skills invites more than one explanation. One is that families differ in their encouragement of academic mastery; children who have been encouraged consistently from the early years will be more highly motivated throughout their school career. This explanation would account for much of the data were it not for the fact that people who are closely related have more similar intelligence scores. That observation means that something more than family encouragement is at work, and that extra something is probably a property of the child's biology.

The exact nature of the biological contribution to scores on intelligence tests is real but, at the moment, a complete mystery. Most citizens who read that intelligence is inherited do not appreciate that the estimate of the heritability of intelligence depends on the degree to which children or adults with high and low IQ (intelligence quotient) scores are included in the sample studied. Heritability is always higher when a trait has a great deal of variability. If there is little variability, for example, in being born with five fingers, heritability is low. That fact means that the heritability of intelligence will be high when the sample has some individuals with very low scores and some with very high scores, and low if everyone has an IQ between 95 and 100. Further, if, as is likely, the biological bases for low IQ scores are different from the biological bases for high IQ scores, different genes will be responsible for very different scores on intelligence tests. We know this is true for children born with Down syndrome or the inability to hear.

I do not question the popular assertion that inherited profiles of brain physiology affect cognitive functioning. But I suggest that "intelligence" is not the best term to describe the complex products of those biological processes. Kurt Godel displayed exceptional intellectual talent when he demonstrated that some true statements about numbers could not be proven. But he showed severely compromised rational abilities when he insisted that people were poisoning his food and refused to eat anything unless his wife first sampled the food. The English language acknowledges the different forms cognitive talents can assume in its selective use of the words "smart," "well educated," "adaptive," "verbally fluent," "creative," "wise," and "clever."

The most frequently reported symptoms of human illnesses refer to complaints of fatigue and discomfort. Yet fatigue and discomfort can be caused by an extraordinarily diverse group of biological conditions, including viruses, bacteria, tumors, lesions, disturbed body chemistry, and ruptures of blood vessels. This diversity is the reason no biologist suggests that humans inherit a vulnerability to fatigue or discomfort but argue, instead, that humans inherit distinct genetic susceptibilities to specific illnesses. Humans do not inherit a "level of general health," even though a scientist could devise such a measure by evaluating the integrity of each organ system and computing an average value. This analogy is apt because, like IQ, vulnerability to most diseases is inversely correlated with social class. People with less than a high school education, who usually have lower incomes, are more vulnerable to most diseases than well-educated, financially more secure adults. But scientists do not conclude that the genes of poor people make them more vulnerable to most diseases; rather, they acknowledge the critical role of personal habits, diet, availability of medical care, and psychological mechanisms linked to a person's social class. The heritability of the scores on one set of questions in a popular intelligence test is close to zero among poor children. But the heritability of the scores to the same questions among children raised in middle-class homes is close to 0.5 because genetic factors assume greater prominence when environmental conditions—poor prenatal care, prematurity, fetal exposure to drugs, and frequent illness in childhood—are minimized. The same is true for conduct disorder.[26] Further, poor children perform less well on tests of language and control of impulsivity but perform as well as middle-class children on tests of short-term memory and perceptual abilities. Therefore their cognitive compromise is specific and not general; the latter is implied by the statement that many poor children have "low intelligence."

The relation between intelligence and the amount of "gray matter" (neuronal tissue) in different brain sites supports this claim. Scores on an intelligence test are primarily a function of language abilities, reasoning skill, and quality of working memory (regarded as primary talents) and secondarily a function of the desire to do well and to avoid mistakes. Children who reflect carefully on each answer before offering it obtain higher scores on tests than those who answer impulsively, even though advocates of the concept of intelligence regard this trait as secondary to the primary talents. It will be disconcerting to these advocates to learn that the variation in the IQ scores of a group of adolescents was related to differences in the amount of gray matter in the areas that mediate a reflective approach and unrelated to gray-matter volumes in the areas mediating language ability, reasoning, and working memory.[27]

The arbitrariness of IQ scores can be appreciated by imagining that a mysterious force reduced the IQ of everyone in the world by ten points. The estimates of heritability and the correlations between IQ scores and academic grades would remain exactly as they were before the strange force arrived. Such an outcome would be impossible for any other natural phenomenon. If human resistance to disease were changed by reducing everyone's white cell count by 10 percent, serious health consequences would follow. I am certain that inherited biological factors affecting brain physiology contribute to the more similar scores of identical, compared with fraternal, twins on tests of intelligence. The nub of the disagreement is over the inference to be drawn from that fact. This is not a trivial issue. Ptolemy and Kepler knew similar facts about the stars and planets, but Ptolemy decided that the Sun revolved around the Earth, whereas Kepler concluded that the Earth moved.

Despite the legitimate critiques of the controversial book *The Bell Curve: Intelligence and Class Structure in American Life* (1994), most critics found fault with the authors' conclusions but not with their claim that the concept of intelligence was useful.[28] Richard Herrnstein, one of the authors of *The Bell Curve* and a former colleague in the Harvard psychology department, had written a highly provocative essay in a 1970 issue of the *Atlantic Monthly*. Herrnstein argued for the strong heritability of IQ scores and resurrected the eugenicists' worry, popular during the first decade of the twentieth century, that because the poor with lower IQ scores were having more children than the middle class, the difference in fecundity implied that the quality of the American mind was deteriorating.

This essay surprised me for several reasons. First, I knew that Herrnstein had devoted his career to testing Skinner's ideas with animals, and I guessed he had never administered an intelligence test. I had given many intelligence tests as part of my work at the Clifford Beers Clinic in New Haven and appreciated the contextual factors that can influence a score. For example, one question on a popular IQ test asks, "What should you do to make water boil?"

African-American children living in poor neighborhoods in Baltimore do not hear the phrase "should you do" in speech at home; hence, they do not understand the question and answer incorrectly. But they do answer correctly if the examiner rephrases the question to "How do you get water to boil?" I called Herrnstein and asked if I could chat with him about his article. I relayed my criticisms politely, but he defended the essay, and no minds were changed.

The law school, having heard of our disagreement, arranged for a public debate on this issue in the winter of 1971. Thirty-five years later, in December 2004, Steven Pinker and Louis Menand held a public debate at Harvard on the degree of determinism contained in the human genome. The dividing issue has not changed, but the controversy now went far beyond intelligence to include all human properties. This tension will not go away, even though everyone acknowledges that psychological characteristics emerge from the sculpting by society of the propensities biology provides.

In an essay written for the *Saturday Review of Literature*, I argued that every society selects some qualities, usually those possessed by a small proportion of the community, as signs of an inner property the community values because the property contributes to economic prosperity, safety, stability, or the muting of uncertainty. Medieval Europeans and colonial Puritans chose piety, the Chinese selected filial loyalty, and the Spartans favored courage. Fewer societies chose the cognitive talents of reasoning, memory, and verbal skills until industrialization arrived in Europe and North America.

Americans argue over whether children are born with different intellectual capacities or attain them through family experiences and good schooling. These opposing arguments are identical in substance to the interpretations of differences in the capacity for religiosity held by Muslims in Morocco and Indonesia. The Moroccans believe that some children are born with a greater capacity for an intense religious experience. The Javanese, by contrast, believe that greater religiosity is attained through long periods of meditation. And these two societies, like our own, discover the few in their communities who fit the description of the pure and permit them special ascent. We, like the Greeks, Moroccans, and medieval Christians, must celebrate some feature that can function as a basis for the awarding of power and privilege. Intelligence is an excellent candidate, for it implies alertness, language sophistication, and the ease with which the skills and ideas needed in a technical society are learned. Moreover, intelligence is a characteristic of a person that, like fingerprints, is not associated with an individual's religion, region, or eating habits. Intelligence is America's version of saintliness, religiosity, courage, or moral purity, and it works. It works so well that when social scientists construct an intervention project, such as Head Start, they usually evaluate its benevolent effects by giving the children an intelligence test. That practice announces the belief that a child's intelligence is the most essential dimension to be changed. If an intervention did not alter that property, it is presumed that it was probably not worthwhile.

Legitimate power is held unequally in every society. Each community must invent a rational strategy that appears just in order to explain why only some are entitled to the prize. But we should be honest about the basis for the allocation of power and rid ourselves of the delusion that those who temporarily occupy high positions have the biologically best brains. Sir Robert Filmer made this argument in 1680 to rationalize the right of kings to govern. John Locke's political philosophy was shaped by a critique of Filmer's thesis. The suggestion that senators, bankers, generals, and CEOs have biologically "better" brains than a random sample of the population fits neither the mood of objectivity hammered out during the past three hundred years of modern scientific research nor the historical fact that the use of power for benevolent or malevolent ends is usually independent of a person's vocabulary, mathematical skill, or analogical ability. It is even possible to defend the heretical suggestion that, for many contemporary occupations, but not all, scores on tests of intelligence should not be the primary attribute on which a candidate is screened. Many Americans would prefer physicians who were more caring, even if that meant that they were of slightly lower intelligence. Of course, a person's brain affects his or her psychological functioning. But we should not exploit that hard-won fact to rationalize the distribution of secular power, which is the product of political and sociological events. Defense of such a strategy exploits fair science for dark purposes.

A Plea for Specificity

One afternoon about ten years ago, I met a retired Swiss pediatrician with a rich background in brain development who wished to learn about the growth of psychological competences. The mutuality of our interests and our complementary backgrounds were apparent, and Norbert Hershkowitz and I spent more than six years surveying what scientists had learned about brain maturation in humans and other primates and determining which of those facts might explain the times of emergence of the human psychological properties that mature over the first decade of life. We were especially interested in working memory, fear of the unfamiliar, a moral sense, forms of consciousness, and integration of past with present. The product of our collaboration appeared in the spring of 2005 in *A Young Mind in a Growing Brain*.

One of the important lessons gleaned from the many hundreds of technical papers was the stark contrast between the extraordinary specificity of brain function and the vague generality of psychological concepts. Almost every time one biologist suggests a relation between two aspects of brain function, or between a brain profile and a psychological outcome, another soon discovers that that the claim was too general.

The specificity frustrates those hungry for broad conclusions that might capture newspaper headlines. For example, related strains of mice in which a particular gene had been eliminated were tested on two similar procedures believed to reflect a state of fear. One was avoidance of the brightly lit areas in a black circular platform with open and closed quadrants. A mouse is placed initially in a dark, closed quadrant, and scientists measure the total time spent in any of the lit, open quadrants. Mice prefer to stay in the dark, closed quadrants; therefore, an animal that spends little time in the open quadrants is presumed to be more fearful. A second index of fear is failure to explore an unfamiliar area; animals who explore less are presumed to be more fearful. Despite the apparent similarity in the behaviors in the two situations, there was absolutely no relation between these two measures of fear.[29] Neuroscientists were also surprised to learn that rats trained to become immobile (called freezing) to a conditioned stimulus that had been paired with a brief electric shock to their left eyelid learned this reaction when the amygdala on the right side of the brain was intact but did not learn to freeze when a drug inactivated the right amygdala. (When the shock was delivered to the right eyelid, the rat needed an intact amygdala on the opposite or left side.) Thus, even the statement "Animals require an intact amygdala to learn a conditioned freezing reaction" is too general.[30]

Owls provide a final, exquisite illustration of specificity. The average diameter of the black spots on the underside feathers of a female owl is positively related to the competence of the immune system of her offspring, but surprisingly, the number of black spots is not.[31] These facts, and many others, force biologists to be "splitters" when they explain their evidence.

Contemporary psychologists and psychiatrists, by contrast, tend to be "lumpers," preferring abstract constructs to highly constrained ones. Compare the specificity of the diameter, but not the number, of the melanin spots on the owls with unspecified psychological terms like "arousal," "self-esteem," "intelligence," "secure attachment," and "anxiety." Psychologists and psychiatrists are fond of the word "stress," even though the biological reactions following a threat to the body are different from those evoked by worrying over an examination or a job interview.[32] The reaction of the cardiovascular system to a difficult cognitive task, as well as the pain that follows immersion of the hand into ice-cold water, are muted if someone is tested with his or her pet dog or cat present in the same room compared with being alone.[33] The ambiguity of the term "stress" is revealed by the fact that many African-American women live with extreme economic hardship, the responsibility of being the single head of a family, and the racism that remains in America. Yet suicide rates in 1999–2000 for this group were lower than the rates for black males as well as for white males and females. Only 1 percent of all suicides during that period were committed by African-American women. By contrast, white males, who confront less objective social stress, have the highest suicide rate.[34]

The age when young children solve a cognitive problem is often a function of tiny details in the testing procedure. Preschool children tested in a small room (four by six feet) without any windows fail to use a landmark (in one case it was a single blue wall) to help them determine where an adult had hidden an object. But children of the same age did use the blue wall as a landmark if tested in a larger room (eight by twelve feet). Simply changing the size of the room led to a different conclusion.[35] A detail as seemingly innocuous as restraining a cat's head, compared with leaving the cat free to move, leads to an underestimate of the animal's ability to locate the source of a brief sound.[36]

A more accurate understanding of the relation between brain and mind will require acceptance of the principle that the relation is always dependent on the context in which someone is acting. Richard Shweder, an anthropologist at the University of Chicago who spoke at the Harvard conference on morality, offered a lovely example of the importance of context. Shweder and his wife, who were living temporarily in the town of Orissa, India, where Shweder was doing fieldwork, were entertaining three guests one evening. Because the guests had different statuses in the community, Shweder had to guarantee that the food served was acceptable to all of them. So he went to the local temple to acquire food others had placed there earlier in the day because anyone can eat a food once a god has removed its essence. After the guests departed, some rice remained, and Shweder's wife diced chicken into a bowl and served it to her husband. Surprisingly, Shweder reported feeling disgust and an inability to eat the food. The moral standard of the temple town in which he was working had become part of his code. But his reaction of disgust could occur only in Orissa. Shweder would have had no problem eating diced chicken in a bowl of rice had he been in his dining room in Chicago.

Insistence on the utility of broad states like fear, arousal, or consciousness is aesthetic, makes experimentation easier, and permits scientists to be indifferent to the species and methods used in their research. It is not a coincidence that beauty and convenience are the primary criteria mathematicians use to decide which equations deserve celebration. The mathematical physicist Paul Dirac believed that the beauty of a mathematical solution should always take precedence over correspondence with evidence when the two are inconsistent. However, the natural phenomena that human minds try to understand existed long before we evolved with an appreciation of beauty and a desire for convenience. Most of the current psychological concepts proposed to explain behavior, belief, and emotion are too pretty to be true. They remain appealing because they satisfy a desire for simple, parsimonious explanations. Both behaviorism and psychoanalysis owe their initial popularity to the hope that a small number of highly abstract psychological concepts could explain a large number of human properties. Both theories lost their favored status when they failed to predict or to explain most of the phenomena of interest.

Kenneth Spence, a professor at the University of Iowa (the Byzantium to

Yale's Vatican in the 1950s), suggested that people's scores on a questionnaire that asked them about their anxious feelings was a sensitive index of their level of arousal (or drive level) and therefore a good predictor of the ease of learning a conditioned response. In Spence's lab, the measure of learning was the ease of acquiring a conditioned eye blink. A high score on a similar scale today is regarded as a sensitive index of anxiety and a predictor of the likelihood of developing symptoms, such as extreme shyness with strangers or panic attacks. The words have changed, but the ingenuous hope that contextually unspecified concepts, such as drive, arousal, and anxiety, would be theoretically useful has not fared well under the harsh light of evidence.

The problem can be stated succinctly. Scientists make up words intended to explain a class of phenomena; for example, they invented the term "anxiety" to explain why some people who avoid social gatherings report feeling uncomfortable when they meet strangers. The next move is crucial. Investigators construct a laboratory procedure they believe will generate evidence that reveals the hidden nature of the phenomenon and represents a defining property of the precious explanatory word. Some psychologists wishing to measure level of anxiety in those who avoid crowds record the magnitude of the eye blink reflex to a loud sound while the person is looking at pictures of threatening scenes because both the avoidance of crowds and abnormally large eye blinks are presumed to be consequences of an excitable amygdala. And it is believed that an excitable amygdala creates a state of anxiety. But if "shame" were a better word to explain the avoidance of strangers, the rationale for measuring eye blinks would be weakened because there is less reason to believe that an excitable amygdala is a defining feature of shame. This suggestion is not totally hypothetical. Japanese adults who avoid strangers say that they wish to avoid the embarrassment that accompanies interactions that make the other person uncomfortable. And Latin American psychiatrists use the term *susto* to describe the feeling of someone who, frightened by an unexpected encounter with a stranger, concludes that he or she has lost some of his or her vital spirit. English has no obvious synonym for *susto* because concern with having violated a personal standard is, along with the surprise of the encounter, a critical feature of this concept. Thus, selecting the best explanatory word is critical. If the scientist happens to pick the wrong concept, much effort will be wasted. Spence's choice of "level of arousal" proved to be unproductive. Natural scientists chose useful words when they selected "energy" and "electron" but erred when they invented "phlogiston" and "ether." Early-twentieth-century biologists, who did not yet know the chemical structure of DNA, used the word "mutation" to describe a change in a hypothetical gene. Contemporary scientists, who understand the relation between base pairs and amino acids, prefer the term "substitution," which has gentler connotations. I suspect that many of the popular words used by psychologists and psychiatrists will not prove to be fruitful because, like the terms "beauty," "truth," and "good," they fail to specify the contexts in which the concepts are applicable.

Two Kinds of Scientists

Most scientists balance an interest in a particular aspect of nature with the desire to discover an irrefutable fact, but they vary in the relative attractiveness of each of these prizes. I intend no pejorative evaluation of the two kinds of scientists to be described. One type, found more often among physicists, chemists, and biologists, wants facts that are maximally certain because discovery of a reliable relation, or the elegant proof of a hypothesis, releases a feeling of intellectual potency. The domain of discovery is often less important than the victory the mind seized. If Rosalind Franklin had been prevented from studying the crystal structure of DNA, she would have found another problem and probably would have made an equally significant discovery. If David Hubel were unable to record activity in the brains of cats and monkeys, he, too, would have found another domain in which to exploit his extraordinary talents. The trophy for these scientists, like hunters who finally find and shoot the deer they were tracking all day, is an unambiguous fact. The successful exploitation of talent, technical skill, and perseverance that announces to self and others a mind of exceptional brilliance permits a unique pleasure. Most physicists, chemists, and molecular biologists believe that the best way to attain this pleasure is to work only on clearly stated problems that have definite answers. If the question is fuzzy, avoid it. If Darwin had access to this wisdom, he certainly would not have joined the Beagle voyage. Not only did he not have a well-stated question, but it is not clear what problem he thought he would solve when he set sail.

The second type, more common among social scientists, is characterized by a curiosity directed at a particular aspect of nature. These discoveries also require talent, but the opportunities for pleasure are restricted to domains with special symbolic significance for the investigator. I suspect that if Alexander Thomas and Stella Chess could not have probed the variation in human personality, they would not have investigated fear in rats or monkeys. The illumination of a particular class of question, even if not crisply stated, is the incentive among these scholars who seek a glimpse of any rare, or unusually beautiful, butterfly, are open to surprises, and accept the impermanence of their observations. I confess to being a butterfly chaser. If I had been told in 1950 that I would not be allowed to study the development of children, I probably would have taken my uncle's advice and attended law school. I wanted to know why I felt uneasy, why some humans hated with intensity, why my younger brother was so different from me, and why men and women seemed to march to different pipers. I remember the look of disappointment on Frank Beach's face when I told him, in my final year at Yale, that I was looking for a faculty position in child psychology because of my deeper interest in human development than in animal sexual behavior.

Tolerance for Ambiguity

Most scholars can be placed on a continuum that reflects their degree of comfort, or discomfort, with ambiguity. Howard Kendler, an important behaviorist during my graduate years, confessed in a memoir that he was bothered by the ambiguity in the papers of the social psychologist Kurt Lewin when he was a student at the University of Iowa in the 1940s.[37] The apparent certainty that Kenneth Spence's approach promised was more appealing. When Kendler reported this personal bias to Abraham Maslow, his undergraduate professor, Maslow noted that the preference for certainty fit the young man's personality. Kendler interpreted Maslow's remark as a compliment. Variation in the tolerance for ambiguity separates hunters from butterfly chasers. At one end are historians and paleontologists; to their right are social scientists; in the middle are biologists; and at the opposite end are chemists, physicists, and mathematicians who feel uneasy with conclusions that begin with words like "maybe" or "perhaps." Einstein, a prototypic hunter, was bothered by the lack of determinism in quantum mechanics. My suggestion that biological evidence considered alone cannot explain all behaviors and emotions does not appeal to hunters.

Sadly, the hunters with rifles are driving the children chasing butterflies from the forest, even though rifles are not a very good way to catch butterflies. A James Thurber story described a woman who wrote to a pet counselor that her husband had brought home a dog that after only a week had chased the family into a small bedroom they were now afraid of leaving. The woman enclosed a photo of the dog and asked for advice. The pet counselor replied, "Your husband brought home a bear. Bears belong in zoos. Cordially, The Pet Counselor."

It is not clear why ambiguity is anathema to most natural scientists. This attitude may be traceable, in part, to the Greek decision to make elemental structures, Plato's forms or Democritus's atoms, the building blocks of nature rather than sources of energy, as the Chinese did. One possibility is that because agricultural activity in small hamlets was the primary activity in ancient Chinese society, the unpredictability of drought, flood, and storms, which affected their crops, made nature the central source of uncertainty. And wind and rain seemed to arise from changes in the balance of energy rather than from particular things. If uncertainty is a seminal characteristic of nature, ambiguity is less anomalous—it is the way things should be.

For the Greeks, who enjoyed a more benign environment, disruption of social harmony within the polis was the important source of uncertainty. Harmony requires each citizen to adhere strictly to the ethical rules of the society. There can be no ambiguity over whether an individual should be honest, brave, and loyal. Each person must follow certain moral laws as each atom follows natural laws.

Of course, not all natural scientists are hunters troubled by ambiguity. Bohr invented the concept of complementarity to explain why a photon could behave as a wave or a particle depending on the experimental setting. Scientists who had heard Bohr lecture, including Einstein, felt that he always seemed unsure of what he was saying. Bertrand Russell and Alfred North Whitehead represent the classic odd couple. In a passage from *Portraits from Memory*, Russell wrote, "It was Whitehead who was the serpent in this paradise of Mediterranean clarity. He said to me once: 'You think the world is what it looks like in fine weather at noon day; I think it is what it seems like in the early morning when one first wakes from deep sleep.' I thought his remark horrid, but could not see how to prove that my bias was any better than his. At last he showed me how to apply the technique of mathematical logic to his vague and higgledy-piggledy world, and dress it up in Sunday clothes that the mathematician could view without being shocked. This technique, which I learnt from him delighted me, and I no longer demanded that the naked truth should be as good as the truth in its mathematical Sunday best."[38]

There is a fable of a king who asked his wisest advisers to reduce to one word all the knowledge in the many volumes in the palace library. After years of toil the scholars brought the king a piece of paper on which was written the single word "maybe."

Respect or Celebrity

The hunters and butterfly chasers also vary in the relative salience of two other prizes colleagues award for creative scientific work. One goal is gaining a position of greater respect among the colleagues of one's discipline. François Jacob described Martin Pollock and Jacques Monod arguing a theoretical point at the Pasteur Institute in Paris as "two trained roosters beak to beak vying with humor and sarcasm. Not because of nationalism, but through a will to power, a desire for intellectual domination."[39] Two Nobel laureate chemists have been feuding recently over the priority of an idea that surfaced more than forty years ago because the demonstration of originality is a requisite for the gift of peer respect.

The knowledge that colleagues will defer to those who have demonstrated unusual levels of scientific brilliance allows these privileged individuals to assume that they will dominate interactions with those who occupy positions lower on the ladder of respect. Put plainly, the accomplished investigator imagines that colleagues will be reluctant to challenge his or her authority. This pleasure might share features with an alpha male chimpanzee that anticipates that other males will retreat when he approaches. A New Yorker cartoon in December 2004 illustrated a very large man behind a desk talking to a very small one standing before the desk. The caption reads, "Just as your family means a lot to you, Henderson, power means a lot to me." Citizens of

Sumatra use the word *malu* to describe how one feels when in the presence of a person who is unusually talented, powerful, or rich.

Sadly, some scientists reach their eighth decade still unsatisfied with the level of status or respect they have attained. I recall a retirement dinner to honor an eminent scientist attended by hundreds of former students and colleagues. After an hour of praise the master of ceremonies called on the honorand. To my surprise, his first words were not "Thank you," but "I almost left this university twenty-five years ago." Imagine a wife or husband on their fiftieth anniversary telling the many guests at a party celebrating their long marriage, "I almost divorced my husband/wife twenty-five years ago."

A second prize for a productive scientific career is admiration from the larger community of strangers, many of whom are not scientists. The knowledge that many thousands of strangers are aware of self's scientific achievements, even if they do not understand them, provides a somewhat different pleasure that is closer to a child's feeling when a parent or teacher praises and, in so doing, announces that he or she values the child. These investigators imagine that many in the society, colleagues as well as strangers, will admire them. The pleasure accompanying the belief that self is respected by members of one's professional group is subtly different from the pleasure of imagining self as admired by people one will never meet. Eugène Delacroix described the feeling that accompanies "living in the minds of others" as intoxicating.[40] Alan Lightman, who teaches both physics and creative writing, confessed that he prefers writing to work in a physics laboratory because of its promise of greater celebrity.[41] Most scientists want both respect and celebrity but are motivated more strongly by the first prize. A small number, who must have both, cannot relinquish either delight. Alfred Kinsey and John Watson are two examples.

Human groups are characterized by a status hierarchy in which those with less status envy those with more and the latter are aware of the envy and resentment of the former. Many communities invent ways to minimize variation in status, wealth, and property to reduce the tension. Australians like the phrase "Lop off the tall poppies." The scientists in each discipline understand that celebrity provokes envy; hence, knowing that one might be resented by peers curbs the ambitions of those who desire community admiration. The extraordinary increase in the number of scientists over the past fifty years has weakened the force of this restraint. Most scientists will never meet more than 10 percent of those working in their discipline. The greater the diversity, the weaker the restraint on seeking celebrity because fewer scientists worry excessively about the opinions of all colleagues in their discipline. Darwin, by contrast, was aware that all naturalists, and many in the educated public, would judge his ideas, and his concern with their reactions led him to delay completion of On the Origin of Species.

There has been an extraordinary expansion of science over the past century and a half. There were twenty-seven Harvard faculty members in 1869; by 1910 the faculty exceeded seven hundred. When the number of scientists in the world was small, many educated citizens felt an obligation to be aware of the dominant issues being debated. Thomas Jefferson and John Adams exchanged letters on the relation between mind and brain that cited the writings of leading philosophers and scientists. Adams was skeptical of a materialist interpretation of mind, whereas Jefferson, who admired science, thought that natural science would illuminate thought and morality.[42] I cannot imagine any pair of twentieth-century American presidents exchanging opinions on this theme.

The fact that more scientists are alive today than have ever lived has sharpened the differences between hunters and butterfly chasers. Before the establishment of graduate programs in science (the first one was at the Johns Hopkins University in the 1870s), far fewer twenty-year-olds chose science as a life vocation, and many who did were motivated by strong passions. The biographies of Galileo, Kepler, Newton, Pasteur, Darwin, Wallace, and Krebs, none of whom had postdoctoral fellows and million-dollar grants, reveal their enormous ambitions. Their passion for research seemed to be driven by desires they could not deny. Many Europeans who pursued science before the end of the nineteenth century were independently wealthy and regarded by the community as gentlemen — Darwin is a classic example.

Science has become a vocation, not just a calling, and many twenty-one-year-olds choose science because it is a secure, satisfying job with a clear set of rules for advancing to the next rung on the academic ladder and acquiring the prizes that define success. The first task for investigators in the formative phase of their career is to obtain a grant, from the government or a private philanthropy, to pay research assistants, graduate students, and bring overhead money to the university. I know many scientists who seem prouder of the amount of grant money they have garnered than the facts they have discovered. When obtaining a grant becomes the primary goal, investigators are forced to tailor their research to fit the biases of the anonymous judges who award the funds. These conditions lead, inevitably, to caution and to research proposals that are maximally immune from peer criticism. The primary purpose of scientific research is to discover some relation in nature with theoretical or practical importance. The current structure of science forces many to subordinate these goals to the procurement of research funds. A marriage motivated by love for another is quite different from a marriage promising wealth.

The increase in the number of subspecialties, and in the number of investigators in each, has led to a fragmentation of science in which each local interest group is the source of the rules declaring which practices and forms of evidence are, and which are not, acceptable. Neither Darwin nor Wallace would have received government support today because neither would have presented a crisply stated hypothesis whose validity could be tested. When scientists seeking funds must please a dozen colleagues who are simultaneously strangers and competitors, rather than patrons who identify with their protégés, they are tempted to rein in their imagination and accommodate to constraints that most scientists born before 1900 found it easier to ignore. The current system is necessary because there are too many scientists for the resources available. To honor an egalitarian ethic that treats all applicants equally, the evaluators must establish rational criteria, especially a well-stated hypothesis, preliminary work, and a clear description of the statistical analyses to be performed, so that those awarding the funds can feel assured that their decisions were fair. The problem is that the consistent application of these "fair" criteria leads to the rejection of much research that would have made an original contribution.

Every rationale for research support has advantages and disadvantages. A system that seems fair because all applicants know the rules for writing applications, and assume they have an opportunity for success, is a salient imperative in our society. Unfortunately, it competes with the desire to make an original discovery. But we may have to live with the current conditions for awhile. History, always the sculptor of social change, altered the structure of nineteenth-century science by increasing the number of investigators, placing them in large, bureaucratic institutions, forcing them to compete with one another for money, status, and celebrity, and making it necessary to scream rather than whisper when one was lucky enough to uncover one of nature's secrets. Compare the repeated caveats in Darwin's masterful argument for evolution with many contemporary books written for the public on the power of genes, the influence of parents, or the causes of crime. The current arrangements for the support of science, less than a hundred years old, force many investigators to be more risk averse than they would like or should be. A tourist strolling in a section of a city where a large building was being constructed asked three masons what they were doing. The first replied, "I'm laying bricks." The second said, "I'm building a wall." The third answered, "I'm building a cathedral." I wish the current structure of the sciences permitted more investigators to build cathedrals.

Summing Up

A career in science resembles the psychological development of a person. A small number of early assumptions are preserved for a lifetime, a larger number are rejected, and, if chance is kind, some new ideas are added to the network that guides the next question. I have always believed that the unexpected and the unfamiliar, whether sensations, thoughts, or feelings, are the central provocateurs of activity in brain and mind. This premise explains why the male rats in my thesis learned to make the correct turn in the maze, even though their only reward was a few moments of genital rubbing. It also explains why dopamine-producing neurons in the rat brain become active when a conditioned stimulus signals that a larger-than-expected amount of liquid is about to be delivered. The significance of novelty also explains why the human amygdala is activated by unfamiliar faces with neutral expressions as well as by faces with fearful expressions and sexual scenes.[43] Both the fearful faces and the erotic pictures are unexpected by adult volunteers lying in a scanner who did not anticipate that the friendly scientist would show them these unusual pictures.

I also remain convinced that the child's symbolic interpretations of experience, not the events a camera would record, control the most important judgments about self and other. The early research on the young child's symbolic constructions of gender was motivated by that notion. Finally, the human preoccupation with "good" and "bad," affirmed by our study of the second year, is a third assumption that has preserved its usefulness over many years.

But observations since 1950 permitted me to reject three flawed premises that had burdened earlier reflections. I was convinced as a graduate student that biology was irrelevant, family experiences during the opening years had permanent formative power, and the semantic concepts in journals and conversations referred to real things in the world. Yes, I confess, with embarrassment, that I believed the concepts "ego," "anxiety," and "learn" fit nature like a glove.

These simple notions have been replaced with six more recent assumptions that seem to be in closer correspondence with nature's plans. Temperamental biases are more potent than I had imagined, the lawful maturation of brain constrains the age when the universal properties of our species appear, the events of the opening years do not set the clay of personality firm, the knowledge contained in perceptual structures is very different from the knowledge stored in words and sentences, the meaning and truth value of every scientific concept cannot be separated from the evidence on which the concept is based, and, last, the economy, social structure, and beliefs of a historical era, like the fence restraining a baboon troop at a zoo, limit each person's understanding of the world to a small space in which each day is lived.

Psychology has made extraordinary progress since my graduate years but has still not achieved consensus on its fundamental entities and their functions.[44] Whatever these concepts turn out to be, their names will not be the same as the terms used to describe the underlying brain processes that were necessary for their emergence. Because the context in which an agent acts affects the entities and functions selected from a large number of possibilities, scientists must reject context-free concepts. They must write and speak in full sentences rather than continue to apply the same telegraphic utterances—learn, remember, categorize, stressed, regulate, attached—to mice, monkeys, and humans. The continued resistance to this restriction on the use of language generated a sadness that might have been the basis for a dream on a summer night in 1984: I was in Philadelphia with a boyhood friend who had attended the University of Pennsylvania and later became a lawyer. We had extra time and I decided to buy a car that I needed. I went to a Ford dealer and bought a used car that, despite its many poorly repaired dents, was attractive. The dealer failed to ask me for a check, and my friend and I went off with the car without paying for it. We parked the car in a hotel garage, convinced we would not be found. To my surprise, the dealer called the next day to say that he was coming to the hotel to be paid, and I did not understand how he located us at the hotel. When the dealer arrived and I paid him, a fish appeared on his face.

One interpretation felt correct moments after awakening. The used car with dents symbolized my perception of psychology's difficulty in producing the robust, significant findings characteristic of the natural sciences. I had chosen psychology out of affection for its aims. I wanted to understand the human mind in order to alleviate the ills of society but hoped that its frailties might not be discovered. The reason for the fish on the dealer's face is that Pisces is my astrological sign.

I do not enjoy the role of critic. The moral arrogance of those who sermonize renders this posture low on my list of attractive activities. So let's turn the penny over to see the shinier side of psychological efforts during the past fifty years. The behaviorists contributed to three nontrivial advances. First, they discovered important principles of conditioning that Pavlov did not anticipate. The significance of the conditioning stimulus, especially its unexpectedness, the schedule of delivery of rewards, and the special biological properties of each species were fresh facts that now have a secure place in contemporary work. They permitted Eric Kandel to elucidate the chemistry of conditioned gill withdrawal in the sea snail, for which he earned a Nobel Prize, facilitated the invention of therapeutic strategies that have benefited patients, and allowed pharmacologists to evaluate the effectiveness of drugs designed to alleviate psychiatric symptoms.

The generation of scientists who initiated the cognitive revolution unpackaged the boxes labeled "perception," "memory," and "inference" to reveal a variety far richer than midcentury investigators would have predicted. Although the list of discoveries is too long to detail, four warrant mention. We now appreciate that the separate features of a sensory event are initially processed in different places in the brain and are integrated milliseconds later in other sites. These observations motivate new questions, especially how that integration occurs, what the differential contributions of the right and left hemispheres are, and why the location and the features of an object initially activate different circuits. The brain treats the questions "Where is it?" and "What is it?" as different inquiries. The first students of perception concentrated on the intensity of a stimulus rather than its pattern of features and place in the environment. Few, if any, nineteenth-century psychologists would have guessed that the timbre and rhythm of a spoken sentence undergo a more elaborate analysis in the right hemisphere while the sentence's meaning is more thoroughly massaged by the left. If Robert Fantz had known in 1960 that infants pay more attention to the elements in the upper rather than the lower half of the visual field, he would have designed different experiments.

The probing of inference, which had been ignored because laboratory rats showed little evidence of this competence, has illuminated its role in moral development, economic decisions, and the syndrome of autism. The elegant studies that parsed "memory" into its components (short term, working, long term, procedural, declarative, and implicit) deserve high praise. No contemporary psychologist would assume, as Hermann Ebbinghaus did in 1913, that memorizing lists of nonsense syllables would yield the essential principles of the variety in human memory. These discoveries have permitted clinicians to discriminate among varied types of senile memory failures and between these patients and a football player who suffered a concussion.

The analysis of what had been broad domains into many separable components is the critical feature in the extraordinary progress psychology has enjoyed over a short slice of history. Experimental proof of the ancient intuition that the human mind uses at least three tools—schemata, semantic networks, and motor programs—to carry out its responsibilities is a fourth mark of progress that requires scientists to specify "what" is understood, together with the method used for that inference, when they write that an animal, infant, or college student "knows" something about the world. But the analysis will remain incomplete until it includes the context in which a psychological process proceeds. If the size of the testing room determines whether a young child will or will not use a single blue wall to find the location of a hidden toy and the presence of a pet dog influences the bodily reaction to a challenge, then we have far to go before we sleep. Our history is still in a formative phase.

The history of each scientific discipline is marked by a change in the most urgent questions asked. These changes can be the result of a new technology, a novel theory, or the discarding of an older question because of damaging evidence. The decision to study consciousness during psychology's first stage was based on its historical link to philosophy rather than theory or technology. Pavlov's discovery of the conditioned reflex and a ready supply of rats made the question "What are the mechanisms of learning?" a dominant query. The passion behind this work was sustained by the political need to refute the eugenicists, who were demanding sterilization of certain European immigrants, and to support those advocating benevolent family experiences and universal education. Many of the important discoveries made during the fifty-year reign of behaviorism are now established parts of contemporary psychology. But because conditioning could not explain human thought and emotion, it was inevitable that a competitor would appear. Chomsky's ideas on language, Piaget's research on children's reasoning, and the availability of computers that permitted measurement of very fast response times and reliable presentation of stimuli catapulted a family of new questions into prominence. Among the more important were: How do humans acquire language? What is the nature of memory? and How do emotions affect human decisions?

Although these cognitive concepts were fuzzy, technology, like a prince on a stallion, came to the rescue by providing powerful amplifiers and brain scanners that promised to reveal which brain sites were the foundations of the psychological functions. As a result, the psychological puzzles were replaced with such queries as "What is happening in the brain when language, memory, and decision are ongoing processes?" I do not question the importance of knowing what profiles of brain activity occur when a person recalls the author of a book, imagines a frightening incident, or thinks about a sick relative. But the brain state produced by most events is a joint product of the person's past history and the event, and the former is not always "knowable" from the brain evidence. It is hard to imagine any future technology that could reveal the perceptions and beliefs created during my sabbatical year on Lake Atitlán that had such a profound effect on my views of development. That knowledge will have to be described with a psychological vocabulary.

I noted earlier that children who spent their first decade with parents who did not graduate from high school showed distinct psychological profiles of language and impulsivity. No pattern of brain activity could reveal the sequence of emotions, beliefs, and values produced by their ten years of experience in these families. The brain profiles can only reveal some of the consequences of those experiences. It will be more accurate, and more efficient, to describe the relation between those experiences and later outcomes in sentences that contain psychological concepts. Thus, the dark shadow hovering over this fourth stage in the history of psychology is the assumption that if one knew with certainty the circuits activated when a person was reading a poem, there would be no need for psychological terms to describe the meanings and feelings that accompanied comprehension. I believe that this assumption is flawed. We will always require psychological terms for the semantic and schematic representations activated when someone reads, "Do not go gently into that good night." The brain profiles created by the sights, sounds, and smells of spring in New England cannot replace a psychological description of my rush of feelings the morning in May when the dogwood tree on my lawn blossoms. A complete understanding of brain is not synonymous with a full understanding of mind.

EIGHT

Coda

Although most estimates of the future prove to be wildly incorrect, it is hard to subdue the temptation to be prophet. I am encouraged in this harmless game by recalling two predictions I made in 1983 in the fourth edition of the *Handbook of Child Psychology*. I suggested that future investigators would acknowledge the importance of brain maturation and include biological measures in their research. Both guesses were correct. By limiting the temporal horizon to the year 2060 (about two generations), I should be able to avoid the appearance of excessive foolishness. The most secure prediction, which I regret, is that psychology will fission into two fields, as happened to physics in the 1920s and to biology in the 1970s when new methods generated novel evidence and the ability to ask fresh questions.

One group will study the biological foundations of sensation, perception, the establishment of conditioned associations, the registration and retrieval of information, and motor performance. These phenomena are currently the first chapters of introductory textbooks and were the concern of many of the first psychologists. The extraordinary advances in genetics, neuroscience, and molecular biology will attract talented men and women who enjoy working on problems that promise crisp answers—the hunters. This division has already occurred in a few of our universities.

The complementary group will resemble Harvard's Department of Social Relations when I joined the faculty in 1964. These scholars, who will primarily but not exclusively probe human behaviors, emotions, and beliefs,

will explicitly acknowledge the contribution of history and culture and will contain psychologists, sociologists, anthropologists, and a few historians and economists. This division between the small and the large is inevitable, because methods determine evidence and evidence gives meaning to concepts. The current incommensurability between biological measures of emotions and beliefs and verbal reports of ambivalence toward one's work means that, at least for the near future, the scientists pursuing these two phenomena will work in separate places.

Today's papers on the heritability of intelligence or anxiety disorder, based on heritability equations that assume that genetic and environmental forces are additive, will be replaced with descriptions of the contributions of very particular genes to the growth and activity of neuronal circuits in equally particular sites in the brain. I can imagine a paper titled "The Consequences of the FOXP2 Gene on the Activity of Interneurons in the Superior Temporal Gyrus." Analogously, contemporary reports on the effects of surrogate rearing of infants will be replaced with an acknowledgment of the culture and historical era, and a future paper might be titled, "A Comparison of the Effects of Surrogate Rearing of Infants in Rural Indonesia, Zaire, and Australia on Quality of Peer Friendships in the First Half of the Twenty-first Century." Some discoveries of the two groups will eventually be synthesized by imaginative minds. But we must be patient.

This division of labor does not mean that scientists concerned with human development, personality, social behavior, and psychopathology will fail to take advantage of biological measures. The next cohort of psychologists and psychiatrists will routinely gather biological data to separate those with similar behavioral profiles into one category that does and one that does not possess a certain biology. Behaviorally shy, timid adolescents who show greater right- rather than left-hemisphere activation, high heart rates, and high levels of cortisol will be distinguished from equally timid adolescents who lack these features. Most current psychiatric categories will be historical relics, and new terms that combine emotion, behavior, history, social context, and biology will be invented. Adults who avoid strangers and possess two short forms of the gene in the promoter region for the serotonin transporter receptor will be differentiated from equally phobic adults with two long forms of this gene. It is even likely that different therapies will be prescribed for these two types.

The two scholarly groups will recognize that most relations between psychological or biological measures in humans must be contextualized in at least five ways. Scientists will routinely restrict their inferences to specific types of people (male or female, young or old, introvert or extravert, anxious or depressed); specific long-term histories (associated with social class, culture, ethnicity); the immediate context (familiar or unfamiliar, challenging or relaxed); the season of the year and time of day; and always the source of the evidence. This austere limitation is required by the facts. Low-reactive males and high-reactive females display very different profiles to the same event. I have described the profound effects of social class and culture, and some biological measures—cortisol and melatonin, for example—vary across seasons of the year, which implies that some relations between brain activity and behavior will be different in January than in July. Similar constraints apply to research on animals. Future scientists will write full sentences, and no journal in 2060 will contain papers titled "A Theory of Learning," "The Meaning of Reward," or "The Consequences of Fear" intended to apply to all animals. Few of today's decontextualized concepts will survive these stringent rules. A century ago, "will," "constitutional defect," and "libido" dotted the technical literature. A half-century later "habit strength," "drive reduction," "need," and "minimal brain damage" filled journal pages. All were swept away in the flood of better evidence. I suspect that a majority of currently popular concepts will suffer a similar fate. This is not a criticism of the efforts of so many who combined high talent with hard work. The reativity of each generation is limited by the methods it inherits and the available facts it can trust. Newton refined Copernicus; Einstein transformed Newton. Darwin's ideas were improved by the evolutionary synthesis that recognized the complementarity of mutation and the ecological conditions that produce speciation.

Members of both disciplines will begin the planning of a study by focusing first on the phenomena they wish to understand rather than brood about the meanings of abstract words and the ways to measure their referents. They will, for example, try to illuminate the reasons for insomnia, lack of pleasure, and loss of appetite in adolescents living in poverty rather than wonder how to measure depression. They will try to understand why the dopamine-producing neurons in the midbrain of the rat are activated by a light that signals a larger amount of liquid than they have been receiving rather than reflect on what brain profile defines reward.

Finally, future students interested in the role of evolution will recognize that optimizing inclusive fitness is not the only principle human behavior obeys, because the emergence of a moral sense added a second basis for choice. Humans want to survive and to beget the next generation, but they also want to remain in close contact with the definition of "good" that their culture taught them. But that definition is dependent on historical events that cannot be predicted. The inability to know the future, a frustrating source of uncertainty in the life sciences, and especially in studies of human behavior, is the wall in the labyrinth that will not fall until history, signaling its vulnerability, allows our hero to pass into the next room to confront another barrier on the endless journey to the center, where truth, reclining on a silk couch, waits patiently to be touched.

A unique combination of six improbable events shaped the intellectual themes in my less than auspicious journey. They were, in chronological order: (1) growing up a firstborn son in a small town in New Jersey in the 1930s, (2) the town library having Donald Hebb's book in the spring of 1950 when I was deciding between a career in biochemistry or one in psychology, (3) the rejection by two psychologists of Lester Sontag's invitation to come to the Fels Institute so that I was able to conduct the longitudinal project, (4) the request to join a group of consultants in Guatemala, (5) the minister of the church in Boston's Chinatown who, in return for rescuing the daycare project, asked us to enroll Chinese-American infants, and (6) Tom James's trusting generosity when he funded Cynthia Garcia-Coll's thesis research on temperament.

Equally significant was the good fortune that brought an extraordinary group of talented students and colleagues to my laboratories over the past forty-eight years. Had any one of these events failed to occur, my tiny mural would be shamefully incomplete. The probability of all of them occurring is so low that the combination can be regarded as a freak sequence. I remain acutely conscious of the extraordinary privileges I have enjoyed and grateful for such a bountiful share of good luck.

1 Choice and Indoctrination

1. A. Lightman and R. Brawer, *Origins: The Lives and Worlds of Modern Cosmologists* (Cambridge, MA: Harvard University Press, 1990).

2. F. Jacob, *The Statue Within: An Autobiography*, trans. F. Phillip (New York: Basic Books, 1988), 21–22.

3. J. E. Wideman, *Brothers and Keepers* (New York: Holt, Rinehart and Winston, 1984).

4. G. F. Kennan, *Sketches from a Life* (New York: Pantheon Books, 1989).

5. D. O. Hebb, *The Organization of Behavior: A Neuropsychological Theory* (New York: Wiley, 1949).

6. E. O. Wilson, *Sociobiology* (Cambridge, MA: Belknap Press of Harvard University Press, 1975).

7. I. P. Pavlov, *Lectures on Conditioned Reflexes*, trans. W. H. Gantt (London: Laurence and Wishart, 1928).

8. D. A. Dewsbury, "The Chicago Five: A Family of Integrative Psychobiologists," *History of Psychology* 5 (2002): 16–37.

9. C. L. Hull, *Principles of Behavior: An Introduction to Behavior Theory* (New York: Appleton-Century, 1943).

10. G. Gorer, "Theoretical Approaches," in M. Mead and M. Wolfenstein, eds., *Children in Contemporary Cultures*, 31–36 (Chicago: University of Chicago Press, 1955).

11. C. Kluckhohn, *Mirror for Man: The Relation of Anthropology to Modern Life* (1949; reprint, Tucson: University of Arizona Press, 1985); T. Parsons, *Toward a General Theory of Action* (New Brunswick, NJ: Transaction, 1970).

12. K. Lorenz, "The Comparative Method in Studying Innate Behavior Patterns," *Symposium Society, Experimental Biology* 4 (1950): 221–268.

13. P. E. Griffiths, "Instinct in the '50s: The British Reception of Konrad Lorenz's Theory of Instinctive Behaviour," *Biology and Philosophy* 19 (2004): 609–631.

14. J. M. Toro, J. B. Trobalon, and N. Sebastian-Galles, "Effects of Backward Speech and Speaker Variability in Language Discrimination by Rats," *Journal of Experimental Psychology: Animal Behavior Processes* 31 (2005): 95–100.

15. A. Hodges, *Alan Turing: The Enigma* (New York: Simon and Schuster, 1983).

16. J. Diamond, *Guns, Germs, and Steel: The Fates of Human Societies* (New York: W. W. Norton, 1997).

17. J. B. Watson, "Psychology as the Behaviorist Views It," *Psychological Review* 20 (1913): 158–177.

18. S. Pinker, *The Blank Slate: The Denial of Human Nature in Modern Intellectual Life* (New York: Viking, 2002).

19. K. R. Popper, *Conjectures and Refutations: The Growth of Scientific Knowledge* (1962; reprint, London: Routledge, 1989); J. Dollard and N. E. Miller, *Personality and Psychotherapy: An Analysis in Terms of Learning, Thinking, and Culture* (New York: McGraw-Hill, 1950).

20. P. Lagerqvist, *The Eternal Smile, and Other Stories* (New York: Hill and Wang, 1971).

21. N. Chomsky, *Language and Mind* (New York: Harcourt Brace and World, 1968); J. Piaget, *The Psychology of Intelligence* (London: Routledge and Kegan Paul, 1950).

22. J. H. Flavell, *The Developmental Psychology of Jean Piaget* (Princeton, NJ: Van Nostrand, 1963).

23. J. Garcia and R. Koelling, "Relation of Cue to Consequences in Avoidance Learning," *Psychonomic Science* 4 (1966): 123–124.

24. K. Breland and M. Breland, "The Misbehavior of Organisms," *American Psychologist* 16 (1961): 681–684.

25. F. G. Gosling, *Before Freud: Neurasthenia and the American Medical Community, 1870–1910* (Urbana: University of Illinois Press, 1987).

26. S. Freud, *Collected Papers*, trans. Joan Riviere, 5 vols. (London: Hogarth Press and Institute of Psycho-Analysis, 1953–1956); Freud, *New Introductory Lectures on Psychoanalysis* (New York: Norton, 1965).

27. K. Atkinson-Leadbeater, W. M. Nuttley, and D. van der Kooy, "A Genetic Dissociation of Learning and Recall in *Caenorhabditis elegans*," *Behavioral Neuroscience* 118 (2004): 1206–1213.

28. L. Kohlberg, *The Philosophy of Moral Development: Moral Stages and the Idea of Justice* (New York: Harper and Row, 1981).

2 Setting a New Foundation

1. G. A. Miller, E. Galanter, and K. H. Pribram, *Plans and the Structure of Behavior* (New York: Holt, Rinehart and Winston, 1960).

2. D. Purves, S. M. Williams, S. Nundy, and R. B. Lotto, "Perceiving the Intensity of Light," *Psychological Review* 111 (2004): 142–158.

3. H. Munsterberg, *Frühe Schriften zur Psychologie* (New York: Springer Verlag, 1990).

4. J. H. Plumb, "The New World of Children in Eighteenth-Century England," *Past and Present* 67 (1975): 64–95.

5. H. Wagatsuma, "Some Aspects of the Contemporary Japanese Family: Once Confucian, Now Fatherless?" *Daedalus* 106 (1977): 181–210.

6. J. W. Giles and G. D. Heyman, "Young Children's Beliefs about the Relationship between Gender and Aggressive Behavior," *Child Development* 76 (2005): 107–121.

7. C. E. Osgood, G. J. Suci, and P. H. Tannenbaum, *The Measurement of Meaning* (Urbana: University of Illinois Press, 1957).

8. H. Barry and A. S. Harper, "Three Last Letters Identify Most Female First Names," *Psychological Reports* 87 (2000): 48–54; C. Whissell, "Cues to Referent Gender in Randomly Constructed Names," *Perceptual and Motor Skills* 93 (2001): 856–858.

9. A. Mehrabian, "Characteristics Attributed to Individuals on the Basis of Their First Names," *Genetic, Social, and General Psychology Monographs* 127 (2001): 59–88.

10. E. C. Tolman, *Behavior and Psychological Man* (Berkeley: University of California Press, 1966).

11. M. J. Guitton and Y. Dudai, "Anxiety-like State Associates with Taste to Produce Conditioned Taste Aversion," *Biological Psychiatry* 56 (2004): 901–904.

12. G. A. Miller and P. N. Johnson-Laird, *Language and Perception* (Cambridge, MA: Belknap Press of Harvard University Press, 1976).

13. H. C. Heims, H. D. Critchley, R. Dolan, C. J. Mathias, and L. Cipolotti, "Social and Motivated Functioning Is not Critically Dependent on Feedback of Autonomic Responses," *Neuropsychologia* 42 (2004): 1979–1988.

14. V. Woolf, *The Virginia Woolf Reader: An Anthology of Her Best Short Stories, Essays, Fiction, and Nonfiction* (San Diego, CA: Harcourt Brace Jovanovich, 1984).

15. J. Kagan and G. S. Lesser, *Contemporary Research in Thematic Apperceptive Methods* (Springfield, IL: Charles Thomas, 1961).

16. M. D. S. Ainsworth and S. M. Bell, "Attachment, Exploration, and Separation: Illustrated by the Behavior of One-Year-Olds in a Strange Situation," *Child Development* 41 (1970): 49–67; N. Eisenberg, R. A. Fabes, I. K. Guthrie, B. C. Murphy, P. Maszk, R. Holmgren, and K. Suh, "The Relations of Regulation and Emotionality to Problem Behavior in Elementary School Children," *Development and Psychopathology* 8 (1996): 141–162; M. K. Rothbart, D. Derryberry, and M. I. Posner, "A Psychobiological Approach to the Development of Temperament," in J. R. Bates and T. W. Wachs, eds., *Temperament*, 83–116 (Washington, DC: American Psychological Association, 1994).

17. J. Kagan and H. A. Moss, *Birth to Maturity: A Study in Psychological Development* (New York: Wiley, 1962).

18. J. I. Lacey and B. C. Lacey, "Verification and Extension of the Principle of Auto-nomic Response-Stereotopy," *American Journal of Psychology* 71 (1958): 50–73.

19. A. J. Leggett, "The Quantum Measurement Problem," *Science* 307 (2005): 871–872.

3 Flirting with Biology

1. E. H. Erikson, *Childhood and Society* (New York: Norton, 1950).

2. J. Bowlby, *Attachment and Loss*, Vol. 1, *Attachment* (New York: Basic Books, 1969).

3. B. Whiting and J. W. M. Whiting, *Children of Six Cultures: A Psycho-cultural Analysis* (Cambridge, MA: Harvard University Press, 1975).

4. R. L. Fantz and S. B. Miranda, "Newborn Attention to Form and Contour," *Child Development* 46 (1975): 224–228.

5. J. S. Rigden, *Rabi, Scientist and Citizen* (New York: Basic Books, 1987).

6. S. Heaney, *Seeing Things* (New York: Noonday Press/Farrar, Straus and Giroux, 1991).

7. C. Darwin, "Notebooks," cited in H. E. Gruber, *Darwin on Man* (London: Wildwood House, 1974), 400.

8. J. Kagan, *Change and Continuity in Infancy* (New York: Wiley, 1971).

9. K. R. Scherer, M. R. Zentner, and D. Stern, "Beyond Surprise: The Puzzle of Infants' Expressive Reactions to Expectancy Violation," *Emotion* 4 (2004): 389–402.

10. P. W. Bridgman, *The Logic of Modern Physics* (New York: Macmillan, 1927).

11. C. E. Shannon and W. Weaver, *The Mathematical Theory of Communication* (Urbana: University of Illinois Press, 1949).

12. K. H. Onishi and R. Baillargeon, "Do Fifteen-Month-Old Infants Understand False Beliefs?" *Science* 308 (2005): 255–258.

13. C. Milosz, *A Year of the Hunter*, trans. M. G. Levine (New York: Farrar, Straus and Giroux, 1994).

14. "The World in 2005," *Economist*, January 2005, 62.

15. L. J. Ji, Z. Zhanz, and R. E. Nisbett, "Is It Culture or Is It Language?" *Journal of Personality and Social Psychology* 87 (2004): 57–65.

16. C. Lutz, "The Domain of Emotion Words on Ifaluk," *American Ethnologist* 9 (1982): 113–128.

17. J. Van Os, C. B. Pedersen, and P. B. Mortensen, "Confirmation of Synergy between Urbanicity and Familial Liability in the Causation of Psychosis," *American Journal of Psychiatry* 161 (2004): 2312–2314.

18. T. T. Haug, A. Mykletun, and A. A. Dahl, "The Association between Anxiety, Depression, and Somatic Symptom in a Large Population: The Hunt-II Study," *Psychosomatic Medicine* 66 (2004): 845–851.

19. D. Sabatinelli, M. M. Bradley, J. R. Fitzsimmons, and P. J. Lang, "Parallel Amygdala and Inferotemporal Activation Reflect Emotional Intensity and Fear Relevance," *NeuroImage* 24 (2005): 1265–1270.

20. M. D. Bauman, P. Laveney, W. A. Mason, J. P. Capitanio, and D. G. Amaral, "The

Development of Social Behavior Following Neonatal Amygdala Lesions in Rhesus Monkeys," *Journal of Cognitive Neuroscience* 16 (2004): 1388–1411.

21. J. Kaufman, B. Z. Yang, H. Douglas-Palumberi, S. Hooshyer, D. Lipschitz, J. H. Krystal, and J. Gelertner, "Social Supports and Serotonin Transporter Gene Modulate Depression in Maltreated Children," *Proceedings of the National Academy of Sciences* 101 (2004): 17316–17321.

4 Accepting Biology and History

1. A. Firkowska, A. Ostrowska, M. Sokolowska, Z. Stein, and M. Susser, "Cognitive Development and Social Policy," *Science* 200 (1978): 1357–1362.

2. M. Schiff, M. Duyme, A. Dumaret, J. Stewart, S. Tomkiewicz, and J. Feingold, "Intellectual Status of Working-Class Children Adopted Early into Upper-Middle-Class Families," *Science* 200 (1978): 1503–1504.

3. E. E. Werner and R. S. Smith, *Vulnerable but Invincible: A Longitudinal Study of Resilient Children and Youth* (New York: McGraw Hill, 1982).

4. S. H. Broman, P. C. Nichols, and W. Kennedy, *Preschool IQ: Prenatal and Early Developmental Correlates* (New York: Wiley, 1975).

5. W. Kessen, *New York Times Book Review*, Dec. 10, 1978.

6. M. A. Novak and H. F. Harlow, "Social Recovery of Monkeys Isolated for the First Year of Life: 1. Rehabilitation and Therapy," *Developmental Psychology* 11 (1975): 453–465.

7. R. Helson and R. S. Crutchfield, "Creative Types in Mathematics," *Journal of Personality* 38 (1970): 177–197.

8. F. J. Sulloway, *Born to Rebel: Birth Order, Family Dynamics, and Creative Lives* (New York: Pantheon, 1996).

9. J. H. Flavell and H. M. Wellman, "Metamemory," in R. Kail and J. Hagen, eds., *Perspectives on the Development of Memory and Cognition*, 3–34 (Hillsdale, NJ: Erlbaum, 1977).

10. J. Kagan and N. Herschkowitz, *A Young Mind in a Growing Brain* (Mahwah, NJ: Erlbaum, 2005).

11. R. W. Brown, *A First Language: The Early Stages* (Cambridge, MA: Harvard University Press, 1973).

12. M. Tomasello, M. Carpenter, J. Call, T. Behne, and H. Moll, "Understanding and Sharing Intention" (Unpublished paper. Max Planck Institute for Evolutionary Anthropology, Leipzig, 2005).

13. D. G. Kemler-Nelson, M. B. Holt, and L. C. Egan, "Two- and Three-Year-Olds Infer and Reason about Design Intentions in Order to Categorize Broken Objects," *Developmental Science* 7 (2004): 543–549.

14. J. Kaminski, J. Call, and J. Fischer, "Word Learning in a Domestic Dog: Evidence for 'Fast Mapping,' " *Science* 304 (2004): 1682–1683.

15. G. M. Edelman, *The Remembered Present: A Biological Theory of Consciousness* (New York: Basic Books, 1989).

NOTES TO PAGES 122–152

. B. F. Skinner, *Beyond Freedom and Dignity* (New York: Knopf, 1971).

17. M. Lewis and J. Brooks-Gunn, *Social Cognition and the Acquisition of Self* (New York: Plenum Press, 1979).

18. J. Kagan, *The Second Year: The Emergence of Self-Awareness* (Cambridge, MA: Harvard University Press, 1981).

5 Human Morality

1. G. E. Moore, *Principia Ethica* (Cambridge: Cambridge University Press, 1993).

2. R. Rorty, *Philosophy and the Mirror of Nature* (Princeton, NJ: Princeton University Press, 1979).

3. J. Kagan, *The Nature of the Child* (New York: Basic Books, 1984).

4. J. Kagan and S. Lamb, eds., *The Emergence of Morality in Young Children* (Chicago: University of Chicago Press, 1987).

5. R. A. Shweder, N. A. Much, M. Mahaptra, and L. Park, "The Big Three of Morality (Autonomy, Community, and Divinity) and the Big Three Exemplars of Suffering," in J. A. Brandt and P. Rozin, eds., *Mortality and Health*, 293 (New York: Routledge and Kegan Paul, 1997).

6. L. Kohlberg, *The Philosophy of Moral Development* (San Francisco: Harper and Row, 1981).

7. C. Gilligan, *In a Different Voice: Psychological Theory and Women's Development* (Cambridge, MA: Harvard University Press, 1982).

8. H. Wellington, ed., *The Journal of Eugene Delacroix: A Selection* (London: Phaidon Press, 1951), 16.

9. M. C. Ashton, K. Lee, and L. R. Goldberg, "A Hierarchical Analysis of 1,710 English Personality-Descriptive Adjectives," *Journal of Personality and Social Psychology* 87 (2004): 707–721.

10. S. Lamb, "First Moral Sense: An Examination of the Appearance of Morally Related Behaviors in the Second Year of Life," *Journal of Moral Education* 22 (1993): 97–109.

11. J. Briggs, *Never in Anger: Portrait of an Eskimo Family* (Cambridge, MA: Harvard University Press, 1970); M. M. Katz, "Gaining Sense at Age Two in the Outer Fiji Islands" (Ph.D. diss., Harvard University, 1981).

12. G. Sereny, *Cries Unheard: The Story of Mary Bell* (London: Macmillan, 1999).

13. Wellington, ed., *Journal of Delacroix*, 16.

14. F. A. Hayek, *The Road to Serfdom* (Chicago: University of Chicago Press, 1994).

15. R. G. Douthet, *Privilege: Harvard and the Education of the Ruling Class* (New York: Hyperion, 2005).

16. K. Ishiguro, *The Unconsoled* (New York: Knopf, 1995).

17. E. Canetti, *The Memoirs of Elias Canetti* (New York: Farrar, Straus and Giroux, 1999).

18. C. Darwin, "Notebooks," cited in H. E. Gruber, *Darwin on Man* (London: Wildwood House, 1974), 400.

19. S. Brody, "Blood Pressure Stress Reactivity Is Less after Penile-Vaginal Intercourse Than after Other or No Sexual Activity" (Paper presented at the Forty-fourth Annual Meeting of the Society for Psychophysiological Research, Santa Fe, NM, 2004), S 20–21.

20. B. Schlink, *The Reader*, trans. C. B. Janeway (New York: Pantheon Books, 1997).

21. Douthet, *Privilege*.

22. A. Janik and S. Toulmin, *Wittgenstein's Vienna* (New York: Simon and Schuster, 1973); L. Wittgenstein, *Tractatus Logico-Philosophicus* (London: K. Paul, Trench, Trubner, 1922).

23. Briggs, *Never in Anger*.

24. D. Callahan, *What Price Better Health? Hazards of the Research Imperative* (Berkeley: University of California Press, and New York: Milbank Memorial Fund, 2003).

25. J. L. Rodgers, D. F. Harris, and K. B. Vickers, "Seasonality of First Coitus in the United States," *Social Biology* 39 (1992): 1–14.

26. M. White, *Science and Sentiment in America: Philosophical Thought from Jonathan Edwards to John Dewey* (New York: Oxford University Press, 1972).

27. E. Fromm, *The Fear of Freedom* (London: Routledge, 2001).

6 Acknowledging Temperament

1. P. J. Greven, *Child-rearing Concepts, 1628–1861: Historical Sources* (Itasca, IL: F. E. Peacock, 1973).

2. J. Kagan, R. B. Kearsley, and P. R. Zelazo, *Infancy: Its Place in Human Development* (Cambridge, MA: Harvard University Press, 1978).

3. A. Thomas, S. Chess, H. G. Birch, M. Hertzig, and S. Korn, *Behavioral Individuality in Early Childhood* (New York: New York University Press, 1963); A. Thomas and S. Chess, *Temperament and Development* (New York: Brunner/Mazel, 1977).

4. J. P. Scott and J. L. Fuller, *Genetics and the Social Behavior of the Dog* (Chicago: University of Chicago Press, 1965).

5. T. C. Schneirla, "An Evolutionary and Developmental Theory of Biphasic Processes Underlying Approach and Withdrawal," in N. R. Jones, ed., *Nebraska Symposium on Motivation*, vol. 7, 1–44 (Lincoln: University of Nebraska Press, 1959).

6. R. E. Adamec and C. Stark-Adamec, "Limbic Hyperfunction, Limbic Epilepsy, and Interictal Balance," in B. K. Doane and K. P. Livingston, eds., *The Limbic System: Functional Organization and Clinical Disorders*, 129–145 (New York: Raven, 1986).

7. K. Coleman, L. A. Tully, and J. L. McMillan, "Temperament Correlates with Training Success in Adult Rhesus Macaques," *American Journal of Primatology* 65 (2005): 63–71.

8. P. Duhem, *La Théorie physique, son objet et sa structure* (Paris: Chevalier et Rivière, 1906); Duhem, *The Aim and Structure of Physical Theory*, trans. P. P. Wiener (Princeton, NJ: Princeton University Press, 1954).

9. S. J. Nasr, A. Popli, and B. Wendt, "Medical Comorbidity in Affective Disorder," *Biological Psychiatry* 57 Suppl. (2005): 109S.

10. I. Figueira, E. Possidente, C. Marques, and K. Hayes, "Sexual Dysfunction: A Neglected Complication of Panic Disorder and Social Phobia," *Archives of Sexual Behavior* 30 (2001): 369–377.

11. J. M. Hettema, C. A. Prescott, M. Myers, M. C. Neale, and K. S. Kendler, "The Structure of Genetic and Environmental Risk Factors for Anxiety Disorders in Men and Women," *Archives of General Psychiatry* 62 (2005): 182–189.

12. L. La Gasse, C. P. Gruber, and L. P. Lipsitt, "The Infantile Expression of Avidity in Relation to Later Assessments of Inhibition and Attachment," in J. S. Reznick, ed., *Perspectives on Behavioral Inhibition*, 159–176 (Chicago: University of Chicago Press, 1989).

13. J. Kagan, *Galen's Prophecy: Temperament in Human Nature* (New York: Basic Books, 1994); G. Shamir-Essakow, J. A. Ungerer, and R. M. Rapee, "Attachment, Behavioral Inhibition, and Anxiety in Preschool Children," *Journal of Abnormal Child Psychology* 33 (2005): 133–143.

14. J. Kagan and N. Snidman, *The Long Shadow of Temperament* (Cambridge, MA: Belknap Press of Harvard University Press, 2004).

15. R. N. Emde and J. K. Hewitt, eds., *Infancy to Early Childhood: Genetic and Environmental Influences on Developmental Change* (New York: Oxford University Press, 2001).

16. F. Crick, *Of Molecules and Men* (Seattle: University of Washington Press, 1966).

17. L. N. Trut, "Early Canid Domestication: The Farm-Fox Experiment," *American Scientist* 87 (1999): 160–169.

18. C. Kunzl and N. Sachser, "The Behavioral Endocrinology of Domestication: A Comparison between the Domestic Guinea Pig (*Cavia aperea f. porcellus*) and Its Wild Ancestor, the Cavy (*Cavia aperea*)," *Hormones and Behavior* 35 (1999): 28–37; P. Saetre, J. Lindberg, J. A. Leonard, K. Olsson, U. Pettersson, H. Ellegren, T. F. Bergström, C. Vilà, and E. Jazin, "From Wild Wolf to Domestic Dog: Gene Expression Changes in the Brain," *Molecular Brain Research* 126 (2004): 198–206.

19. S. L. Gortmaker, J. Kagan, A. Caspi, and P. A. Silva, "Daylength during Pregnancy and Shyness in Children: Results from Northern and Southern Hemispheres," *Developmental Psychobiology* 31 (1997): 107–114.

20. Z. Benderlioglu and R. J. Nelson, "Season of Birth and Fluctuating Asymmetry," *American Journal of Human Biology* 16 (2004): 298–310.

21. N. A. Fox, K. H. Rubin, S. D. Calkins, J. R. Marshall, R. J. Coplan, S. W. Porges, J. N. Long, and S. Stewart, "Frontal Activation Asymmetry and Social Competence at Four Years of Age," *Child Development* 60 (1995): 1770–1784; N. A. Fox, H. A. Henderson, K. H. Rubin, S. D. Calkins, and L. A. Schmidt, "Continuity and Discontinuity of Behavioral Inhibition and Exuberance: Psychophysiological and Behavioral Influences across the First Four Years of Life," *Child Development* 72 (2001): 1–21; S. P. Putman and C. A. Stifter, "Behavioral Approach-Inhibition

in Toddlers: Prediction from Infancy, Positive and Negative Affective Components, and Relations with Behavior Problems," *Child Development* 76 (2005): 212–216.

22. X. Chen, G. Cen, D. Li, and Y. He, "Social Functioning and Adjustment in Chinese Children: The Imprint of Historical Time," *Child Development* 76 (2005): 182–195.

23. J. Cheever, *The Journals of John Cheever* (New York: Knopf, 1991); J. Strouse, *Alice James: A Biography* (Boston: Houghton Mifflin, 1980).

24. B. J. Rice, J. Woolston, E. Stewart, B. D. Kerker, and S. M. Horwitz, "Differences in Younger, Middle, and Older Children Admitted to Child Psychiatric Inpatient Services," *Child Psychiatry and Human Development* 32 (2002): 241–261.

25. T. S. Eliot, *The Waste Land, and Other Poems* (New York: Harcourt Brace World, 1934).

26. C. Jung, *Psychological Types* (New York: Harcourt Brace, 1926).

27. H. Weiner, *Perturbing the Organism: The Biology of Stressful Experience* (Chicago: University of Chicago Press, 1992).

28. H. Wellington, ed., *The Journal of Eugene Delacroix: A Selection* (London: Phaidon Press, 1951), 16.

29. R. Brown, *Against My Better Judgment: An Intimate Memoir of an Eminent Gay Psychologist* (New York: Harrington Park Press, 1996).

30. J. P. Sanchez-Navarro, J. N. Martinez-Selva, and F. Roman, "Emotional Response in Patients with Frontal Brain Damage," *Behavioral Neuroscience* 119 (2005): 87–97.

31. K. Dervic, M. A. Oquendo, M. F. Grunebaum, S. Ellis, A. K. Burke, and J. J. Mann, "Religious Affiliation and Suicide Attempt," *American Journal of Psychiatry* 161 (2004): 2303–2308; K. S. Kendler, X. Q. Liu, C. O. Gardner, M. E. McCullough, D. Larson, and C. A. Prescott, "Dimensions of Religiosity and Their Relationship to Lifetime Psychiatric and Substance Use Disorders," *American Journal of Psychiatry* 160 (2003): 496–503.

32. J. D. Flory, S. B. Manuck, K. A. Matthews, and M. F. Muldoon, "Serotonergic Function in the Central Nervous System Is Associated with Daily Ratings of Positive Mood," *Psychiatry Research* 129 (2004): 11–19.

33. J. A. King, W. L. De Oliveira, and N. Patel, "Deficits in Testosterone Facilitate Enhanced Fear Response," *Psychoneuroendocrinology* 30 (2005): 333–340.

34. A. H. Rellini, K. M. McCall, P. K. Randall, and C. M. Meston, "The Relationship between Women's Subjective and Physiological Sexual Arousal," *Psychophysiology* 42 (2005): 116–124.

7 Celebrating Mind

1. R. Hoffmann, "Hi O Silver," *American Scientist* 89 (2001): 311.

2. E. D. Adrian, *The Physical Background of Perception* (Oxford: Clarendon Press, 1947).

3. K. G. Noble, M. F. Norman, and M. J. Farah, "Neurocognitive Correlates of Socio-economic Status in Kindergarten Children," *Developmental Science* 8 (2005): 76–87.

4. T. Furmark, F. Ahs, C. Linnman, A. Pissiota, A. Michelgard, A. Hellqvist, S. Herne-falk, K. Flyckt, L. Appel, M. Bani, E. M. Pich, S. Zancan, and M. Fredrikson, "Amygdalar Activity during Emotional Perception and Experience in Subjects with Social Phobia," *Biological Psychiatry* 57 (2005): 169S; A. E. Guyer, C. S. Monk, E. B. McCoure, E. E. Nelson, R. Roberson-Nay, A. D. Adler, E. Zarahn, D. S. Pine, and M. Ernst, "Developmental Differences in Attention Related Amygdala Response to Emotional Facial Expression," *Biological Psychiatry* 57 (2005): 8S.

5. M. Brazdil, M. Dobsik, M. Mikl, P. Hlustik, P. Daniel, M. Pazourkova, P. Krupa, and I. Rektor, "Combined Event-related fMRI and Intracerebral ERP Study of an Auditory Oddball Task," *NeuroImage* 15 (2005): 285–293.

6. K. A. Kiehl, M. C. Stevens, K. R. Laurens, G. Pearlson, V. D. Calhoun, and P. F. Liddle, "An Adaptive Reflexive Processing Model of Neurocognitive Function," *NeuroImage* 25 (2005): 899–915.

7. A. S. Fox, T. R. Oakes, S. E. Shelton, A. K. Converse, R. J. Davidson, and N. H. Kalin, "Calling for Help Is Independently Modulated by Brain Systems Under-lying Goal Directed Behavior and Threat Perception," *Proceedings of the National Academy of Sciences* 102 (2005): 4176–4179.

8. S. B. Manuck, J. D. Flory, R. E. Ferrell, and M. F. Muldoon, "Socio-Economic Status Covaries with Central Nervous System Serotonergic Responsivity as a Func-tion of Allelic Variation in the Serotonin Transporter Gene-linked Polymorphic Region," *Psychoneuroendocrinology* 29 (2004): 651–668.

9. J. Kaufman, B. Z. Yang, H. Douglas-Palumberi, S. Houshyar, D. Lipschitz, J. H. Krystal, and J. Gelertner, "Social Supports and Serotonin Transporter Gene Mod-erate Depression in Maltreated Children," *Proceedings of the National Academy of Sciences* 101 (2004): 17316–17321.

10. I. Gauthier and K. N. Curby, "A Perceptual Traffic Jam on Highway N170: Inter-ference between Face and Car Expertise," *Current Directions in Psychological Science* 14 (2005): 30–33; D. J. Veltman, W. E. Tuinebreijer, D. Winkelman, A. A. Lammertsma, M. P. Witter, R. J. Dolan, and P. M. Emmelkamp, "Neurophysio-logical Correlates of Habituation during Exposure in Spider Phobia," *Psychiatry Research* 132 (2004): 149–158.

11. D. Cox, E. Meyers, and P. Sinha, "Contexually Evoked Object-Specific Responses in Human Visual Cortex," *Science* 304 (2004): 115–117.

12. D. J. Grelotti, A. J. Klin, I. Gauthier, P. Skudlarski, D. J. Cohen, J. C. Gore, F. R. Volkmar, and R. T. Schultz, "fMRI Activation of the Fusiform Gyrus and Amyg-dala to Cartoon Characters but Not to Faces in a Boy with Autism," *Neuropsycho-logia* 43 (2005): 373–385.

13. T. T. Rogers, J. Hocking, A. Mechelli, K. Patterson, and C. Price, "Fusiform Acti-

vation to Animals Is Driven by the Process, Not the Stimulus," *Journal of Cognitive Neuroscience* 17 (2005): 434–445.

14. B. King-Casas, D. Tomlin, C. Anen, C. F. Camerer, S. R. Quartz, and P. R. Montague, "Getting to Know You: Reputation and Trust in a Two-Person Economic Exchange," *Science* 308 (2005): 78–83.

15. J. Greene and J. Cohen, "For the Law, Neuroscience Changes Nothing and Everything," *Philosophical Transactions of the Royal Society of London B* 359 (2004): 1775–1785.

16. K. L. Briggman, H. D. I. Abarbanel, and W. B. Kristan, Jr., "Optical Imaging of Neuronal Populations during Decision-Making," *Science* 307 (2005): 896–901.

17. A. N. Whitehead, *Science and the Modern World* (New York: Macmillan, 1928).

18. R. Kittler, M. Kayser, and M. Stoneking, "Molecular Evolution of *Pediculus humanus* and the Origin of Clothing," *Current Biology* 13 (2003): 1414–1417.

19. M. Rivera-Gaxiola, G. Csibra, M. H. Johnson, and A. Karmiloff-Smith, "Electrophysiological Correlates of Cross-Linguistic Speech Perception in Native English Speakers," *Behavioral Brain Research* 111 (2000): 13–23.

20. S. L. Brenner, T. P. Beauchaine, and P. D. Sylvers, "A Comparison of Psychophysiological and Self-Report Measures of BAS and BIS Activation," *Psychophysiology* 42 (2005): 108–115.

21. J. R. Harris, *The Nurture Assumption: Why Children Turn Out the Way They Do* (New York: Free Press, 1998).

22. K. Wynn, "Addition and Subtraction by Human Infants," *Nature* 358 (1992): 749–750.

23. F. Galton, *Hereditary Genius: An Inquiry into Its Laws and Consequences* (London: Macmillan, 1869).

24. H. Gardner, *Frames of Mind: The Theory of Multiple Intelligences* (New York: Basic Books, 1983).

25. A. Diamond, M. Prevar, G. Callender, and D. P. Druin, "Prefrontal Cortex in Children Tested Early and Continuously for PKU," *Monographs of the Society for Research in Child Development* 62 (1997): 1–207.

26. E. Turkheimer, A. Haley, M. Waldron, B. D'Onofrio, and I. I. Gottesman, "Socioeconomic Status Modifies Heritability of IQ in Young Children," *Psychological Science* 14 (2003): 623–628.

27. S. Frangou, X. Chitins, and S. C. Williams, "Mapping IQ and Gray Matter Density in Healthy Young People," *NeuroImage* 23 (2004): 800–805.

28. R. J. Herrnstein and C. Murray, *The Bell Curve: Intelligence and Class Structure in American Life* (New York: Free Press, 1994).

29. M. N. Cook, V. J. Bolivar, M. P. McFadyen, and L. Flaherty, "Behavioral Differences among 129 Substrains: Implications for Knockout and Transgenic Mice," *Behavioral Neuroscience* 116 (2002): 600–611; J. L. Cameron, "Linkage Analysis in a Nonhuman Primate Population to Identify Genes Underlying Anxious Behaviors," *Biological Psychiatry* 57 (2005): 8S.

30. H. T. Blair, V. K. Huynh, V. T. Vaz, J. Van, R. R. Patel, A. K. Hiteshi, J. E. Lee, and J. W. Tarpley, "Unilateral Storage of Fear Memories by the Amygdala," *Journal of Neuroscience* 25 (2005): 4198–4205.

31. A. Roulin, "Proximate Basis of the Covariation between a Melanin-Based Female Ornament and Offspring Quality," *Oecologia* 140 (2004): 668–675.

32. S. S. Dickerson, T. C. Gruenewald, and M. E. Kemeny, "When the Social Self Is Threatened: Shame, Physiology, and Health," *Journal of Personality* 72 (2004): 1191–1216.

33. A. K. Blascovich and W. B. Mendes, "Cardiovascular Reactivity in the Presence of Pets, Friends, and Spouses: The Truth about Cats and Dogs," *Psychosomatic Medicine* 64 (2002): 727–739.

34. S. J. Garlow, D. Purselle, and M. Heninger, "Ethnic Differences in Pattern of Suicide across the Life Cycle," *American Journal of Psychiatry* 162 (2005): 319–323.

35. A. E. Learmonth, L. Nadel, and N. S. Newcombe, "Children's Use of Landmarks: Implications for Modularity Theory," *Psychological Science* 13 (2002): 337–341.

36. D. J. Tollin, L. C. Populin, J. M. Moore, J. L. Ruhland, and T. C. T. Yin, "Sound-Localization Performance in the Cat: The Effect of Restraining the Head," *Journal of Neurophysiology* 93 (2005): 1223–1234.

37. H. Kendler, "A Personal Encounter with Psychology (1937–2002)," *History of Psychology* 5 (2002): 52–84.

38. B. Russell, *Portraits from Memory and Other Essays* (New York: Simon and Schuster, 1956).

39. F. Jacob, *The Statue Within: An Autobiography*, trans. F. Phillip (New York: Basic Books, 1988).

40. H. Wellington, ed., *The Journal of Eugene Delacroix: A Selection* (London: Phaidon Press, 1951), 16.

41. A. Lightman, *A Sense of the Mysterious: Science and the Human Spirit* (New York: Pantheon, 2005).

42. D. N. Robinson, "Jefferson and Adams on the Mind-Body Problem," *History of Psychology* 6 (2003): 227–238.

43. C. E. Schwartz, C. E. Wright, M. L. Shin, J. Kagan, and S. L. Rauch, "Inhibited and Uninhibited Children 'Grown Up': Adult Amygdala Response to Novelty," *Science* 300 (2003): 1950–1953.

44. J. Kagan, *Three Seductive Ideas* (Cambridge, MA: Harvard University Press, 1998); Kagan, *Surprise, Uncertainty, and Mental Structures* (Cambridge, MA: Harvard University Press, 2002).